BASIC
WOODWORKING

BASIC
WOODWORKING

James Summers & Mark Ramuz

Watson-Guptill Publications / New York

First published in the UK in 1997 by
Collins & Brown Ltd.
London House, Great Eastern Wharf, Parkgate Road
London SW11 4NQ

First published in the United States in 1997 by Watson-Guptill
Publications, a division of BPI Communications, Inc.,
1515 Broadway, New York, N.Y. 10036

Library of Congress Cataloging-in-Publication Data:
Summers, James, Ramuz, Mark.
     Basic Woodworking
James Summers and Mark Ramuz.
     p. cm.
Includes index

Editorial Director: Sarah Hoggett
Project Editor: Peter Brooke-Ball
Editor: Ian Kearey
Assistant Editor: Corinne Asghar
Designed by: Alan Marshall
Art Director: Roger Bristow
Senior Art Editor: Julia Ward-Hastelow
Designer: Suzanne Metcalfe-Megginson
Photography: John Freeman
Projects made by: Pearl Dot Limited
Illustrators: David Ashby, Keith Field

Printed in Great Britain by Butler & Tanner, Frome

1 2 3 4 5 / 00 99 98 97 96

James Summers manages Pearl Dot Ltd., a London-based company
that designs and makes contemporary furniture to commission.
He is a trained cabinet-maker and one of a small team of designers
based at the workshop.

Mark Ramuz is an enthusiastic woodworker and has written about
all aspects of the craft for many years. He is group editor of the
magazines *The Woodworker* and *Practical Woodworking* and has
co-authored a book on making wooden birdhouses.

CONTENTS

ABOUT THIS BOOK 6

THE BEAUTY OF WOOD 8
Wood and How to Work with It 10
Softwoods 12
Hardwoods 14
Board and Sheet Materials 16

TOOLS AND TECHNIQUES 18
A Woodworker's Toolkit 20
Measuring and Marking Tools 22
Measuring and Marking Techniques 24
Saws for Woodworking 28
Sawing Techniques 30
Drills and Bits 32
Drilling Techniques 34
Chisels and Cutting Tools 36
Cutting and Shaping Techniques 38
Planes and Rasps 40

Planing Techniques   42
Clamps and Vises   46
Clamping Techniques   48
Tools for Fixing   50
Fixings, Fittings and Adhesives   52
Fixing Techniques   54
Hanging and Fastening Techniques   56
Sanding and Finishing Tools   58
Sanding and Finishing Techniques   60
Wood Finishes   62
Power Saws   64
Power Sanders   66
Power Planes   68
Power Drill Attachments   70
Simple Joint Techniques   72
Dowel Joints   78

THE PROJECTS   80
Bird House   82
Bulletin Board   84
Shoe Storage Rack   86
Picture Frame   88
Bird Feeder   90

Knife Block   92
Spice Rack   94
Shelving Unit   96
Plant Box   100
Occasional Table   104
Towel Rack   108
Workbench   112
Children's Toy Chest   116
Trellis   120
Dish Rack   124
Blanket Chest   128
Child's Desk   132
Garden Bench   136
Computer Workstation   140
Picnic Table   144
Corner Cupboard   148
Hardwood Stool   152

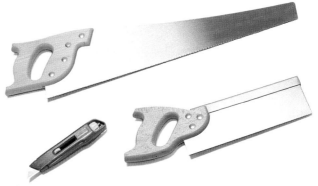

GLOSSARY   156
INDEX   158
ACKNOWLEDGMENTS   160

ABOUT THIS BOOK

Basic Woodworking is a practical, step-by-step guide to carpentry and cabinet-making for both beginners and those who want to improve their skills. As well as illustrating tools and techniques, it includes designs for numerous household and garden projects.

The Beauty of Wood
The opening section contains valuable information on wood and man-made boards. It explains how trees are converted into planks and explains the differences between softwoods and hardwoods. It also offers advice on how to select and choose the best wood.

Tools and Techniques
The Tools and Techniques section introduces all the tools you need to work and manipulate wood. Step-by-step photographs and illustrations, combined with professional hints and tips explain how to use the tools. There is also advice on storing and maintaining tools.

Ranges of tools available

TOOLS AND TECHNIQUES
All the important woodworking tools are illustrated. By following the clear step-by-step photographs on how to use the tools, you will be able to get the best from them.

Good working practises
This caption gives sound advice on the safest and best way to use tools so that you minimize the chances of hurting yourself or spoiling the workpiece.

Boxed features
Panels like this explain how to use particular devices or gadgets that enable you to get the most from your tools.

SAWING TECHNIQUES

Sawing is an easy woodworking skill to master once you have established a few basic rules. With practice, the rules become habitual and you make clean, accurate cuts every time.

BEFORE YOU start sawing, make sure that you choose an appropriate type of saw for the job in hand (*see pages 28-29*). Anchor the workpiece securely to a workbench so that it cannot wobble or move, and start the cut slightly to the waste side of the cutting line. The width of a saw cut, although small, can make the difference between a tight joint and a loose joint.

While you saw, keep your dominant eye (usually the right eye) in line with the saw blade. The exception to this rule is when using a coping saw, when it is not always possible to keep your eye lined up with the blade.

Lean forward and support your body weight with your free hand. Keep your eye in line with the saw blade.

Grasp the handle lightly. An outstretched finger helps to steady the saw.

GOOD SAWING TECHNIQUE
Let the saw do most of the hard work for you. If you force a saw, it will wander off the cutting line.

Use a panel saw for boards and large pieces of wood and a tenon saw for more intricate work where accuracy is crucial.

Hold the edge of a board to prevent it from lifting when you pull the saw backwards.

Supporting the workpiece
Always clamp the wood or board you are working on to a workbench. It is equally important to support the waste wood as well because if you allow it to just fall away as you finish the cut, it will almost certainly tear the wood, possibly leaving an ugly scar on the underside.

Keep as much of the workpiece on the bench as possible and improvise supports for the waste. Try using a clamp to prevent a thin section of board from flapping (see far right) or prop a large offcut on a table to stop it from snapping off. Hold the offcut in the final stages of sawing or, if possible, ask an assistant to hold it steady for you as you cut through.

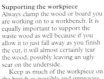

Starting the cut
Start the saw cut gently. Guide the side of the saw with your thumb but keep it out of the line of the teeth.

Supporting the offcut
Clamp the offcut to prevent it from flapping. Support a large offcut on a table to stop it from snapping off.

30

Cutting a tenon
When you cut a tenon, it is best to saw down the grain in stages. If you saw straight down the grain with one cut, your saw will probably wander off the cutting line and the tenon will be crooked.

After you have marked the tenon (*see pages 24-27 and 72-77*), cut the shoulders with a back saw. Next, clamp the workpiece upright and, holding your saw at an angle of around 45°, saw down one check to the shoulder. Do the same to the second check before reversing the wood in the clamp and sawing down the other sides at an angle of 45°. Finally, saw down both the checks horizontally to remove the waste.

Cutting the first side of the tenon
Hold your saw at an angle of 45° and cut down as far as the shoulder. Keep the saw to the waste side of the cutting line.

Repeat with the second side
Before turning the workpiece around, saw down the second check, once again holding the saw at an angle of around 45°.

Finishing the cut
When you have made two 45° cuts in each check, saw horizontally down to the shoulder cut to remove the waste.

Cutting with a coping saw
To cut a shape out of the middle of a board, first drill a starter hole in the waste area of wood. Thread the coping saw blade through the hole and slot it into the frame.

Saw to the waste side of the cutting line and when you want to change the direction of the cut, gently turn the frame. If you need to adjust the blade further, twist the top and bottom blade supports on the frame. Make sure that the blade is held straight at all times.

Coping saw blades are brittle, so never try to force the saw along. If the workpiece starts to vibrate, move your clamps as near as possible to the cutting line.

Handling a coping saw
Firmly clamp the workpiece and keep the saw blade at right-angles to the wood as you cut out the curve.

USING A MITER BOX
Clamp the miter box in, or on to, your workbench so that it cannot swivel around or move, and then place an offcut in the bottom. Mark the piece of wood you want to cut and set it in the box on top of the offcut. Insert a back saw into the appropriate slots and line up the blade just to the waste side of your cutting line. Hold the timber (wood) steady with one hand, or clamp it in position, and saw through the workpiece.

Inserting an offcut
Place an offcut in the bottom of the box to bring the workpiece up to the level of the slots and to protect the base.

Cutting the miter
Hold the workpiece steady with your free hand and line up the back saw blade to the waste side of your cutting line. Saw gently and make sure you cut right through to the offcut underneath before removing the workpiece.

31

Step-by-step pictures
All the crucial woodworking skills are illustrated with clear photographs so that you can see exactly what is going on.

Using specialized tools
All common tools, including those that are designed to do specific tasks, are included.

The projects

This section contains easy-to-follow drawings for a variety of household and garden items. Clear illustrations and instructions guide you step-by-step through each project.

The 'Project Planner' panels at the beginning of each project pinpoint the crucial stages so that you know at a glance, what skills are involved . 'What You Need' panels contain details of the tools and materials needed, and 'Cutting Lists' give precise measurements for the wood needed for each project. The 'See Also' panels contain cross-references

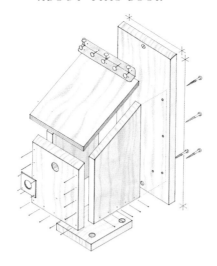

Detailed artworks

so you can remind yourself of the techniques needed for each project.

The simplest projects come first in the book and the more difficult ones lie towards the back. Begin by making the easier designs and progress to the more difficult ones as your confidence grows. Many of the projects can be made from either softwood or hardwood. Softwood is recommended for beginners as it is easier to work and is less expensive.

Imperial and metric measurements have been used throughout. As conversions are not precise, use either one system or the other consistently.

THE PROJECTS
All the projects have an easy-to understand text that explains how to carry out the crucial stages. Photographs illustrate the critical steps.

Detailed artworks
These show you exactly how the components of each project slot together. Each drawing is labelled with dimensions.

Finished project photography
A photograph shows you what each project looks like after it has been assembled. Some projects should be painted while others are best left bare.

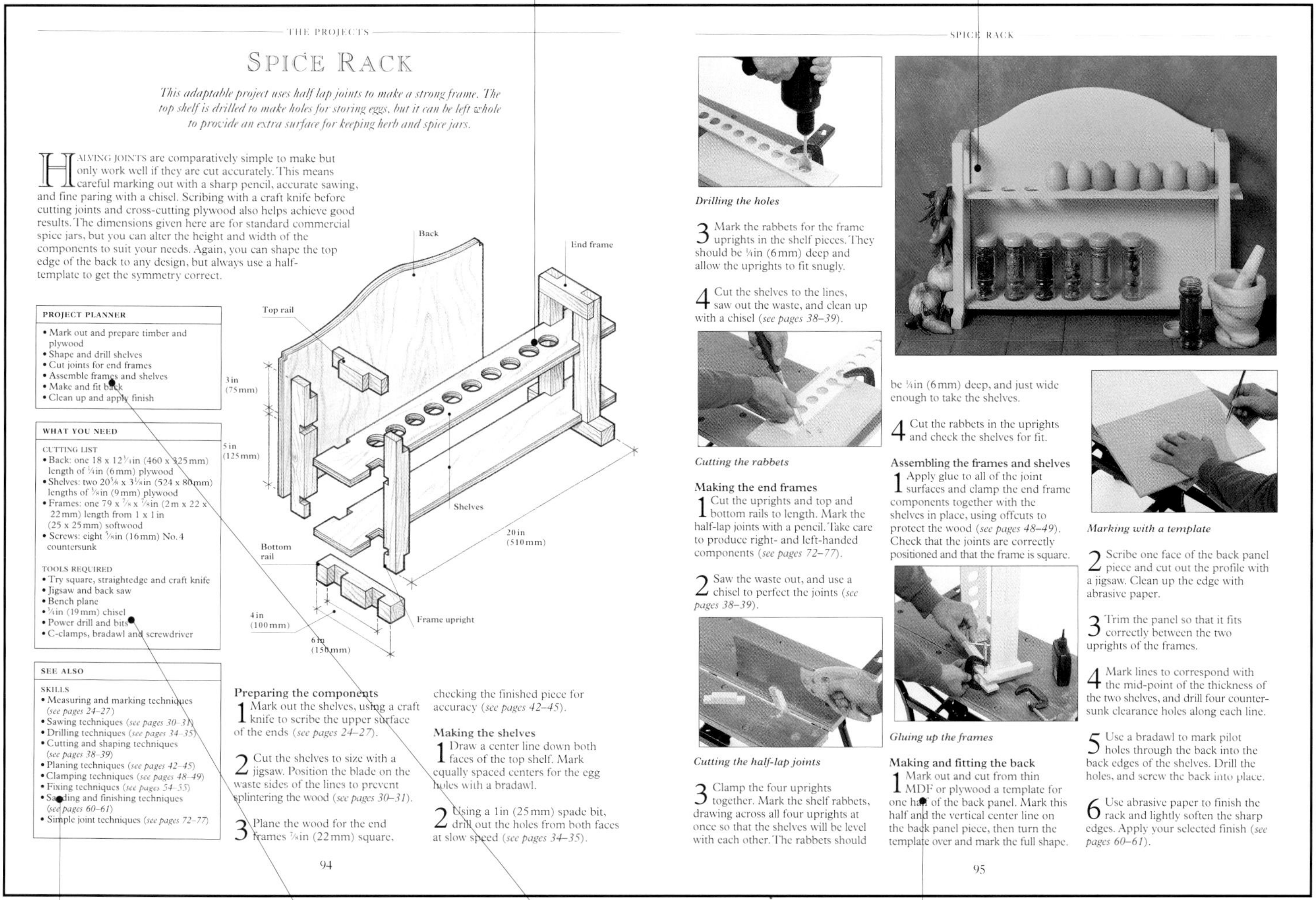

SPICE RACK

This adaptable project uses half lap joints to make a strong frame. The top shelf is drilled to make holes for storing eggs, but it can be left whole to provide an extra surface for keeping herb and spice jars.

HALVING JOINTS are comparatively simple to make but only work well if they are cut accurately. This means careful marking out with a sharp pencil, accurate sawing, and fine paring with a chisel. Scribing with a craft knife before cutting joints and cross-cutting plywood also helps achieve good results. The dimensions given here are for standard commercial spice jars, but you can alter the height and width of the components to suit your needs. Again, you can shape the top edge of the back to any design, but always use a half-template to get the symmetry correct.

PROJECT PLANNER
- Mark out and prepare timber and plywood
- Shape and drill shelves
- Cut joints for end frames
- Assemble frames and shelves
- Make and fit back
- Clean up and apply finish

WHAT YOU NEED

CUTTING LIST
- Back: one 18 x 12¾in (460 x 325mm) length of ¼in (6mm) plywood
- Shelves: two 20⅝ x 3⅛in (524 x 80mm) lengths of ⅜in (9mm) plywood
- Frames: one 79 x ⅞ x ⅞in (2m x 22 x 22mm) length from 1 x 1in (25 x 25mm) softwood
- Screws: eight ⅝in (16mm) No.4 countersunk

TOOLS REQUIRED
- Try square, straightedge and craft knife
- Jigsaw and back saw
- Bench plane
- ¾in (19mm) chisel
- Power drill and bits
- C-clamps, bradawl and screwdriver

SEE ALSO

SKILLS
- Measuring and marking techniques (see pages 24–27)
- Sawing techniques (see pages 30–31)
- Drilling techniques (see pages 34–35)
- Cutting and shaping techniques (see pages 38–39)
- Planing techniques (see pages 42–45)
- Clamping techniques (see pages 48–49)
- Fixing techniques (see pages 54–55)
- Sanding and finishing techniques (see pages 60–61)
- Simple joint techniques (see pages 72–77)

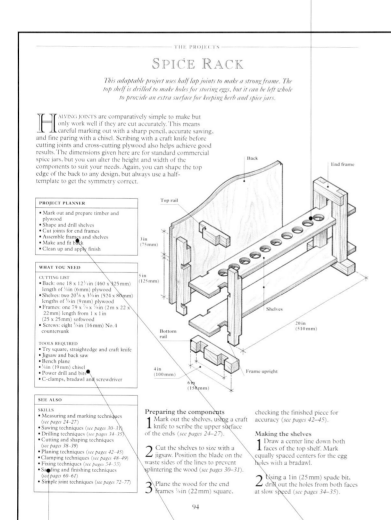

Back

End frame

Top rail

3in (75mm)

5in (125mm)

Shelves

Bottom rail

20in (510mm)

4in (100mm)

6in (150mm)

Frame upright

Preparing the components

1 Mark out the shelves, using a craft knife to scribe the upper surface of the ends (see pages 24–27).

2 Cut the shelves to size with a jigsaw. Position the blade on the waste sides of the lines to prevent splintering the wood (see pages 30–31).

3 Plane the wood for the end frames ⅞in (22mm) square,

checking the finished piece for accuracy (see pages 42–45).

Making the shelves

1 Draw a center line down both faces of the top shelf. Mark equally spaced centers for the egg holes with a bradawl.

2 Using a 1in (25mm) spade bit, drill out the holes from both faces at slow speed (see pages 34–35).

Drilling the holes

3 Mark the rabbets for the frame uprights in the shelf pieces. They should be ¼in (6mm) deep and allow the uprights to fit snugly.

4 Cut the shelves to the lines, saw out the waste, and clean up with a chisel (see pages 38–39).

Cutting the rabbets

Making the end frames

1 Cut the uprights and top and bottom rails to length. Mark the half-lap joints with a pencil. Take care to produce right- and left-handed components (see pages 72–77).

2 Saw the waste out, and use a chisel to perfect the joints (see pages 38–39).

Cutting the half-lap joints

3 Clamp the four uprights together. Mark the shelf rabbets, drawing across all four uprights at once so that the shelves will be level with each other. The rabbets should

be ¼in (6mm) deep, and just wide enough to take the shelves.

4 Cut the rabbets in the uprights and check the shelves for fit.

Assembling the frames and shelves

1 Apply glue to all of the joint surfaces and clamp the end frame components together with the shelves in place, using offcuts to protect the wood (see pages 48–49). Check that the joints are correctly positioned and that the frame is square.

Gluing up the frames

Making and fitting the back

1 Mark out and cut from thin MDF or plywood a template for one half of the back panel. Mark this half and the vertical center line on the back panel piece, then turn the template over and mark the full shape.

Marking with a template

2 Scribe one face of the back panel piece and cut out the profile with a jigsaw. Clean up the edge with abrasive paper.

3 Trim the panel so that it fits correctly between the two uprights of the frames.

4 Mark lines to correspond with the mid-point of the thickness of the two shelves, and drill four countersunk clearance holes along each line.

5 Use a bradawl to mark pilot holes through the back into the back edges of the shelves. Drill the holes, and screw the back into place.

6 Use abrasive paper to finish the rack and lightly soften the sharp edges. Apply your selected finish (see pages 60–61).

'See Also' boxes
These refer you to relevant skills covered in the Tools and Techniques section of the book.

'What You Need' boxes
These include detailed cutting lists as well as lists of all the tools you require to make the projects.

'Project Planner' boxes
These show you at a glance what the various stages in making a project are.

Numbered step-by-step
All the stages to making a project are numbered. The most important steps are also illustrated with photographs.

THE BEAUTY OF WOOD

Wood can be manipulated and worked like no other natural material. This section explains the difference between the various types of hardwoods, softwoods and manmade boards that you are likely to use for making projects, and gives advice on how to select the best quality wood.

WOOD AND HOW TO WORK WITH IT

Wood is a complex living material which continues to react to its surroundings long after it has been cut. Knowing more about the raw material will help you select the right wood for each project.

THE ROOTS AND LEAVES of a growing tree are connected by microscopic tubes that run up the trunk and along the branches. Nutrients and water move along these tubes and, as the tree grows, more and more layers of these fibrous, conductive tissues are laid down underneath the bark. As a result, the diameter of the tree increases and the trunk gets longer. In the course of time, the tubes toward the center of the tree become redundant and form what is known as heartwood.

From a woodworker's point of view, the most usable wood comes from the trunk of a tree. Even the largest branches tend to be twisted and laced with knots (the outgrowths of smaller branches) which can make planing and sawing extremely difficult.

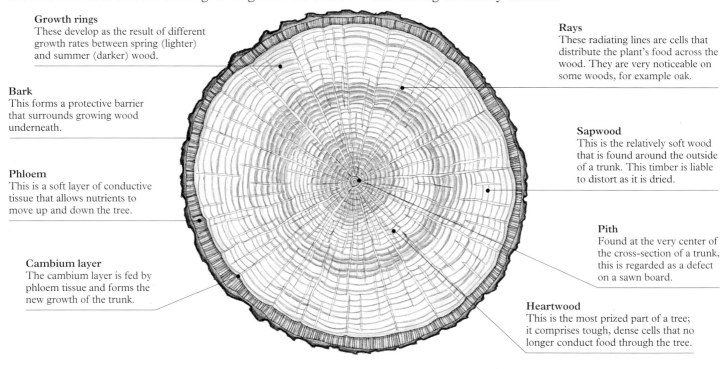

Growth rings
These develop as the result of different growth rates between spring (lighter) and summer (darker) wood.

Bark
This forms a protective barrier that surrounds growing wood underneath.

Phloem
This is a soft layer of conductive tissue that allows nutrients to move up and down the tree.

Cambium layer
The cambium layer is fed by phloem tissue and forms the new growth of the trunk.

Rays
These radiating lines are cells that distribute the plant's food across the wood. They are very noticeable on some woods, for example oak.

Sapwood
This is the relatively soft wood that is found around the outside of a trunk. This timber is liable to distort as it is dried.

Pith
Found at the very center of the cross-section of a trunk, this is regarded as a defect on a sawn board.

Heartwood
This is the most prized part of a tree; it comprises tough, dense cells that no longer conduct food through the tree.

How a tree is sawn

The simplest way to convert a log into boards is to slice through it with a series of parallel cuts. This method is called through-and-through or flat-sawing. The problem with this method, however, is that the resulting boards are prone to warping. An alternative method is to saw each quarter-section of the log into boards. This is called quarter-sawing and involves a more elaborate procedure, but the boards are usually more stable. Another advantage of quarter-sawing is that it is possible to select particular areas of the log for making stout beams.

Ironically, through-and-through sawing tends to produce the most attractive type of timber as the grain shows up clearly. Quarter-sawing usually produces plainer and more uniform lumber.

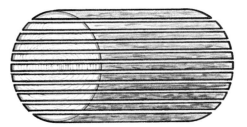

Through-and-through sawing
This method of sawing converts a log into boards with parallel cuts. Almost all the wood is used but the planks are likely to warp.

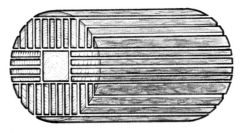

Quarter-sawing
This is costly but the resulting wood tends to be stable and it is possible to vary the thicknesses of the boards.

Shrinkage of wood

All wood shrinks as it dries out but exactly how a plank or board shrinks and warps depends on where it was cut from the log. Boards cut obliquely across the grain, away from the center of the log, warp the most.

Shrinkage
Wood shrinks in different ways, depending on how it was cut from the log in the first place.

Selecting wood

Wood, especially hardwood, is expensive, so it is well worth hunting around to get the best value for money. First, look at the orientation of the rings on the end of a board to see if it was sawn through-and-through or quarter-sawn, bearing in mind that quarter-sawn wood is more stable. Secondly, look carefully along the board to spot any obvious warps or other defects.

Rough sawn and planed lumber

Lumber is sold either rough-sawn or planed. If you buy rough-sawn lumber, you will, of course, have to plane it down yourself.

Planed lumber is often referred to as 'surfaced all sides' or S4S and is usually sold in nominal dimensions. This means that the dimensions are not exact and are likely to be smaller than those given. For example, a planed 1 x 6 in (25 x 150 mm) piece of wood will probably measure about ¾ x 5 ½ in (19 x 140 mm). If you require boards of a size that is non-standard, many suppliers will cut and plane them for you.

Lumber grading

Lumber is usually graded by the time it reaches a retail outlet. Grading is

RECLAIMED WOOD

Old wood is often discarded or burnt once it is thought to have served its time. This is a tragedy as there is often nothing wrong with old wood and it can in fact be superior to new wood as it tends to be more stable. In addition, old wood is usually cheap to buy.

If you are interested in reclaiming wood, check out architectural salvage yards or lumber merchants who specialize in reclaimed wood. Other sources include neighbours who are getting rid of old furniture and shops that are being revamped.

When you salvage wood, always check it for old nails and also watch out for signs of rot.

carried out according to the amount of defects in the wood but different suppliers use different codes and standards. For this reason, always select boards yourself rather than relying on confusing definitions.

Looking for defects

There are many faults that are commonly found in lumber. Some only mar the appearance of the wood but others, such as encased

bark, actually weaken the wood. Spend time checking each board you plan to buy for the faults illustrated below, most of which indicate suspect or worthless wood. The one exception is knots. For some items of furniture, particularly rustic tables and chairs, knots can be appealing. However, for other projects, knots can be a bane as they are difficult to saw through and can leave ugly holes if they fall out.

COMMON TIMBER DEFECTS

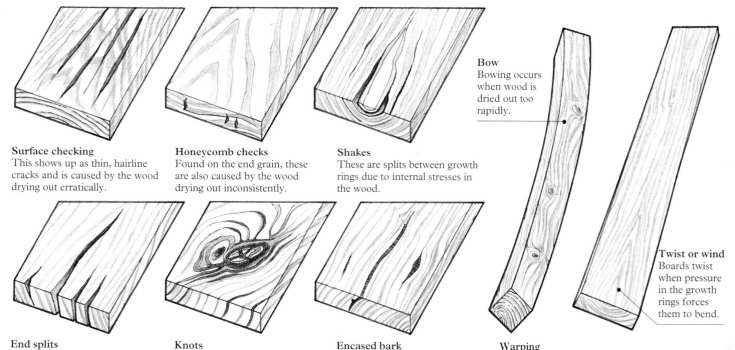

Surface checking
This shows up as thin, hairline cracks and is caused by the wood drying out erratically.

Honeycomb checks
Found on the end grain, these are also caused by the wood drying out inconsistently.

Shakes
These are splits between growth rings due to internal stresses in the wood.

Bow
Bowing occurs when wood is dried out too rapidly.

End splits
If the ends dry out quicker than the rest of the board, splits are the result.

Knots
These are sites where a branch grew from the tree. They are attractive in some woods.

Encased bark
This is the result of a fold in the tree trunk; it can substantially weaken timber.

Twist or wind
Boards twist when pressure in the growth rings forces them to bend.

Warping
Wood warps or twists along its length if it has not been dried properly or if internal stresses are released as it is cut.

SOFTWOODS

Softwood is a generic term for lumber that is cut from coniferous trees. Some species are more suited to furniture-making than others, so it makes sound sense to get to know the various common sorts so that you can make wise decisions when selecting and buying.

AS A GENERAL RULE, softwoods are relatively lightweight and are less expensive to buy than hardwoods (*see pages 14–15*) because they are fast-growing and can be cultivated. However, there are a few exceptional softwoods. Yew, for example, is a slow-growing softwood and its wood is dense and hard!

Many commercial softwoods, such as European redwood and Western red cedar, come from 'renewable sources'. In other words, as soon as a tree is cut down, a new sapling is planted in its place. This means that the environment is not damaged in the long term. 'Farming' of this type takes place in Northern America as well as in Europe and New Zealand.

Although softwoods are not as durable as many of the hardwoods, some have exceptional qualities that make them ideal for specific jobs. Western red cedar, for

Cedar of Lebanon
(*Cedrus libani*)
DENSITY: *35 lb/cu. ft (550 kg/m³)*

This type of cedar has a fragrant scent that has been exploited by cabinetmakers for generations. It is honey-brown in color with well-defined growth rings. It is not a particularly strong wood but it is durable, easy to work, and takes a fine finish. Sometimes grown in European and North-American parks as a decorative tree, the finest quality still comes from the Middle East.

Douglas fir
(*Pseudotsuga menziesii*)
DENSITY: *33 lb/cu.ft (530 kg/m³)*

Also called Columbian and Oregon pine (although not botanically a pine at all), Douglas fir is one of the most used softwoods, particularly in North America. It is pale, reddish-brown in color and has a straight grain that is easy to saw, plane and sand. Douglas fir is a strong wood and is moderately resistant to decay. It is grown commercially in North America and Europe and is one of the main sources of plywood.

European redwood
(*Pinus sylvestris*)
DENSITY: *32 lb/cu.ft (512 kg/m³)*

This is probably the most widely used softwood in Europe. It is generally pale in color with well defined growth rings but the heartwood at the center of the tree is reddish, hence its name. Easy to work, European redwood is used in the construction industry as well as in furniture-making. It is grown commercially in Scandinavia and Russia and is similar to the American red pine.

Hemlock
(*Tsuga heterophylla*)
DENSITY: *31 lb/cu.ft (500 kg/m³)*

Hemlock can vary in color from almost white to a golden red. It has a straight grain with well defined growth rings and is easy to work to a fine finish. Although it is used to make furniture, hemlock is mainly grown as a substitute for Douglas fir and is much in demand for the construction of houses and for plywood. The chief source of hemlock is North America.

Parana pine
(*Araucaria angustifolia*)
DENSITY: *33 lb/cu.ft (530 kg/m³)*

Parana pine is generally a deep straw color but often has deep red streaks. It is evenly textured and has virtually no visible growth rings or knots. For these reasons, it is a popular wood for furniture-making. As it is available in long lengths, it is also used to make mouldings and staircases. The Parana pine is very similar to the Monkey Puzzle tree and is exported from Brazil.

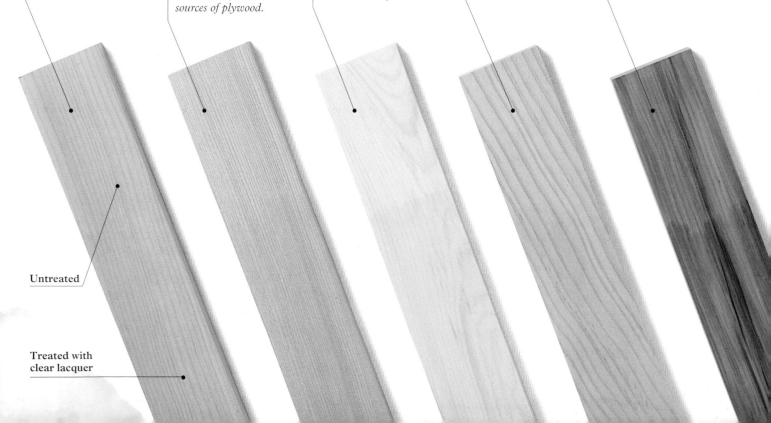

Untreated

Treated with clear lacquer

instance, is a light, almost spongy wood but it contains natural insect and fungi repellents. These chemicals render the wood almost impervious to rot and decay so it is ideal for use outside.

Most softwoods tend to be light in color and many also have knots. In some species, such as yew, knots are highly prized as they are usually stable and give the wood character. In other species, like European redwood, knots are, however, a nuisance. Resinous ('live') knots seep resin that can ruin the finish of a piece of work unless they are sealed with a film of shellac (*see page 61*); dry knots can work loose and fall out, leaving unsightly holes in the wood.

Western red cedar (Thuja plicata)
DENSITY: *23 lb/cu.ft (368 kg/m³)*
This is the lightest softwood in general commercial use. Reddish-brown in color, it has conspicuous growth rings and a straight grain. It is resistant to decay but is a brittle wood so is of limited use in furniture-making. It also has a slightly pungent smell that is not endearing. Western red cedar is grown commercially in North America where it is often used to make clapboards and siding.

Yew (Taxus baccata)
DENSITY: *42 lb/cu.ft (672 kg/m³)*
When it is first sawn, yew heartwood is a beautiful red color but fades to a dull brown; the sapwood is almost white in color. The grain is very fine and rarely straight which gives the wood character. Yew is an extremely hard, durable wood and is used to make furniture as well as craft items. As yew is slow-growing it is not grown commercially; it occurs naturally in Europe and parts of Asia and Africa.

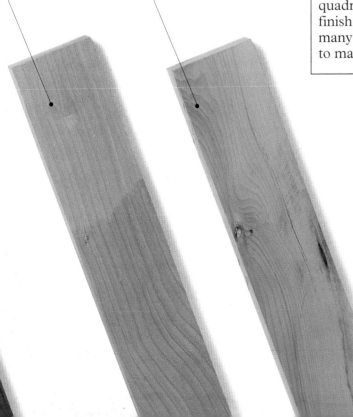

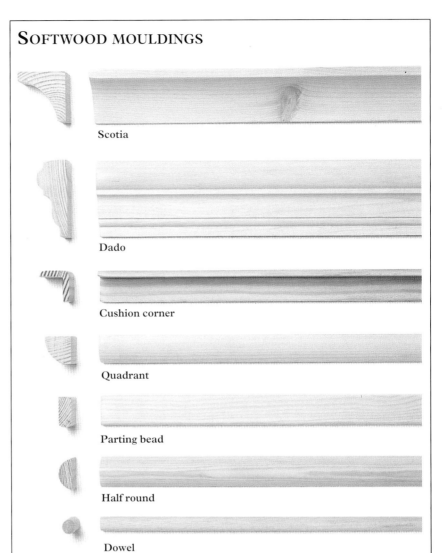

SOFTWOOD MOULDINGS

Scotia

Dado

Cushion corner

Quadrant

Parting bead

Half round

Dowel

Mouldings – decorative or practical strips of wood – are usually, but not always, made from a softwood such as pine. Some mouldings are designed to fulfil a purpose. For instance, parting bead is used to separate the sashes in sash windows. Half round, quadrant and corner mouldings, on the other hand, can be used to finish off pieces or to cover gaps. Dado is just one example of the many sorts of purely decorative mouldings, and dowel can be used to make joints (*see pages 78–79*) and rungs.

Choosing softwood

The least expensive softwoods tend to be easy to work by hand because they are not dense and often have a straight grain. However, the lack of grain makes them appear uninteresting, and it is often best to coat a piece made from softwood with varnish, stain or paint (*see pages 62-63*). If you want to leave the wood bare, select a softwood with character – yew, Parana pine or hemlock, for instance.

For outdoor projects, choose a wood like Cedar of Lebanon, which is exceptionally durable, or redwood. Although Western red cedar is also resistant to fungi and insect attack, it is not strong and is best reserved for fences and shingles. You should treat these two woods, and certainly all other softwoods, with at least two coats of preservative if they are to be placed outside.

HARDWOODS

Hardwoods come from deciduous or broad-leaved trees and they offer a far wider choice of colors, characteristics and overall effects than softwoods. Explore a few different types, and you will begin to appreciate their natural beauty and potential.

HARDWOOD TREES usually grow much slower than conifers and the wood they produce is generally heavier, denser, and more durable. There are, of course, exceptions. The balsa tree is classified as a hardwood but grows very swiftly and produces the lightest of all woods!

It takes tens, if not hundreds, of years for most deciduous trees to grow to maturity, and so hardwood is generally a great deal more expensive than softwood to buy. Against this, you have to weigh up the advantages of hardwoods – they are invariably more attractive when finished than softwoods and last a good deal longer.

Within the family of hardwood trees, there is a distinction between temperate and tropical types. Temperate climates, such as those experienced in most of Europe and North America, generate trees that are

Teak
(Tectona grandis)
DENSITY: *45 lb/cu.ft (720 kg/m³)*
Teak is golden brown in color with a slightly uneven texture and a greasy feel. It is one of the most durable of all woods and is traditionally used in ship-building. It is also commonly used to make outdoor furniture and, because it is resistant to acids, laboratory worktops.

The main sources of teak are Thailand and India, although it is also grown in many other tropical parts of the world.

Iroko
(Chlorophoro excelsa)
DENSITY: *44 lb/cu.ft (700 kg/m³)*
Yellow to deep brown in color, iroko has an irregular grain pattern and an open texture. It shares many properties with teak, and is often used as a teak substitute, but is not so oily.

As iroko is available in large boards, it is sometimes used to make table tops but is more usually reserved for garden furniture. The principal source of iroko is West Africa.

Utile
(Entandrophragma utile)
DENSITY: *30 lb/cu.ft (480 kg/m³)*
Reddish-brown with a coarse texture and an interlocking grain, utile is an outstanding wood that is much sought after for furniture-making. As it is a strong wood, it is used to make window frames and doors. Plywood is often faced with veneers of utile. The main exporting region for utile is West Africa.

Sapele
(Entandrophagma cylindricum)
DENSITY: *44 lb/cu.ft (700 kg/m³)*
Reddish-brown with a coarse but very even grain, sapele occasionally has an attractive mottled appearance and is very strong and durable. In many respects it is similar to mahogany and is used to make all kinds of furniture, both indoors and out. As a veneer, sapele is often put to good use on pianos and doors. The bulk of sapele comes from West African countries

African mahogany
(Khaya spp.)
DENSITY: *30 lb/cu.ft (480 kg/m³)*
Pale-pink to red-brown, this mahogany has a medium texture and a characteristic striped appearance.

Although it is a comparatively light hardwood, it is used for making all sorts of furniture as well as veneers. Recycled wood is often of better quality than new lumber. African mahogany grows in all parts of the continent.

Untreated

Treated with clear lacquer

subject to annual cycles of growth and dormancy. This growth pattern is evident as annual rings or grain in the wood's structure. Tropical regions such as Central Africa, Malaysia and Brazil sustain trees that are almost constantly growing and the wood is therefore more evenly textured.

Choosing hardwoods

Deciding on color and texture are the two obvious steps you have to take when selecting a hardwood. There is no shortage of choice as you can buy hardwoods in shades from white, through a range of browns and reds, to black. Textures vary too: some woods, such as beech, have flecks while others, like oak, have a characteristically strong grain. However, before you make your choice, consider the country of origin of the wood. Temperate hardwoods are harvested from regions that are generally more capable of regeneration than those taken from tropical countries.

Looking for faults

When you buy a board of hardwood, check its condition. Wood that has been artificially dried in kilns is less stable than wood that has been left to dry out (season) naturally. Some hardwoods take many years to season properly and if they are worked too soon they are likely to distort. Look for any obvious splits, cracks and warps which are particularly common in tropical woods that have been imported into a dry climate.

Unlike softwood, hardwood is usually sold rough-sawn so make sure you buy lumber that is slightly larger than you actually require. This will allow you some leeway when you plane down and prepare the wood for a project.

Elm
(Ulmus spp.)
DENSITY: 34 lb/cu.ft
(540 kg/m³)
Light reddish-brown with very distinct annual growth rings, elm has a coarse texture. It is an attractive wood and is used to make tables and cupboards as well as English Windsor chairs. There are several types of elm that range across the whole of the northern hemisphere, from North America to Japan. They all share similar characteristics.

Cherry
(Prunus spp.)
DENSITY: 40 lb/cu.ft
(640 kg/m³)
When it is first cut, cherry is a pale, pinkish-brown but, on exposure to air, it darkens and can become almost mahogany-red. It has a fine texture and is straight-grained. Two sorts are used commercially – European and American. European cherry is usually only available in limited quantities. Both kinds are decorative woods and are much sought after by cabinetmakers.

English oak
(Quercus robur)
DENSITY: 45 lb/cu.ft
(720 kg/m³)
Mid-tan to brown in color, English oak has a distinctive grain and has been used for centuries in all manner of construction, including boat-building and furniture. It combines strength and durability with good looks and is very pleasing to work provided your tools are sharp. Like most temperate hardwoods, it is very prone to shrinkage while seasoning (which can take a considerable time) and is particularly subject to splitting.

Beech
(Fagus spp.)
DENSITY: 43 lb/cu.ft
(690 kg/m³)
Beech can range from pale brown to pink in color. It has a smooth and even grain texture and, in Europe, rivals oak as the most used commercial hardwood. It is an outstanding wood for furniture and is also often used for making chopping blocks and numerous other culinary and household items. The various types of beech grow readily all over the northern hemisphere.

Ash
(Fraxinus spp.)
DENSITY: 45 lb/cu.ft
(720 kg/m³)
Straight and boldly grained, ash is creamy-white with occasionally darker heartwood. Its elasticity and toughness have made it almost indispensable for agricultural vehicles, shafts, handles, ladders, and sporting equipment. It is also a pliable wood and can be bent into curves. Ash is an important commercial hardwood and grows readily in North America and Europe.

BOARD AND SHEET MATERIALS

*The quality of man-made sheet materials has improved dramatically in recent years
and this has made life considerably easier for woodworkers who no longer have to
join planks together to make wide boards.*

TODAY, most lumber merchants sell a range of sheet materials which can be sawn and shaped for numerous applications. Man-made boards can be divided into three categories – fiberboards, particle boards and laminates. All of these have their advantages and disadvantages but generally they are cheaper than solid wood, more stable when exposed to changes in temperature and humidity, and are stronger when compared to solid wood of the same thickness.

Sheet materials are usually sold as 8 x 4 ft (2.44 x 1.2 2m) boards but you can often buy half- or quarter-boards and you may even be able to get offcuts for small jobs. The various types of board available are usually graded. For example, plywood is generally graded from A to D, with A having the best quality veneer. Surface appearance is not the only thing to look for when buying. Boards that are going to be exposed to dampness – for instance in the kitchen or outside in the garden – should be resistant to moisture penetration. Most fiber and particle boards are available in moisture resistant (MR) grades and robust, exterior-grade plywoods are generally called Water and Boil Proof (WBP).

BUYING AND STORING BOARDS

- Avoid boards that have been left exposed to the elements, as the core may have swollen.
- Check that the edges haven't been scratched or bruised in storage.
- Do not buy boards that have any unsightly knots or splits.
- Buy boards of a quality appropriate for the particular job and buy water-resistant sheets if it is necessary.
- Store boards upright, preferably clear of the floor on battens.

Exterior-grade, pine-faced plywood
Made by gluing wafers of wood together in a sandwich, plywoods are exceptionally strong. Pine-faced boards are relatively inexpensive and come in thicknesses ranging from ⅛in (3 mm) to 1⅛in (30 mm). Use exterior-grade plywood for outdoor or kitchen projects and, if required, cover the edges with strips of timber.

Pine-faced laminboard
This is an expensive alternative to conventional plywood. The inner core comprises thin strips of solid wood glued side to side; the faces are fine sheets of plywood glued and pressed to the core. Laminboard is very strong and stable and is excellent for projects where the slightest distortion could be a problem.

3-ply board
This is inexpensive and is often used for making drawer bottoms and as the backing in bookcases and cabinets. A solid core of wood is sandwiched between the face (front) and back veneers. When the core is thicker than the outer plywood veneers, the board is called 'balanced'. 3-ply board is not as rigid as boards made from more layers (plies) of wood.

7-ply marine board
This is a plywood made of water-resistant hardwoods which are bonded with a very strong phenolic glue. Marine plywood is not damaged by water, steam, temperature changes or fungi, but it is expensive and is best reserved for jobs where durability is essential. As its name implies, marine plywood is used to make boats.

Sapele-faced blockboard
Blockboard is an extremely rigid laminate. The core, made from strips of solid wood laid edge-to-edge, is sandwiched between plies faced with sapele, an African hardwood. Thicknesses range from ½in (12 mm) to 1in (25 mm). As blockboard has a solid-wood core, screws grip well when they are driven into the edges.

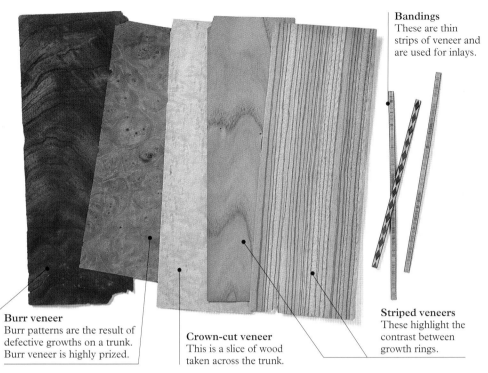

VENEERS

Many types of hardwood are too rare and expensive to be used as solid timber. However, it is possible to achieve the effect of solid, exotic wood by using veneers – thin sections of hardwood which are cut into leaves and are sold individually or in bundles. Veneers are glued and pressed on to a carcass of man-made board or solid timber, but considerable skill is needed to make the job look professional. Veneers should be stored flat in a cool, dry place, otherwise they can start to warp and buckle.

Bandings
These are thin strips of veneer and are used for inlays.

Butt veneer
This is cut from the base of a tree. Irregular growth rings give it its character.

Burr veneer
Burr patterns are the result of defective growths on a trunk. Burr veneer is highly prized.

Crown-cut veneer
This is a slice of wood taken across the trunk.

Striped veneers
These highlight the contrast between growth rings.

Exterior-grade flakeboard
An inexpensive board composed of slivers of wood, glued and pressed together to form a thick layer of shavings which lie parallel with the length of the board. Flakeboard is strong (it is often used as shuttering for concrete) but does not have a perfectly smooth surface. It is best reserved for projects where looks are unimportant.

Melamine-faced chipboard
Chipboard which is coated with melamine provides a decorative surface which is easy to clean. Any number of colors and finishes are available and faced chipboard is commonly used to make kitchen and bedroom furniture. You can hide sawn edges with edging strips. Chipboard can also be faced with hardwood veneers.

Unfaced chipboard
Chipboard is made by bonding and compressing small wood chips together. It has a coarse grain and is not as strong as plywood. Another disadvantage is that it does not hold screws well. However, it is cheap and is adequate for furniture that is to be painted or veneered. Chipboard is available in a variety of thicknesses and a moisture-resistant grade.

Hardboard
Hardboard is produced by chopping up wood shavings into tiny fibers which are then soaked in water. The mix is finally compressed and heated to form a board with a uniform texture. It is sold in thicknesses from 1/16 in (1.5 mm) to 1/2 in (12 mm). Hardboard is slightly flexible but can be used for the backs of cabinets and frames.

Medium-density fiberboard (MDF)
This is one of the newest and most versatile of woodworking materials. MDF is made up of fine particles bonded together with a resin. The close texture can be planed and MDF is a good substitute for solid wood. However, as the surface is so characterless, it is best painted. Thicknesses up to 1¼ in (32 mm) are sold.

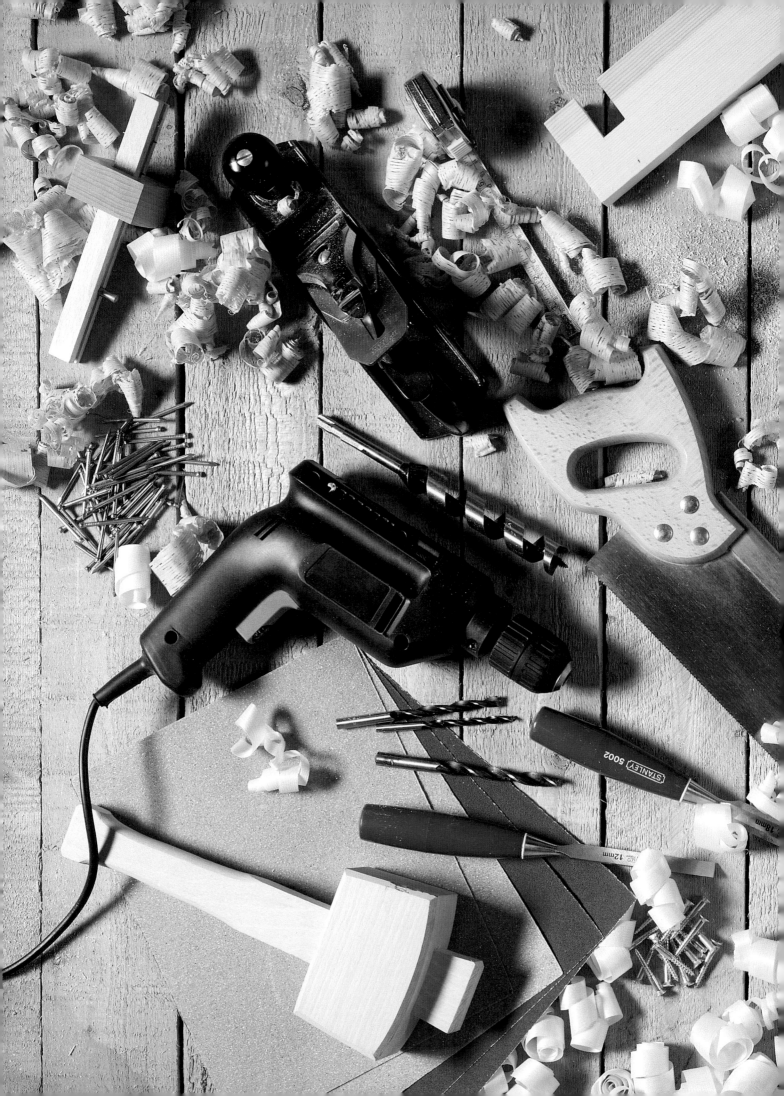

Tools and Techniques

Successful woodworking relies on the ability to use tools efficiently and safely. This section is devoted to illustrating the most essential woodworking tools and shows you how to handle and get the best from them. Build up your collection of tools gradually and practice working with them as often as you can.

A WOODWORKER'S TOOLKIT

Before you can start on any woodwork project, you must have tools. For a modest outlay, you can equip yourself with a few choice items that will prove invaluable over the years and will be used again and again.

A WOODWORKER is never entirely happy with his toolkit – no matter how many tools are in it, there is always something that can be added. It is best to start with the bare essentials before investing in specialist equipment that is invariably expensive. Buy the best quality tools you can afford – there is no reason why they should not last a good few years provided they are well looked after and are stored carefully after use. If possible, choose tools with brass fittings, which will not rust, and consider how each item feels. Select handles that fit your hands and are comfortable to use – this is particularly important when choosing screwdrivers.

Concertina toolbox
Steel boxes are tough and expand to reveal handy compartments; plastic versions are less durable.

Screwdrivers
You will need at least two – one for slot-head screws and one for Phillips-head screws. Shaped (not cylindrical) handles are best.

Adjustable wrench
A medium-sized spanner will cope with most nuts and bolts.

Chisels
A set of four chisels in sizes from ¼in (6mm) to 1in (25mm) will cope with most projects.

Claw hammer
Steel or hickory shafts are best (cheap hammers can be dangerous); 20oz (550gm) is a good weight.

Paint brushes
Good quality brushes last longest and give a smooth finish.

Mortise/Marking gauge
Hardwood gauges last longest.

Screws

Nails

Fixings
Keep a supply of fixings in various sizes.

Panel nails

The essentials
You don't need a vast array of sophisticated equipment to start working with wood. Illustrated on these pages are some of the most useful of all woodworking tools, and you will miss them if you don't have them at hand. A power drill is the only essential electrical tool as it makes light work of boring holes. Treat your tools with respect – keep them sharp, clean and dry – and they will last for years.

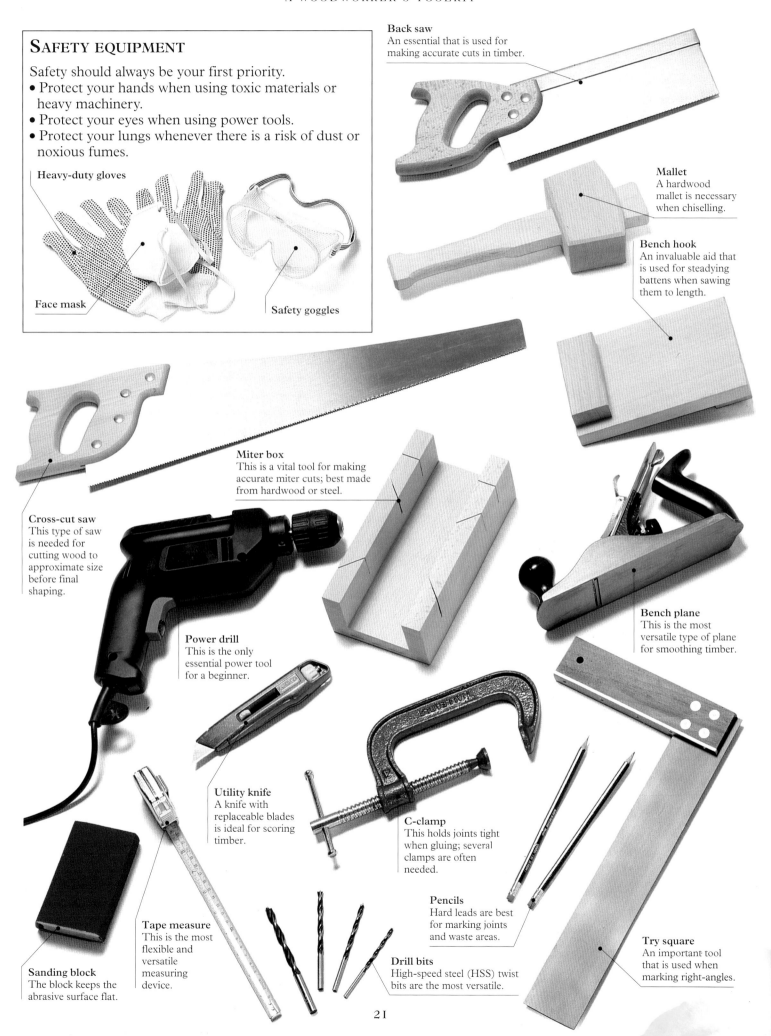

SAFETY EQUIPMENT

Safety should always be your first priority.
- Protect your hands when using toxic materials or heavy machinery.
- Protect your eyes when using power tools.
- Protect your lungs whenever there is a risk of dust or noxious fumes.

Heavy-duty gloves

Face mask

Safety goggles

Back saw
An essential that is used for making accurate cuts in timber.

Mallet
A hardwood mallet is necessary when chiselling.

Bench hook
An invaluable aid that is used for steadying battens when sawing them to length.

Cross-cut saw
This type of saw is needed for cutting wood to approximate size before final shaping.

Miter box
This is a vital tool for making accurate miter cuts; best made from hardwood or steel.

Power drill
This is the only essential power tool for a beginner.

Bench plane
This is the most versatile type of plane for smoothing timber.

Utility knife
A knife with replaceable blades is ideal for scoring timber.

C-clamp
This holds joints tight when gluing; several clamps are often needed.

Pencils
Hard leads are best for marking joints and waste areas.

Sanding block
The block keeps the abrasive surface flat.

Tape measure
This is the most flexible and versatile measuring device.

Drill bits
High-speed steel (HSS) twist bits are the most versatile.

Try square
An important tool that is used when marking right-angles.

MEASURING AND MARKING TOOLS

Good results are reliant on accurate marking and measuring. It is worth investing in a few specialist tools to help you in these two critical tasks. If you buy good-quality tools you will be able to rely on them for many years to come.

THE KEY to successful furniture-making is the ability to mark out timber precisely. You need only a few specialist tools for accurate marking but they must be of good quality. Inferior tools do not last and can be inaccurate. For example, a marking gauge made from inexpensive softwood is likely to warp or twist. Good tool storage is also essential – if vulnerable tools are thrown into a toolbox alongside hammers they are inevitably going to get damaged. The best place to store items such as a try square or sliding bevel is on a

wall-mounted tool rack. You can buy such racks, but it is not difficult to construct a rack to suit your own personal needs and requirements.

Always wipe down tools with steel components, such as a try square, with an oily rag before putting them away in a dry place after use. Pay particular attention to wiping away fingerprint smudges – they invariably contain salt and can encourage rust to develop. Given just a short time, rust can eat away at steel and render straightedges hopelessly inaccurate.

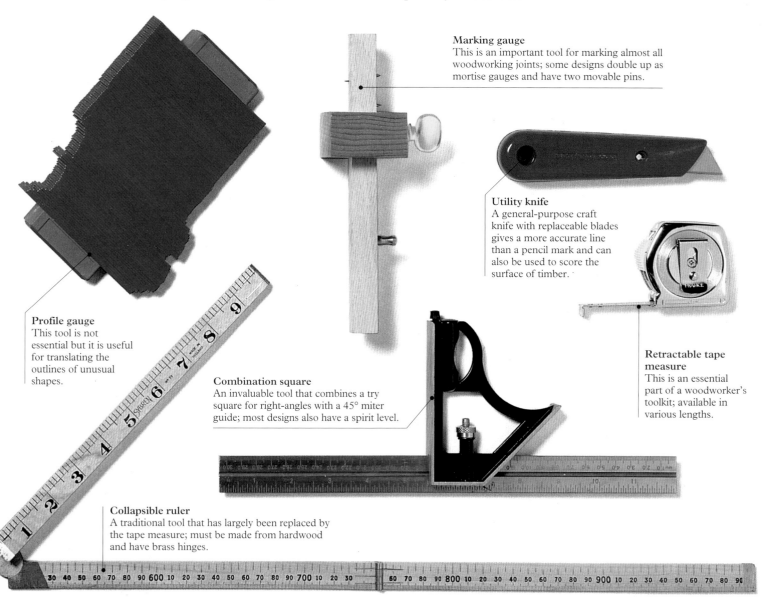

Marking gauge
This is an important tool for marking almost all woodworking joints; some designs double up as mortise gauges and have two movable pins.

Utility knife
A general-purpose craft knife with replaceable blades gives a more accurate line than a pencil mark and can also be used to score the surface of timber.

Retractable tape measure
This is an essential part of a woodworker's toolkit; available in various lengths.

Profile gauge
This tool is not essential but it is useful for translating the outlines of unusual shapes.

Combination square
An invaluable tool that combines a try square for right-angles with a 45° miter guide; most designs also have a spirit level.

Collapsible ruler
A traditional tool that has largely been replaced by the tape measure; must be made from hardwood and have brass hinges.

TOOL MAINTENANCE

- Protect your marking and measuring tools from knocks and always wipe them clean after use; oil bare metal to prevent corrosion.
- Make sure your try square is set at exactly 90° by using it to mark a line across a board from a straight edge. Then reverse the square and check that the steel edge lines up exactly with the first mark.
- Take care of your tape measure: try not to let it bend back on itself and never allow it to snap back into the case as this can loosen the end piece.
- Protect plastic tools like a protractor from getting scratched – smudges and lines can obscure gradations.
- Occasionally oil any tools that have moving parts, such as a sliding bevel. Jointed tools have a tendency to seize up.

Spirit level
This is useful for finding and checking horizontal and vertical lines; available in various lengths.

Plumbline
This is a basic tool for determining a true vertical.

Sliding bevel
Although not essential, a sliding bevel is useful for transferring unusual angles on to a workpiece.

Try square
This is one of the most-used tools in any woodworker's toolkit; used to mark or check right-angles on timber.

Straightedge
A crucial tool that is essential for marking and checking straight lines.

Protractor
This is a convenient tool for measuring and marking angles.

MEASURING AND MARKING TECHNIQUES

*The critical steps of measuring and marking timber are easy to master. Care
and patience are the keys to success. Always remember that the width of a
thick pencil line can make the difference between a tight joint and a flimsy one,
so keep your pencil sharpened to a fine point.*

WHENEVER possible, mark up timber from a face or edge that you know to be straight. If necessary, plane a face perfectly flat first (*see pages 42-45*).

When you mark up components that all have the same dimensions – for example, four table legs – tape or clamp them together and mark them as a group. This reduces the chances of introducing small errors.

Always take note of the old saying, 'measure twice, cut once'. It is hard to rectify mistakes after you have started sawing or cutting.

Use a hard-lead pencil to mark cutting lines and sharpen it to a fine point.

When you use an adjustable try square, make sure you tighten up the screw that locks the rule.

A retractable tape measure is a good tool to use for measuring up boards, but measure and mark twice to eradicate errors.

GOOD MEASURING TECHNIQUE
Keep your head and eyes over the line or mark you are making and use clean, undamaged tools with clear calibrations that are easy to read.

Using a try square
Hold the stock (handle) of the square tight against the edge of the board or plank at the point where you want to draw the line across at right angles. Make sure the blade of the square is flat, and mark the line with the pencil held tight against the steel edge.

Marking with a try square
Make just one pass with the pencil. Try to hold the pencil at a steady angle as you draw it across the face of the wood.

SCORING A CUTTING LINE
Before you saw a piece of timber or a man-made board, score the surface along your marked line with a sharp utility knife. This slices through the topmost fibers and prevents them from splintering and leaving a tattered edge.

Ensure that your utility knife is fitted with a clean, sharp blade and draw it across the face of the workpiece against a steel straightedge. One pass with the knife should be sufficient.

When you make the cut, be sure to position the saw on the waste side of the scored line and you should be left with a neat, clean edge.

Scoring the surface
Hold the knife at right-angles to the wood against a straightedge. Keep your other hand out of the line of the blade.

USING A MARKING GAUGE

Use your marking gauge to scribe any line you want to run parallel to a straight edge. The pin in the shaft of the gauge scribes the line as you run the stock (the movable block on the gauge) up against the side of the straight edge.

Set your gauge by first loosening the screw that secures the stock. Measure the depth of the line you want – from the pin to the stock – either directly from a workpiece or using a rule. Tighten the screw and then hold the stock against the straight edge with the pin pointing down against the timber you want to be marked. Move the gauge up the straight edge in one continuous movement while allowing the pin to score a shallow line.

Measuring off a workpiece
Hold the stock against the side of the timber and slide out the pin. When the pin is aligned with the edge of the wood, tighten the screw to secure the stock.

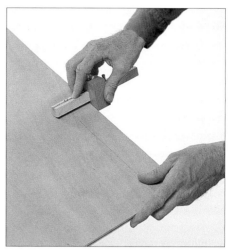

Transferring the measurement
Hold the stock firmly against the straight edge and move it along. Make sure the pin points downwards at an angle against the wood to scribe the line.

Squaring up a piece of wood

If you have to saw up a broad plank or large block of wood, mark cutting lines right the way around the workpiece so that you can check your cut for accuracy on both sides of the wood as you progress. Another reason for marking round or 'squaring up' a piece of wood is to check whether or not the faces and edges are square to each other. Wood from a yard, or even wood you have planed yourself, can appear to be perfectly square when in fact it is not. Squaring up is a foolproof way of finding out.

The first step is to pencil a line at right-angles to one straight edge right across the workpiece using a try square as a guide.

When you have drawn the first line, mark down the sides or edges. To mark an edge, carefully position your try square against a face and line up the steel blade with the first pencil mark.

After marking the sides comes the moment of truth. With the stock of the try square pushed tightly against an edge, draw a line down from one side mark toward the other. If your marking has been accurate and the wood is square, the fourth line should join the two side marks and cross the wood at right-angles.

If the side marks do not line up at right-angles, first check your marking for small inaccuracies. If the marks down the sides are perfectly aligned with the first pencil mark, you can be sure that the wood is not square and needs planing (*see pages 42-45*). With wide boards, a large discrepancy usually implies that the side edges are not perfectly parallel to each other. Carefully measure across the board at four or five points to check whether or not the sides are exactly parallel.

Marking the first face
Hold the try square tight against one edge and make sure the blade is flat. Draw a pencil line right across the face of the wood.

Marking the edges
Line up the blade of the try square with the line across the face. Draw crisp, clean lines down both sides.

Finishing the sequence
To ensure accuracy, hold the pencil point on a side mark and slide the try square up to it before drawing the line.

COMBINATION SQUARE

A combination square comprises a rule which slides through a steel body. The rule can be locked by twisting a screw in the body of the tool. The body has two faces – one angled at 90° to the rule and one at 45°. This means that you can use a combination square to mark and measure both right-angles and miters. When using a combination square, be sure to tighten the screw fully so that the rule cannot slide in and out or laterally.

Marking a miter
Lock the rule in place then position the 45° face against the side of the timber and scribe a line.

Using a mortise gauge
A mortise gauge is a useful tool for marking accurate mortises prior to cutting out joints. It is similar to a conventional marking gauge except that it has one fixed pin and one sliding pin (in fact, most mortise gauges have a single fixed pin on the reverse side so that the tool can be used as a marking gauge as well).

To use a marking gauge first loosen the screw on the stock (the sliding part of the tool). This enables you to move the stock as well as the sliding pin which is fixed to a brass bar set into the body of the tool.

Hold one side of the chisel you want to use to cut the mortise against the fixed pin, then slide the movable pin up until it is in line with the other side of the blade. Hold the sliding pin firm and adjust the position of the stock until it is the distance required from the pins. Tighten up the screw to lock the stock and the sliding pin.

Marking the mortise
Hold the stock firmly against the edge of the timber you are marking and make sure that the two pins are in contact with the timber. Slide the gauge along the timber and the pins will score two parallel lines. Avoid pressing hard on the pins as they could get diverted by the grain.

Setting the pins
Slide the movable pin up until the gap between it and the fixed pin matches the width of the chisel.

Scribing with the gauge
Lock the stock and the movable pin, then slide the gauge against the timber to mark two parallel lines.

Checking edges and faces with a straightedge
You can use a straightedge to check that broad surfaces, as well as edges, are level.

To check an edge, clamp the plank or board vertically in your workbench and position your straightedge on top. Align your eyes with the bottom of the straightedge and look for any signs of light peeping through undulations or dents.

To check a broad surface, lay the board down flat and position the straightedge on top. Again, lower your eyes to the level of the board and look for any gaps under the straightedge. Keep your eyes still and swivel the rule about its center. Continue to move the straightedge across and along the board until you are satisfied that you have covered the entire surface.

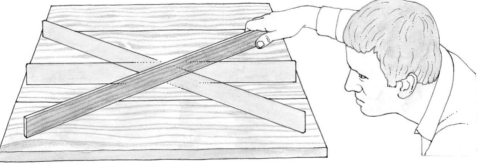

Checking an edge
Place the straightedge on top of the edge and, keeping your eyes level with the rule, look for gaps and undulations.

Checking a broad surface
Swivel the straightedge to cover all parts of the board while looking for low points.

Finding horizontals and verticals

Walls and ceilings can look vertical and horizontal when they are in fact slightly out of true. For this reason, mark accurate guide lines whenever you fix an item of furniture to a wall.

For marking horizontal lines, for example to fit a corner cupboard, it is best to use a spirit level. First pencil in the approximate height you want the guide line to be. Position your spirit level against the mark and adjust it until the bubble in the phial lies between the two lines. Pencil a line across the top of the level. To mark a reverse wall, hold the level against the line you have already drawn and pencil a second line.

To find a true vertical, whether for an indoor or outdoor project, use a plumbline. Simply hold or hang the line up and use it as a guide.

Marking a level in a corner
Set the level against one wall at the height you require and adjust it until the bubble lies between the two lines. Draw a pencil line along the level, right into the corner.

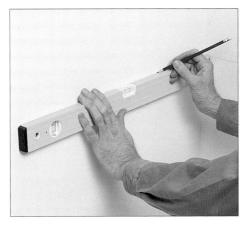

Transferring the level
Place the level on the adjacent wall and adjust its position while keeping the corner end aligned with the pencil line. Mark along the level.

Using a plumbline to find a vertical
To find a true vertical on a wall or for a garden project, hold a plumbline from the uppermost point. Delay making adjustments until the weight is stationary.

MARKING AROUND UNEVEN SURFACES

If you want timber or boards to fit neatly around an awkward outline, the best tool to use when marking up is a profile gauge. You can use a profile gauge to mark around pipework, cornicing, skirting or any other type of moulding. Use a coping saw or jigsaw to cut around the shape once you have transferred the profile to the wood.

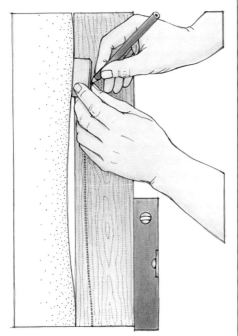

Taking the shape of a moulding
Press the profile gauge tight against the moulding so that the pins of the gauge are pushed into the shape. Make sure you hold the gauge at right-angles to the surface.

Transferring the shape
Lay the gauge on the material to be cut and carefully trace around the profile with a pencil. Don't press on the pins as they are easily moved out of alignment.

Scribing by hand
When making fitted furniture, use a scrap block of wood to scribe the uneven profile of the wall onto the inner face of the timber. Hold a pencil tightly against the block and press against the wall as you move the block over the surface.

SAWS FOR WOODWORKING

You won't get far in woodworking without a saw. In fact, you will probably need at least two – one for reducing wood roughly to size and one for making more accurate cuts.

ALL SAWS cut wood. However, sizes and shapes vary greatly and most saws are made to perform a specific task. For example, different saws are used for cutting across and along the grain.

The two saws that are most frequently used are cross-cut (panel) and tenon saws and these should be the first two saws that you buy; other types can be added to your toolkit gradually as you progress.

Saws should be well looked after. The teeth should be sharpened and set regularly, and it is best to hang them up by the handle rather than storing them away in a box among other tools.

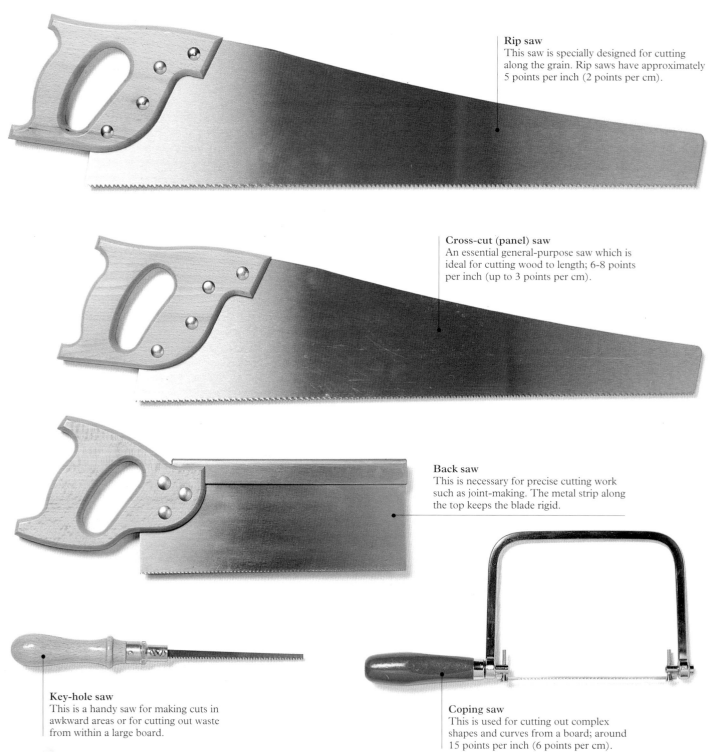

Rip saw
This saw is specially designed for cutting along the grain. Rip saws have approximately 5 points per inch (2 points per cm).

Cross-cut (panel) saw
An essential general-purpose saw which is ideal for cutting wood to length; 6-8 points per inch (up to 3 points per cm).

Back saw
This is necessary for precise cutting work such as joint-making. The metal strip along the top keeps the blade rigid.

Key-hole saw
This is a handy saw for making cuts in awkward areas or for cutting out waste from within a large board.

Coping saw
This is used for cutting out complex shapes and curves from a board; around 15 points per inch (6 points per cm).

Multi-purpose saw

A comparatively recent invention, the multi-purpose saw has hardpoint teeth and can cope with cutting both along and across the grain. Although these saws are excellent for general joinery work, the teeth are too widely spaced and aggressive for very accurate cutting.

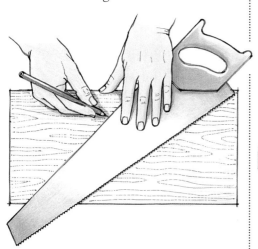

Using a saw as a try square
Some multi-purpose saws have exact 45°
and 90° profiles on the inner handle. These
profiles, although not totally reliable, can
be used for marking cuts.

Miter blocks and boxes

These are made from a hardwood like beech or from hard plastic and are used in conjunction with a back saw for cutting accurate miters. The workpiece is placed in the block or box and the saw is guided by the vertical slots.

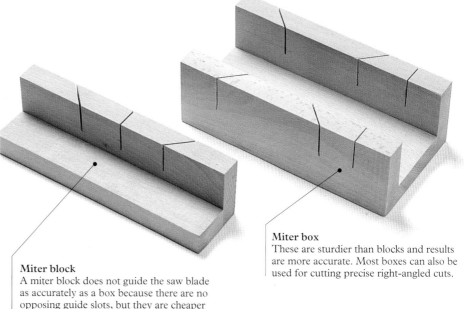

Miter block
A miter block does not guide the saw blade as accurately as a box because there are no opposing guide slots, but they are cheaper and sometimes easier to use.

Miter box
These are sturdier than blocks and results are more accurate. Most boxes can also be used for cutting precise right-angled cuts.

The drawback of wooden blocks or boxes is that the slots can become worn quite quickly and they tend to widen with use. To preserve the life of your block or box, always place the piece you are cutting on top of an offcut so that the base doesn't become damaged.

ALL ABOUT SAW BLADES

Different saws have different teeth. All saw teeth work by shearing off small pieces of wood within the saw cut (known as the kerf), but the shape and size of the teeth vary depending on what the saw is to be used for. Saws such as back or coping saws, that are designed for making narrow, precise cuts, have many small teeth; saws that are made for roughly shaping wood have large, widely set teeth. As anybody who has ever tried will know, it is hard work cutting a large piece of wood with a small saw and almost impossible to cut accurately with a large-toothed saw.

Teeth shapes

A rip saw has teeth that have a steep pitch (angle of the sharpened edge) with plenty of metal behind each cutting edge. Teeth on a cross-cut saw have bevelled leading edges to slice, rather than tear, through the wood fibers.

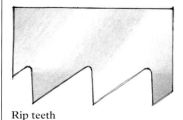

Rip teeth   Cross-cut teeth

Teeth size

Large teeth are found on saws used to cut quickly and efficiently through large pieces of timber. To make finer, cleaner cuts, you need a saw that has a larger number of smaller teeth. Teeth are measured as teeth per inch (TPI) or points per inch (PPI), the metric equivalent being points per cm. Very small saws may have as many as 22 points per inch (9 points per cm).

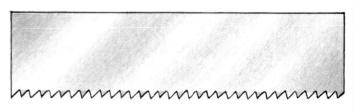

Teeth are measured as points per inch or points per cm.

The set

Teeth are usually 'set' alternately to the left and right so the sawcut is made slightly wider than the blade. This makes cutting more efficient and reduces jamming.

Teeth set alternately to the left and right.

SAWING TECHNIQUES

Sawing is an easy woodworking skill to master once you have established a few basic rules. With practice, the rules become habitual and you make clean, accurate cuts every time.

BEFORE YOU start sawing, make sure that you choose an appropriate type of saw for the job in hand (*see pages 28-29*). Anchor the workpiece securely to a workbench so that it cannot wobble or move, and start the cut slightly to the waste side of the cutting line. The width of a saw cut, although small, can make the difference between a tight joint and a loose joint.

While you saw, keep your dominant eye (usually the right eye) in line with the saw blade. The exception to this rule is when using a coping saw, when it is not always possible to keep your eye lined up with the blade.

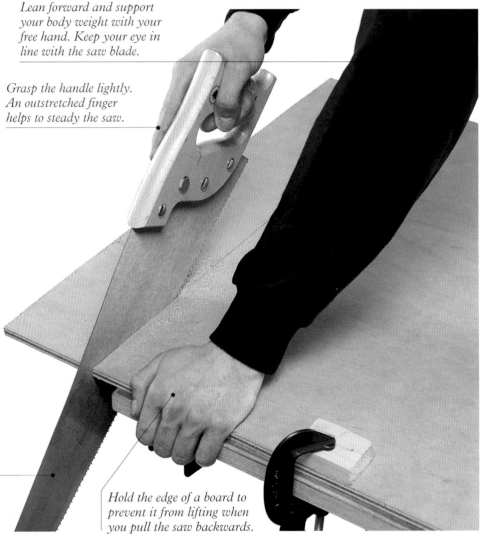

Lean forward and support your body weight with your free hand. Keep your eye in line with the saw blade.

Grasp the handle lightly. An outstretched finger helps to steady the saw.

GOOD SAWING TECHNIQUE
Let the saw do most of the hard work for you. If you force a saw, it will wander off the cutting line.

Use a panel saw for boards and large pieces of wood and a tenon saw for more intricate work where accuracy is crucial.

Hold the edge of a board to prevent it from lifting when you pull the saw backwards.

Supporting the workpiece

Always clamp the wood or board you are working on to a workbench. It is equally important to support the waste wood as well because if you allow it to just fall away as you finish the cut, it will almost certainly tear the wood, possibly leaving an ugly scar on the underside.

Keep as much of the workpiece on the bench as possible and improvise supports for the waste. Try using a clamp to prevent a thin section of board from flapping (see far right) or prop a large offcut on a table to stop it from snapping off. Hold the offcut in the final stages of sawing or, if possible, ask an assistant to hold it steady for you as you cut through.

Starting the cut
Start the saw cut gently. Guide the side of the saw with your thumb but keep it out of the line of the teeth.

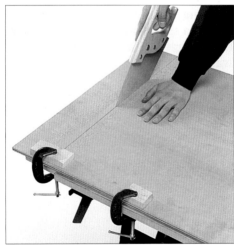

Supporting the offcut
Clamp the offcut to prevent it from flapping. Support a large offcut on a table to stop it from snapping off.

Cutting a tenon

When you cut a tenon, it is best to saw down the grain in stages. If you saw straight down the grain with one cut, your saw will probably wander off the cutting line and the tenon will be crooked.

After you have marked the tenon (*see pages 24-27 and 72-77*), cut the shoulders with a back saw. Next, clamp the workpiece upright and, holding your saw at an angle of around 45°, saw down one cheek to the shoulder. Do the same to the second cheek before reversing the wood in the clamp and sawing down the other sides at an angle of 45°. Finally, saw down both the cheeks horizontally to remove the waste.

Cutting the first side of the tenon
Hold your saw at an angle of 45° and cut down as far as the shoulder. Keep the saw to the waste side of the cutting line.

Repeat with the second side
Before turning the workpiece around, saw down the second cheek, once again holding the saw at an angle of around 45°.

Finishing the cut
When you have made two 45° cuts in each cheek, saw horizontally down to the shoulder cut to remove the waste.

Cutting with a coping saw

To cut a shape out of the middle of a board, first drill a starter hole in the waste area of wood. Thread the coping saw blade through the hole and slot it into the frame.

Saw to the waste side of the cutting line and when you want to change the direction of the cut, gently turn the frame. If you need to adjust the blade further, twist the top and bottom blade supports on the frame. Make sure that the blade is held straight at all times.

Coping saw blades are brittle, so never try to force the saw along. If the workpiece starts to vibrate, move your clamps as near as possible to the cutting line.

Handling a coping saw
Firmly clamp the workpiece and keep the saw blade at right-angles to the wood as you cut out the curve.

Clamp the miter box in, or on to, your workbench so that it cannot swivel around or move, and then place an offcut in the bottom. Mark the piece of wood you want to cut and set it in the box on top of the offcut. Insert a back saw into the appropriate slots and line up the blade just to the waste side of your cutting line. Hold the timber (wood) steady with one hand, or clamp it in position, and saw through the workpiece.

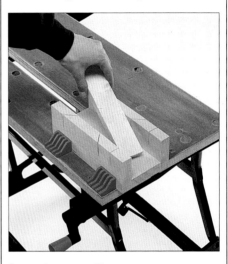

Inserting an offcut
Place an offcut in the bottom of the box to bring the workpiece up to the level of the slots and to protect the base.

Cutting the miter
Hold the workpiece steady with your free hand and line up the back saw blade to the waste side of your cutting line. Saw gently and make sure you cut right through to the offcut underneath before removing the workpiece.

DRILLS AND BITS

You need at least one drill in your toolkit. A power drill is fast and powerful enough to make large holes even in hardwood, but also consider buying a hand drill which is better for more precise, delicate work.

THE MAIN ADVANTAGE of a power drill is its versatility. It can be used to make large or small holes in virtually any material and some models can even be used as screwdrivers. In addition, it is usually possible to fit attachments such as sanding discs to most types (*see pages 70-71*). However, in spite of its obvious convenience, a power drill does have its limitations. You need a power source nearby (unless you use a cordless drill) and you may find it too powerful for refined work.

Hand drills are much slower to use than power drills but this can be an advantage where accuracy and a good finish are essential.

The least expensive way of buying twist and woodwork bits is in sets but special-purpose bits are best bought individually when you need them.

Power drill
Use a power drill to make holes quickly in virtually any material.

Rotary/'hammer' action switch
This enables you to choose between rotary action (for wood) and 'hammer' action (for masonry).

Countersink bit
This is a special-purpose bit for making recesses for screw heads.

Adjustable chuck
The steel jaws inside the chuck grip the bit. Most drill chucks are tightened by a key but this fast-action version does not require one.

Trigger
Squeeze the trigger to turn on the drill.

Drill collar
The collar is a standard size so it can be slotted into most drill stands.

Hand countersink
This is a manual version of the countersink bit.

Bradawl
This is shaped like a sharp screwdriver and is used to make starter holes for screws.

Moulded plastic casing
This enables you to grip the drill like a pistol.

Masonry bit
This is a tungsten carbide-tipped bit for boring holes in masonry.

Hand drill
This is a useful tool for making small screw holes up to 10mm (³/₈in) in diameter. One hand holds and pushes the drill while the other turns the cogged handle which drives the chuck.

Spade bit (wood-boring bit)
This is for making large-diameter holes.

Chuck key holder
This keeps the chuck key within easy reach.

Power-drill bit sets
HSS (High speed steel) twist bits can make holes through soft metals as well as wood. Woodwork bits have sharp spurs on the cutting edges and are excellent for making clean, accurate holes in timber. For a comprehensive range of sizes, buy bits in boxed sets.

Gimlet
This is similar to a bradawl but the screw thread enables it to bore deeper holes.

Twist drills   Woodwork or 'dowel' bits

Special-purpose bits

There are several types of bit that are made to perform specific tasks. You will probably only need a few of these.

The hinge-cutter is designed to bore broad, shallow holes to take the special hinges that are commonly found in chipboard furniture. The plug cutter is a very specialized bit that is used to cut out cylindrical plugs of wood for concealing screw heads below the surface of a workpiece.

The all-in-one bit is one of the most practical of all the special-purpose bits and is available in sizes to match most common screws. This useful bit drills a pilot hole, clearance hole and countersunk recess in one action.

If you are making dowel joints (*see pages 78-79*), it may be worth buying a dowelling kit that contains everything you need: a woodwork bit that has spurs, a depth gauge that slides over the end of the bit, dowelling pins, and pre-cut fluted dowels. You can buy dowelling kits in a variety of sizes.

An auger bit has deep spirals and a screw point that centers the bit accurately and pulls it through the workpiece. Augers are generally used to make deep, precise holes – the long spirals ensure the bit stays aligned as it sinks into the wood. An auger bit for use with a power drill should have a cylindrical shank that can be fitted into a standard type of chuck.

TRADITIONAL HAND BRACE

A hand brace is an excellent tool for drilling large-diameter holes very accurately. To use a hand brace, fit a bit and place the palm of one hand on the top knob. Using your body weight, press down towards the workpiece and, with your other hand, rotate the handle in a clockwise direction.

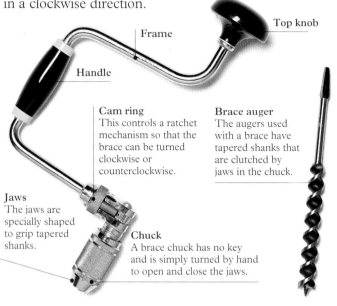

Frame

Top knob

Handle

Cam ring
This controls a ratchet mechanism so that the brace can be turned clockwise or counterclockwise.

Brace auger
The augers used with a brace have tapered shanks that are clutched by jaws in the chuck.

Jaws
The jaws are specially shaped to grip tapered shanks.

Chuck
A brace chuck has no key and is simply turned by hand to open and close the jaws.

Cupboard hinge-cutter
This is used to make the recesses for concealed hinges in chipboard furniture.

Plug cutter
This cuts plugs of wood for covering screw heads.

All-in-one bit
This cuts pilot and clearance holes plus a countersunk recess.

Dowelling bit

Depth marker

Fluted dowel

Dowelling pin

Dowelling kit
This comprises a dowelling bit, depth marker, dowelling pins and fluted dowels.

Auger bits for power drills
These have cylindrical shanks. Use them for making deep holes.

Drill-hole profiles
Different drill bits create different hole profiles, as you can see in the illustration below. A center bit is almost identical to an auger but has a less pronounced spiral.

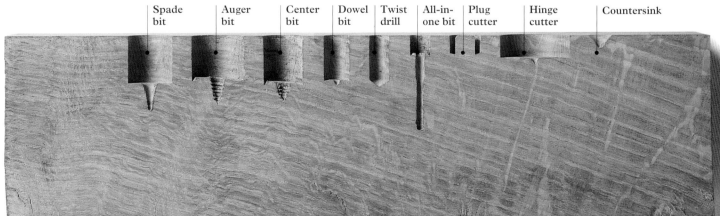

| Spade bit | Auger bit | Center bit | Dowel bit | Twist drill | All-in-one bit | Plug cutter | Hinge cutter | Countersink |

DRILLING TECHNIQUES

Woodworking projects invariably demand clean, precise holes for screws or dowels. Take the time to master a few essential skills and you will drill accurate holes every time.

DRILLING MIGHT APPEAR to be one of the most basic of all woodworking techniques but nevertheless making holes requires patience and care – an imprecise hole can ruin a project.

Using a depth stop

Depth stops are invaluable aids when it comes to drilling holes only part of the way into wood. Off-the-shelf depth stops can be either steel (with grub screws in the side to lock them in place) or rubber and come in various sizes to match the diameters of most drill bits.

Fitting a depth stop
Slide on the depth stop and measure the depth of hole you require from the drill point.

An improvised depth stop
Make your own visual depth stop by wrapping a piece of colored tape around the bit at the depth you require.

GOOD DRILLING TECHNIQUE
Use a sharp bit of the correct size and type and be sure that your drill is set to a medium speed – not fast.

Take care to keep the drill vertical.

Anchor the workpiece with a clamp so that it cannot twist or vibrate as you drill.

Place an offcut underneath the workpiece to protect the bench.

Colored tape wrapped around the drill bit makes a good depth stop.

DRILLING TIPS

Drill into waste timber
Clamp the workpiece over an offcut and slip a scrap of wood under the jaw of the clamp to prevent damage to the workpiece.

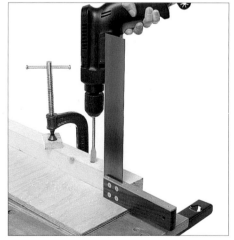

Drilling vertically
Drilling holes at exactly 90° can be tricky. Stand a try square next to the drill and check from the side that the bit is vertical.

Drilling from both sides

Sometimes a hole has to be made all the way through a piece of wood. If one side of the hole is to be covered, you can drill straight through the wood and into a scrap board on the bench. However, if you use a spade bit or an auger (bits with a tip at the end), the wood will splinter as the exit hole is made. To get around this problem and make a clean hole, the solution is to drill the hole from both sides of the workpiece so that the bit never bursts through the wood.

Drill from one side
Drill into the wood from one side. Clamp the wood firmly in a vice or workbench jaws close to the position of the hole.

Drill from the other side
When the tip of the bit protrudes through the wood, remove the bit and drill from the other side.

Using a brace and bit

A brace is designed to drive large, wide drill bits slowly into wood. The cranked shape of the drill produces a substantial amount of turning power that can, most importantly, be controlled easily.

Although braces have largely been superseded by power drills, they still have their uses and many craftsmen prefer to use them when making quality furniture. A brace is ideal for driving wide auger bits (*see page 33*) through hardwood to make clean, accurate holes with straight sides. Practice on offcuts of wood to master using a brace.

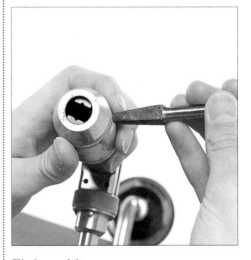

Fitting a bit
Most braces have alligator jaws that can only accept bits which have tapered shanks (they cannot accommodate ordinary twist bits). Turn the handle counter-clockwise, holding the chuck still, to open the jaws.

USING A DRILL STAND

A drill stand enables you to make precise holes every time. With most types of stand, the drill is held firm in a clamped collar which is attached to a vertical column over a steel base. The drill is raised and lowered by pulling a pivoting handle or rotating a lever. The workpiece is clamped underneath the drill on the base, and by adjusting the integral depth gauge on the stand, you can drill extremely accurate holes to a given depth.

Drilling a stopped hole

Lower the drill bit over the workpiece to align its mark, then clamp the workpiece. Adjust the depth gauge, switch on, and lower the drill to make the hole.

Drilling a through hole

Place an offcut underneath the workpiece and anchor both with a vise or clamp. Make sure that the bit cannot pass right through the offcut.

Depth gauge
This governs how far the drill can be lowered.

Feed lever
Pull the lever towards you to lower the drill down to the stand.

Drill collar
This is a clamp that holds the neck of the drill rigid. When fixing a drill, make sure its lead is to one side.

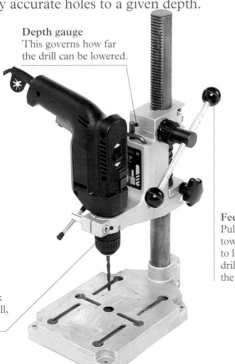

Drilling a hole
Place the palm of your hand over the top handle and turn the cranked handle clockwise. For tough jobs, move your body weight over the brace.

CHISELS AND CUTTING TOOLS

Chisels are among the most essential of all woodworking tools as they are used for making nearly all types of joint. To be effective they need to be sharp, so you will need a sharpening stone as well.

THE MOST economical way of buying chisels is to choose a set of three or four in different sizes. Although you can buy them individually, this can work out to be an expensive option as you will probably need at least three. Look for quality when selecting chisels and, in particular, check that the blades are made from tempered and hardened steel as these give a long-lasting edge. Most modern chisels have shatter-proof polypropylene handles which last indefinitely.

The alternative is to buy chisels with wooden handles, which some people prefer as wood feels more comfortable in the hand.

Store chisels carefully, preferably on a wall-mounted rack where the blades cannot get damaged by other tools, and prevent them from becoming rusty by wiping over them with an oily rag after use. As with all sharp woodworking tools, keep your chisels well out of the reach of children who might be tempted to play with them.

REPLACEABLE WOODEN HANDLES

Wooden handles have a tendency to split or chip. You can, however, hammer inexpensive replacement handles on to the tang (spike) on the end of the chisel blade to give the chisel a new lease of life.

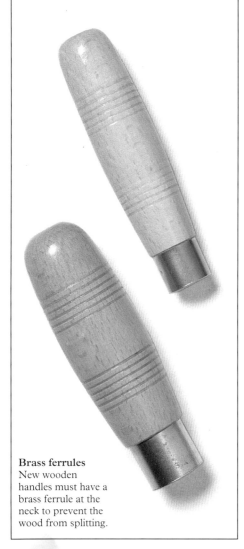

Brass ferrules
New wooden handles must have a brass ferrule at the neck to prevent the wood from splitting.

1 in (25 mm)
bevel-edge chisel

¾ in (18 mm)
bevel-edge chisel

½ in (12 mm)
bevel-edge chisel

5⁄16 in (8 mm)
mortise chisel

Types of blade

There are two basic shapes of chisel blade – firmer and bevel-edge – and both designs are available in a comprehensive range of widths.

Bevel-edge blades have tapered sides which allow you to force the chisel right into the corners of joints that need cleaning up. Bevel-edge chisels were originally designed for hand use only but modern, hardened steel bevel-edge blades can be struck with a mallet. This adaptability makes bevel-edge chisels the most popular type.

The profile of firmer-chisel blades is rectangular. This square section makes them exceptionally strong and inflexible. Firmer chisels are designed to be struck with a mallet and are traditionally used for chopping out the waste from mortises and lock housings.

Choose bevel-edge blades when you buy your first set of chisels. You will find that the blades are strong enough for most tasks. Firmer chisels are really only suitable if you have a lot of deep mortises to chop out or if you need to lever out waste wood from a recess. They are also considerably more expensive than bevel-edge chisels and are not so readily available.

Woodworker's mallet
Mallets have a large head made from a close-grained hardwood that is unlikely to split.

BLADE WIDTHS AVAILABLE

★★ *Recommended sizes for a starter pack*

BLADE WIDTH	FIRMER CHISELS	BEVEL-EDGE CHISELS
¼ in (6 mm)	●	● ★★
⁵⁄₁₆ in (8 mm)	●	●
⅜ in (10 mm)	●	●
½ in (12 mm)	●	● ★★
¾ in (18 mm)	●	●
1 in (25 mm)	●	● ★★
1¾ in (32 mm)	●	●
1½ in (38 mm)	●	●
1¾ in (45 mm)	●	●
2 in (50 mm)	●	●

A tool for striking chisels

Only use a wooden mallet to tap a chisel. Most mallets are made from a hardwood such as beech and are available in various weights. Never use a steel hammer to hit a chisel as it could shatter or splinter even a tough plastic handle.

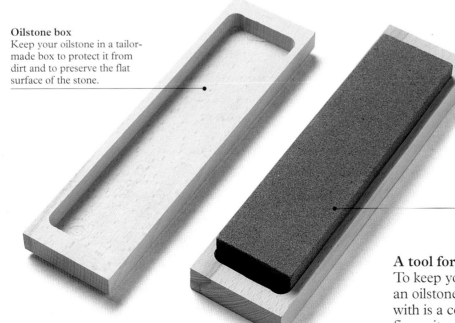

Oilstone box
Keep your oilstone in a tailor-made box to protect it from dirt and to preserve the flat surface of the stone.

Oilstone
An oilstone must be kept in immaculate condition. If you allow it to become pitted or scratched, you will not be able to hone your chisels to a razor-sharp edge.

A tool for sharpening chisels

To keep your chisels sharp you need an oilstone. A good choice to start with is a combination stone that has a fine grit on one side and a medium grit on the other.

CUTTING AND SHAPING TECHNIQUES

To cut out firm, tight joints you must have sharp, clean tools. Make learning how to hone a blade to a keen edge a priority and you will get off to a good start. Surprisingly, sharp tools are also safer to use than blunt ones.

SHARP CHISELS are not only easier to use than blunt ones, but they are also safer. You have to exert undue force on a blunt edge and this can lead to accidents as well as torn wood. Nevertheless, bear safety in mind when chiselling: always secure the workpiece and keep your hands behind the blade.

When paring, guide the chisel with one hand and push with the other.

Choose the widest chisel possible for each job.

Cutting a basic joint

To cut out a simple joint, such as a half-lap joint, saw down the shoulder lines to the required depth before you chop out the waste wood. Chisel first from one side then the other to remove the bulk of the waste, making sure that you hold the chisel with the bevel edge facing down. Finally, take out the residue in the middle of the joint, but this time hold the chisel with the bevel facing upwards.

GOOD CHISELLING TECHNIQUE
Hold your head and body still. Never force a chisel – the blade should slice rather than tear the wood.

Whenever you use a chisel clamp the workpiece to a workbench so that it cannot move.

Chopping out the waste
Hold the chisel with its bevel facing downwards and chop away the waste. Work down the side of the joint to just above the marked depth line.

Removing waste from the other side
Take out the waste on the other side of the joint a little bit at a time. Stop just above the depth line. You should be left with a triangle of waste in the middle.

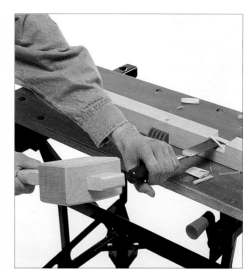

Chiselling to the triangle
Turn your chisel over so that its bevel faces upwards and gently remove the triangle of waste. You are now ready to pare the joint down to the depth line.

Paring to the marked lines

Using a chisel by hand to tidy up a joint is known as paring. To pare across the joint, push the chisel with the palm of one hand and guide and control it with the other. To pare the sides of the joint, hold the chisel vertically and guide the blade carefully with your fingers. Pare away slivers of wood until you reach your marked lines. The sides and bottom of the joint should be smooth.

Tidying the bottom of the joint
Push the chisel, bevel up, with the palm of your hand to shave off thin layers of wood. Pare into the joint from both sides.

Paring the sides straight
Make any adjustments to the sides by pushing down vertically with the blade. Guide the blade with your fingers.

Sharpening a chisel

You can sharpen a chisel in a honing guide (*see page 43*) but it is often quicker and easier to do the job by hand using an oilstone.

Anchor your oilstone to your workbench and pour a few drops of light oil on to the surface. Hold the chisel at an angle of around 30° – this is slightly steeper than the angle of the ground bevel – and move the chisel up and down the stone.

When a thin wire appears on the back of the blade, remove it by turning the chisel over and rubbing the blade flat along the stone.

Honing the blade
Keep the angle of the blade consistent as you move it up and down the entire length of the stone. Add a few more drops of oil if the stone becomes dry.

Wiring off the blade
Remove the wire on the back of the blade by turning the chisel over and rubbing the blade flat against the stone. One or two strokes should be sufficient.

CARING FOR YOUR CHISELS

It pays to look after your chisels: clean, smooth chisels cut slickly and cleanly; rusty chisels with ragged edges tear and damage wood and are a liability.

Store your chisels separately from your other tools, preferably on a wall rack. If you keep them in your general toolbox, they are bound to get damaged. Also make sure they are kept dry or they could become rusty.

Oiling a chisel
Get into the habit of running an oily rag over a chisel every time you finish using it. This wipes off fingerprints and helps to preserve the life of the blade by preventing rust. A cloth spotted with light engineering oil is sufficient.

Using a protective cover
When you buy a new chisel do not throw away the protective cover. Store the chisel with its cover on to maintain the quality of the edge. Covering a sharp edge is also a common-sense safety procedure.

PLANES AND RASPS

*You need at least one plane to smooth down rough lumber and to flatten faces
and edges. Rasps and planer files are less essential and give a cruder finish, but
they are useful for shaping profiles.*

BUYING A NEW PLANE can be difficult because there are so many designs and types from which to choose. Traditional-style planes have wooden bodies but although they are comfortable to use they are invariably very expensive to buy. Steel planes are more common and their extra weight makes them easier to use.

When you buy a plane choose the best quality you can afford. Cheap planes tend to have relatively soft soles

(bases) which can become severely pitted and this can lead to inaccurate planing. In addition cheap planes often have inferior handles that can split or crack.

Always store a plane carefully. When you lay it down, rest it on its side so as not to harm the cutting edge and withdraw the blade into the body of the tool by turning the depth-adjustment screw (see below) when you place it in your toolbox.

Wooden jointer plane

Depth-adjustment screw
This moves the blade assembly in and out and allows you to alter the thickness of shavings.

Wooden bench plane

Regulator
This moves the blade from side to side.

Tension-screw nut
This holds the blade assembly firmly in place.

Metal bench plane

Lateral-adjustment lever
This lever enables you to change the alignment of the blade.

Lever cap
This locks the blade assembly to the body of the plane.

Block plane

Frog-adjusting screw
This adjusts the frog (the part of the plane that supports the blade) so that you can adjust the size of the mouth opening.

Depth-adjustment screw
This raises and lowers the blade to make deep or shallow cuts.

Types of plane

General-purpose planes for smoothing down surfaces are called bench planes. There are three main types of bench plane.

A jointer plane can be up to 22 in (560 mm) long and is used for truing (levelling) long edges and faces of boards. The length of the sole on a try plane ensures that the tool does not ride up and down bumps; instead, the blade levels them.

A jack plane can have a sole up to 15 in (380 mm) long. It can be used for truing boards as well as for final smoothing.

A smoothing plane is usually no more than 12 in (305 mm) long and is specifically designed for trimming surfaces that are already flat. A smoothing plane tends to ride up and down undulations so it is not an ideal tool to use for truing.

As jointer planes are very expensive, your first plane should either be a jack or smoothing plane.

A block plane is a specialist tool designed for shaving down the end grain of a board. The angle of the blade is lower than for bench planes and you can grip the small body with just one hand if necessary. A block plane should probably be the second plane you buy.

Planer files

Planer files, which are available in various lengths and patterns, are essentially part plane and part rasp. A planer file has a series of sharp teeth stamped out of a hardened-steel blade. Shavings pass through the holes in the blade so that the tool does not become clogged like a conventional rasp.

Planer files have an aggressive cut and should not be considered alternatives to planes as the finish they give is relatively rough. They are, however, useful for shaping the edges of boards into profiles. In this respect, a round planer is particularly practical as you can use it to round off edges inside curves and holes – something that no other tool can do as efficiently.

Unlike the blades in planes, planer-file blades cannot be resharpened, but you can fit replacements into the steel or plastic bodies.

RASPS

Rasps cut wood with hundreds of small teeth. The finish they give is invariably coarse so sanding down afterwards is essential. They are crude but useful tools. For example, if you are working on a project where appearances are not important, use a rasp to quickly round off sharp edges. To clean a clogged blade, run diagonally across it with a wire brush.

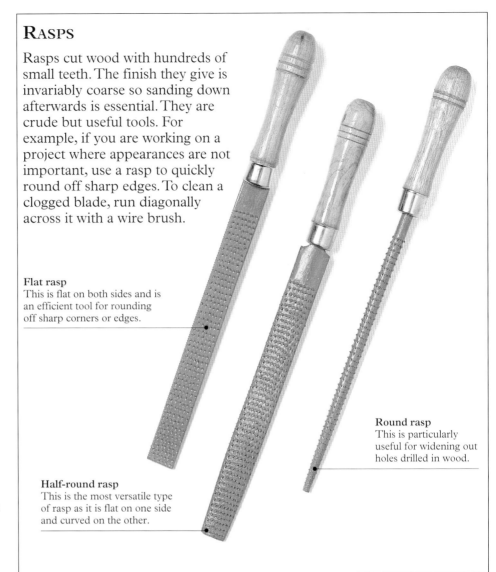

Flat rasp
This is flat on both sides and is an efficient tool for rounding off sharp corners or edges.

Round rasp
This is particularly useful for widening out holes drilled in wood.

Half-round rasp
This is the most versatile type of rasp as it is flat on one side and curved on the other.

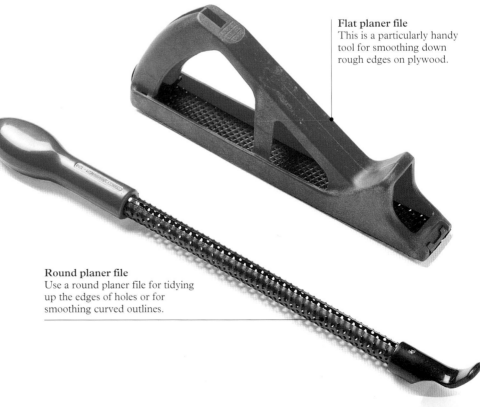

Flat planer file
This is a particularly handy tool for smoothing down rough edges on plywood.

Round planer file
Use a round planer file for tidying up the edges of holes or for smoothing curved outlines.

PLANING TECHNIQUES

*Planing is one of the most satisfying and rewarding of all woodworking skills.
Once you have learned to set your plane correctly and to sharpen the blade to a
razor-sharp edge, mastering the techniques comes with practice.*

ONCE YOU HAVE learned to adjust your plane correctly, and to sharpen the blade to a fine edge, the actual techniques of planing are relatively easy to master.

The most important rule of planing is always to follow the direction of the grain. If you plane against the grain, the blade will jar and the wood will splinter. To gain confidence, practice on offcuts of scrap lumber before you take on a major project.

Press down on the front handle at the beginning of a pass and on the rear handle as you near the end.

Grip the wood in a bench so that the grain slopes away from you to stop the wood tearing.

To produce continuous thin shavings, you may need to use the depth-adjustment nut to alter the depth of cut.

GOOD PLANING TECHNIQUE
Keep your head over the plane as you move it along the wood and always push in a straight line.

The wide vise jaws of a folding bench are ideal for holding a workpiece securely while you plane it.

Components of a bench plane
The modern bench plane is a sophisticated tool with components that allow you to adjust both the depth and alignment of the blade without you having to dismantle the whole assembly. The blade itself has a cap iron bolted to it to curl the shavings and is clamped to the steel support (known as the frog) of the plane by a lever cap. When assembled correctly, none of your plane's components should be loose but you should be able to move the depth-adjustment screw and the lateral-adjustment lever. Practice dismantling and assembling your plane to learn how all the components slot together.

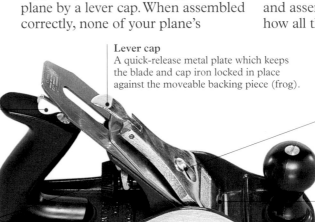

Lateral-adjustment lever
A long metal arm which is moved to the left or right to angle the blade within the mouth of the plane.

Lever cap
A quick-release metal plate which keeps the blade and cap iron locked in place against the moveable backing piece (frog).

Lever-cap screw
A screw which holds the blade, cap iron and lever cap on to the frog. Do not overtighten or the plane will be difficult to adjust.

Depth-adjustment screw
A brass knurled knob which is rotated clockwise or counter-clockwise to move the blade fractionally up or down. The blade should just protrude through the mouth of the sole plate when set up.

Cap iron
This reinforces the blade and curls the shavings.

Adjusting a bench plane

You need to learn how to adjust your plane before you do anything else with it. If the blade is set too deep, it will jar into the lumber and if it is too shallow, it will skate over the surface.

You can alter the depth of cut by turning the brass knob behind the blade. And to change the alignment of the blade, you can push the lateral-adjustment lever one way or the other. However, for major adjustments you may need to reposition the blade within the plane. If you remove the cap iron, make sure when you refit it that it is set close, about 1.5mm (¹⁄₁₆in), to the sharp edge of the blade and is perfectly aligned with it.

Repositioning the blade and cap iron
Before repositioning the blade and cap iron, check that the adjustment lever and nut are in mid-position.

Replacing the lever cap
With the blade in position, insert the lever cap and snap down the lever to lock the whole assembly together.

SHARPENING PLANE BLADES

As with all cutting tools, the edge must be razor-sharp to produce a clean finish. Sharpen your blade on an oilstone and support it in a honing guide to ensure that the bevel is the right angle.

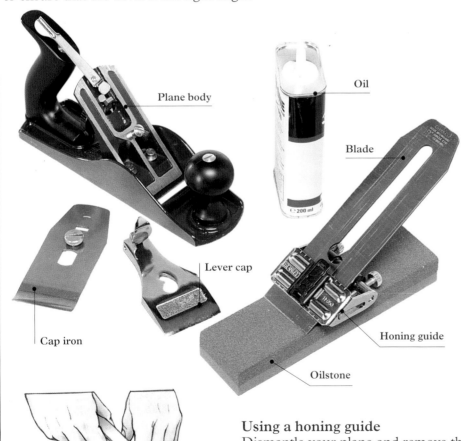

Plane body

Oil

Blade

Lever cap

Cap iron

Honing guide

Oilstone

Sharpening the whole edge
Make sure the edge is honed equally across the width of the blade and try to use the whole length of the oilstone.

Wiring off the blade
Rub the back of the blade over the stone to remove the burr. If you hold the blade flat, the burr should come off as a thin wire.

Using a honing guide

Dismantle your plane and remove the cap iron from the blade. Clamp the blade in the honing guide and smear light oil over the oilstone. Run the guide up and down the stone to sharpen the blade evenly. Sharpening by hand (left) is not so accurate.

Planing a wide board

When smoothing down a wide board, plane diagonally across the board first and finish with shallow passes that run parallel to the grain. If you start by planing along the grain, you will create ugly grooves which tend to become more pronounced the longer you continue.

To make it easier to plane a board flat, round off the edges of the blade by putting more pressure on the sides when you hone it. The curves to the rounded edges need only to be very slight but they will reduce the likelihood of you gouging out unsightly ruts that can be extremely difficult to get rid of.

Plane diagonally across the board
Start with diagonal strokes to level the face of the board.

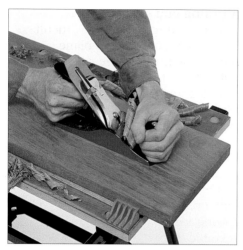

Plane straight along the grain
Set the blade to a fine cut and finish with straight passes.

Planing wood square

You can make many projects with wood that has been planed square by your lumber merchant, but nevertheless it is important to know how to plane the wood square yourself. There are two reasons for this. First, the quality of finish produced by machine tools is greatly inferior to the kind of finish you can achieve with hand tools. Secondly, lumber sold by merchants is usually finished to standard dimensions, and for many projects you need to shave wood down to exact measurements. There is no better way of doing this than with a hand plane.

To plane wood square, start by planing one face flat. Plane in the direction of the grain unless you are dealing with a plank (*see above*). Check your progress at regular intervals by dragging a straightedge along the surface – any gaps under the rule are low points and indicate that the face needs more planing. When you are satisfied that the surface is completely flat, mark it with a pencil. The traditional mark for a planed face is a loop, similar to an inverted 'P'. From now on this marked face will be your constant and your aim should be to make the edges perpendicular to it.

The next step is to plane an edge square to the marked face. Keep the plane horizontal all through the stroke. There can be a tendency to dip the plane as it runs off the end and the result is a curved edge.

Check the angle between the edge and the face regularly with a try square and when you are satisfied that it is a consistent right-angle along the entire length, mark it with a pencil. The traditional mark for a planed edge is a 'V'.

When you have planed one face and one edge, finish by trimming the second edge and finally the remaining face. By the end, the faces should be parallel to each other and square to the edges.

Planing wood square is a considerable skill that takes time to learn, and the only way to master it is to practice. Try squaring up variously-shaped scraps of different wood, from small battens to wide boards and planks.

Mark the face
When you have planed one face flat, mark it along an edge and use it as a constant for the edges.

Check for square
After you have planed the first edge down, check that it is at a right-angle to the face using a try square.

Mark the first edge
Mark the first planed edge with a 'V', then smooth the second edge and lastly the remaining face.

Trimming end grain

End grain is often the most difficult part of a piece of wood to plane smooth. The fibers of the wood are usually at 90° to the surface and are easy to tear, rather than cut.

Before you start, make sure the plane of your blade is very sharp and adjust it to a shallow setting. It is usually best to work the plane carefully towards the center of the board or block. Alternatively, you can clamp a piece of wood to the back of the workpiece to support the vulnerable rear edges and to stop them breaking out when the plane passes over them. This is particularly useful if you use a bench plane as opposed to a block plane.

Planing end grain with a block plane
A block plane is designed for shaving end grain. Work inward from the edges toward the center.

Planing end grain with a bench plane
Use a sharp blade on a shallow setting. Clamp on a backing piece to stop fibers breaking away.

Using a Surform

Surforms are efficient tools for smoothing curved edges, something that is almost impossible to do with a conventional bench plane. You can also use them for finishing off end grain, provided you work from the edges toward the middle.

Always hold long Surforms with two hands. The cutting teeth are arranged in diagonal rows and if you don't grasp the Surform firmly, the blade will tend to glide off at an angle, leaving ugly grooves in its wake. Clear shavings from the blade at intervals to prevent the teeth from becoming clogged. When the teeth become blunt replace the blade.

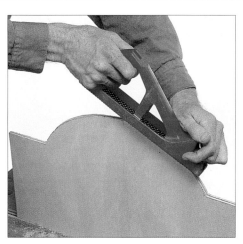

Smoothing off a rounded shape
Hold the Surform body in two hands and push it over the rounded surface in a straight line.

Using a rasp

Rasps give a coarse finish but are nevertheless useful for rounding off sawn edges and for shaping profiles in boards.

Rasps invariably have a sharp metal spike (tang) which is designed to be slotted into a wooden handle. Make sure you fit a handle, if one is required, as a tang could inflict a nasty injury to the palm of your hand as you push the rasp forward.

Rasps only cut on the forward stroke, so push it away from you to cut into the workpiece and steady the tool with your other hand. When you have finished rasping, sand down the edge to get a smooth finish and clean up the rasp with a wire brush.

Rasping inside a curve
Force the rasp with one hand and balance it with the other. Push it diagonally to avoid making grooves.

WAXING THE SOLE

If your plane refuses to glide easily over timber and starts to stick, it is probably because there is too much friction between the sole of the plane and the surface of the wood. One way of reducing the friction created between metal and wood is to rub candle wax over the sole of the plane. This lubricates the wood without leaving marks and makes planing much easier. Apply the candle wax as and when you need it – it is best to rub on a little at a time rather than to cover the whole of the sole.

Waxing the sole with a candle
Rub the end of the candle in a zigzag fashion over the sole of the plane. When the wax wears off, you can repeat the process without any ill effect.

CLAMPS AND VISES

Before you pick up your tools to set to work, the wood or board must be held firmly. The many clamping devices available are designed to cope with different tasks and shapes of lumber.

THE INVENTION of portable folding workbenches means that many of the conventional clamping devices used by traditional craftsmen are no longer essential. Portable workbenches enable you to hold large and small pieces of wood in various ways while you work on them, and they are strongly recommended for anybody starting out in woodworking.

However, a portable workbench is not capable of doing all clamping jobs and you will need to buy a few additional gadgets for holding joints tightly together and for securing wood at angles. C-clamps are exceptionally strong and are also very versatile. As they are often used in pairs, it is a good idea to buy them two at a time and to build up a collection in a range of different sizes.

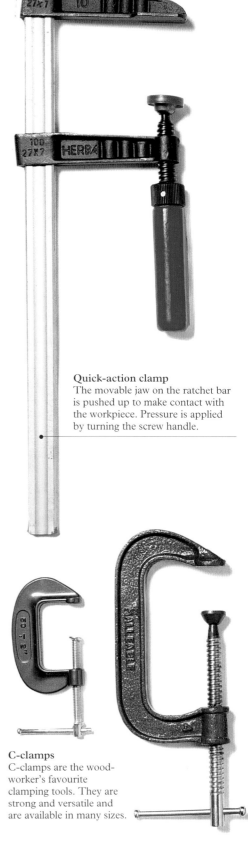

Quick-action clamp
The movable jaw on the ratchet bar is pushed up to make contact with the workpiece. Pressure is applied by turning the screw handle.

C-clamps
C-clamps are the wood-worker's favourite clamping tools. They are strong and versatile and are available in many sizes.

THE FOLDING WORKBENCH

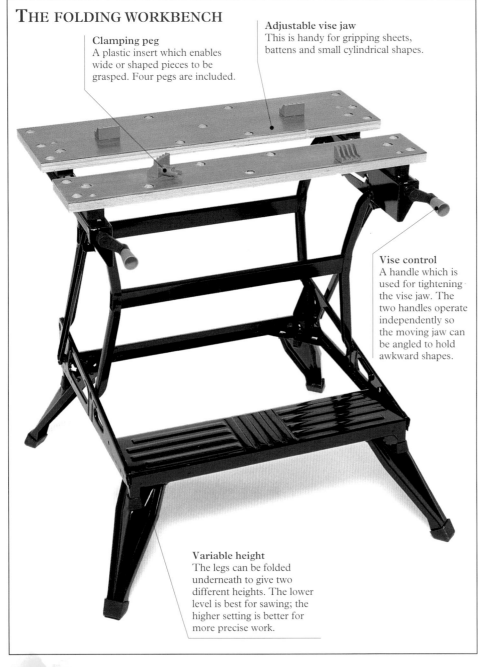

Clamping peg
A plastic insert which enables wide or shaped pieces to be grasped. Four pegs are included.

Adjustable vise jaw
This is handy for gripping sheets, battens and small cylindrical shapes.

Vise control
A handle which is used for tightening the vise jaw. The two handles operate independently so the moving jaw can be angled to hold awkward shapes.

Variable height
The legs can be folded underneath to give two different heights. The lower level is best for sawing; the higher setting is better for more precise work.

One-handed clamp
Useful for complex clamping, this new device has a pump-action trigger which squeezes the jaw heads together.

Miter clamp
This is an essential tool for holding mitered joints together.

Web clamp
This is designed for holding frames together until the glue sets. The strap is drawn around the frame and tightened with a ratchet mechanism.

Bar clamp
This clamp is made for clamping large pieces together. The movable heads can be relocated on the bar.

Clamp heads
Bar clamps can be expensive. Clamp heads fitted to a wooden bar with regularly spaced adjustment holes are a cheaper alternative.

CLAMPING TECHNIQUES

Clamps have two major functions in woodworking: to hold wood steady as it is worked, and to keep pressure on joints until adhesive sets. Always use the clamps and techniques that are appropriate to your work.

To get the tightest fit and strongest possible join, it is essential that joints are clamped firmly until the glue dries. However clamping a joint is not always as simple as it might seem.

First you have to choose the right device for the job in hand (*see pages 46-47*), and there may be other considerations to bear in mind as well – for example, how to prevent parallel boards from warping.

Whenever you clamp wood, even hardwood, insert offcuts of scrap wood between the jaws of the clamp and the workpiece. If you don't protect the workpiece in this way, the clamp will scar or bruise the wood, leaving a blemish which may be very difficult to eradicate.

Joining planks together

If you want to make a large board out of solid wood, you will probably have to join planks together edge-to-edge. This is not as difficult as it might sound, provided that you have several clamps that are long enough to span the width of the board you want to create.

Use a damp cloth to wipe off any adhesive that is squeezed out of the joints.

SUCCESSFUL CLAMPING
Check the alignment of the boards at regular intervals, both during and after applying the clamps.

To distribute the force of each clamp and to prevent the jaws from bruising the wood, insert offcuts.

After screwing up the clamps, systematically tighten each one to apply even tension over the length of the board.

Alternate the growth rings
Keep the overall effect of warping to a minimum by alternating the direction of the growth rings.

Start by selecting planks of equal thickness and width, then check that their edges are flat and smooth so that they butt up against each other

with no gaps. If necessary, plane down the edges until they are perfectly true (*see pages 42-45*).

Next, arrange the planks so that their growth rings alternate. This will minimize warping in the finished board; if all the growth rings follow the same direction, the board is likely to warp into a shallow curve.

Once you have arranged the boards, apply glue to the edges and start clamping them together. If your clamps are rusty, oily or greasy, lay strips of paper across the workpiece to prevent the dirt on the clamps transferring onto the wood. Oily stains in particular can be difficult to remove and may ruin the appearance of the finished article.

Clamping up
After spreading adhesive evenly along the joining edges, tighten up the first clamp. Protect the wood with offcuts of wood.

Space the clamps out about 12 in (305 mm) apart. It is best to alternate the clamps above and below the planks to ensure equal overall tension on the joins. Try to apply similar pressure to all the clamps so as not to distort the board in any way and as you tighten each clamp, check with a rule or straightedge that the boards are flat. After clamping, wipe off any excess adhesive. Once the adhesive has set firm, you can remove all the clamps.

Evening out the tension
Place clamps above and below the boards to balance the pressure applied to the joins.

USING A WEB CLAMP

A web clamp is invaluable for making all types of frames, whether for a picture, a door or a chair. A web clamp comprises a length of nylon strapping which is fed back through a non-slip ratchet device, enabling the strapping to be tightened up around a frame. Most web clamps come complete with right-angled corner supports which ensure that equal pressure can be applied at the corners on a rectangular frame. However, web clamps are not exclusively for rectangular frames, they are extremely versatile tools and can also be used to hold round or awkwardly shaped objects secure.

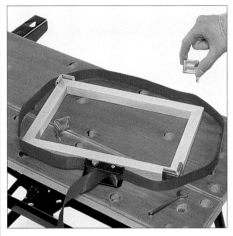

Positioning the corner supports
For rectangular frames, first apply glue to each joint and then place a metal support at each corner. Loop the strap right around the workpiece.

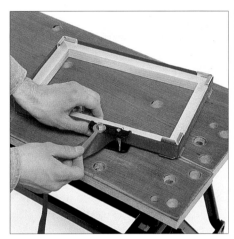

Tightening the ratchet
Tighten up the web clamp by turning the ratchet mechanism with a spanner. Wipe off any surplus glue with a damp cloth before it has a chance to dry.

CHOOSING THE RIGHT CLAMP

Before making a joint, consider what sort of clamp would be best for holding it together until the adhesive sets. Always use small clamps for delicate joints and, if necessary, invest in a special kind of clamp – such as a miter clamp – to deal with a task that no other clamp could do as effectively.

Clamping on a portable workbench
A portable workbench can be used to clamp together reasonably small joints as well as wide boards if the plastic inserts are used. Apply even force at each end of the bench.

Using a miter clamp
Successful miter joints need careful support at the gluing-up stage. Right-angle miter clamps hold the two pieces to be joined at an angle of exactly 90°.

Using a C-clamp
C-clamps come in many sizes and can be used to force halving and numerous other joints together. Always use packing pieces to protect the wood.

TOOLS FOR FIXING

Hammers and screwdrivers are essential tools, and you will need a selection of both to complete most projects. Choose good-quality tools that will provide years of service.

YOU ARE UNLIKELY to use many items in your toolbox more frequently than your hammers and screwdrivers. Because they are so crucial to woodworking, it is well worth investing in the best quality tools you can afford as they should last for many, many years. Cheap screwdrivers are easily bent and the blades can be rendered worthless if they are forged from soft, easily distorted steel. Cheap hammers can be a liability – a weak shaft or a loose head could inflict a serious injury.

Store your hammers and screwdrivers in a dry place to prevent them from rusting, and don't use screwdrivers to open cans of paint!

POWER SCREWDRIVERS

The great attraction of power screwdrivers is that they take the sweat out of twisting in screws. You can choose from many designs and they are no longer prohibitively expensive. When buying one, check that a selection of bits is included.

If you plan to use the screwdriver frequently, it pays to get a good-quality model with a motor that is powerful enough to cope with heavy tasks. All power screwdrivers have a reverse facility which enables you to unscrew, as well as tighten, fixings.

Forward/reverse rocker switch

Locking switch

Interchangeable screwdriver bit

Jack-plug socket for recharging lead

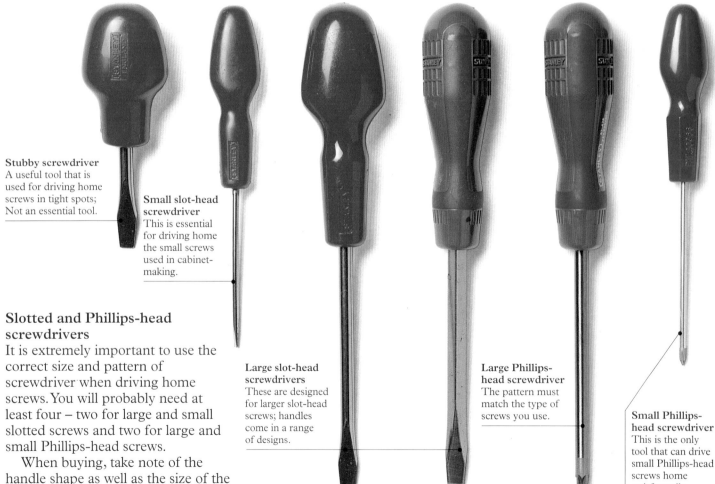

Stubby screwdriver
A useful tool that is used for driving home screws in tight spots; Not an essential tool.

Small slot-head screwdriver
This is essential for driving home the small screws used in cabinet-making.

Large slot-head screwdrivers
These are designed for larger slot-head screws; handles come in a range of designs.

Large Phillips-head screwdriver
The pattern must match the type of screws you use.

Small Phillips-head screwdriver
This is the only tool that can drive small Phillips-head screws home satisfactorily.

Slotted and Phillips-head screwdrivers

It is extremely important to use the correct size and pattern of screwdriver when driving home screws. You will probably need at least four – two for large and small slotted screws and two for large and small Phillips-head screws.

When buying, take note of the handle shape as well as the size of the screwdrivers. Screwdrivers with shaped handles are easier and more comfortable to work with.

Hammers

You will probably need to have at least two hammers – one for tapping in panel pins and one suitable for more heavy-duty work.

Hammer shafts are traditionally made from wood but it is now possible to get all-steel hammers which are extremely durable. The chief advantage of wooden shafts is that they are more comfortable to use, but make sure that the shaft is strong and preferably made from a hardwood such as hickory. You can buy replacement wooden hammer shafts which are easily fixed with steel wedges.

For pulling out nails, you will need either a pair of pincers or a claw hammer, and for sinking panel pin heads, you will require a nail set.

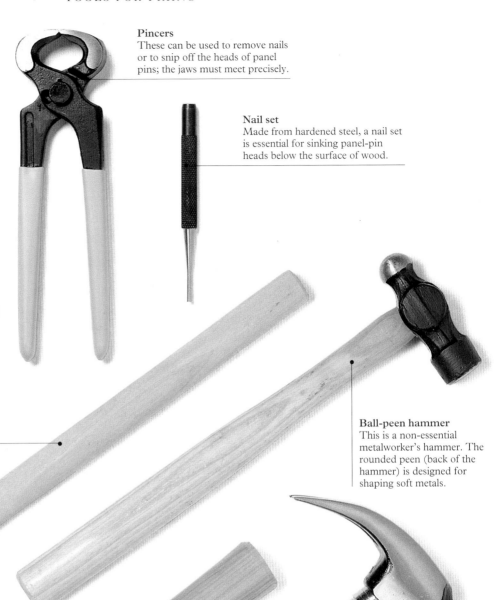

Pincers
These can be used to remove nails or to snip off the heads of panel pins; the jaws must meet precisely.

Nail set
Made from hardened steel, a nail set is essential for sinking panel-pin heads below the surface of wood.

Pin hammer
This is the best tool to use for tapping in panel pins.

Ball-peen hammer
This is a non-essential metalworker's hammer. The rounded peen (back of the hammer) is designed for shaping soft metals.

Continental-pattern hammer
The shaped peen at the back of the hammer can be used to tap in panel nails.

Clawhammer
This is an excellent general-purpose hammer.

USING A CLAWHAMMER

Using a clawhammer to pull nails
Rest the head of the hammer on an offcut before levering out the nail.

FIXINGS, FITTINGS AND ADHESIVES

Fixings are used to hold pieces of wood together or to attach metalwork, such as hinges, to a workpiece. Fittings include catches, hinges and handles, and are available in styles to suit all types of furniture.

TO ASSEMBLE and complete a project you need fixings – usually woodscrews – and most probably, an adhesive of some kind as well. In addition, you may also require wallplugs, knock-down fittings, and hinges and catches. When you buy either a fixing or fitting, you should first consider its strength, but appearance may be important, too.

Woodscrews

Woodscrews are usually made from steel or brass. Brass screws should be reserved for fixing lightweight fittings like hinges, as the metal is relatively soft. For outdoor projects, use plated or stainless-steel screws.

A screw is measured in terms of length and also by shank thickness, or gauge. For greatest strength, use screws of the largest diameter and greatest length that is practical. Gauges range from 0 to 20, 20 being the thickest. Thick screws give the strongest grip. The most commonly used gauges are 6, 8 and 10.

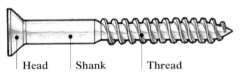

Traditional woodscrew
This has a single thread along the shank. A traditional screw is excellent for joining wood but not chipboard or MDF.

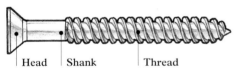

Twin-thread woodscrew
This is a relatively new type of screw that has a narrow shank and two deep threads. It grips well in chipboard, MDF and solid wood.

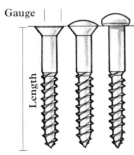

Screw sizes
The length of a screw is defined as the distance between the tip of the screw and the rim of the head. The thickness of the shank is expressed as a gauge number ranging from 0 to 20.

WOODWORKING ADHESIVES

Choose an adhesive that is specifically designed for gluing wood. Many general-purpose adhesives claim to stick to wood but few of them are very efficient.

Polyvinyl acetate (PVA) woodworking adhesive is excellent for most jobs as it gives a strong bond and is easy to use. It is also relatively inexpensive. You can buy 'quick-setting' PVA adhesive as well as waterproof types that are recommended for outdoor projects.

Hot-melt woodworking adhesives are applied with a 'gun' that has to be connected to a power supply. The adhesive gives a reasonably strong bond but is best applied in dabs to tack wood in place.

Urea-formaldehyde glues give a stronger bond but must be mixed up in advance. They are also expensive.

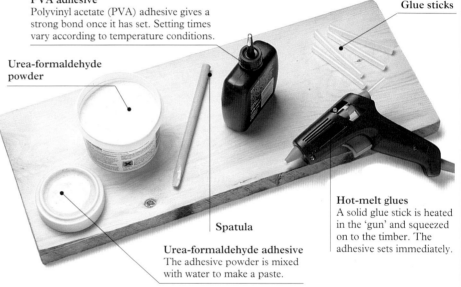

PVA adhesive
Polyvinyl acetate (PVA) adhesive gives a strong bond once it has set. Setting times vary according to temperature conditions.

Urea-formaldehyde powder

Glue sticks

Spatula

Urea-formaldehyde adhesive
The adhesive powder is mixed with water to make a paste.

Hot-melt glues
A solid glue stick is heated in the 'gun' and squeezed on to the timber. The adhesive sets immediately.

Types of screwhead

Countersunk screwheads are the best choice for woodworking as they can be recessed into the wood to lie flush with the surface. Alternatively, they can be sunk deeper into the wood and disguised with filler. Raised and roundhead screws are designed for fixing metal or sheets of hard plastic to wood. Their heads stay above the surface and they can be used as decorative features.

Screwheads either have a slot, to receive a flat screwdriver, or a recessed cross to receive a Phillips-head screwdriver. Phillips-head screws have the advantage that the screwdriver is less likely to slip and damage the head, but it is crucial to use a screwdriver of the correct size.

Screwhead types
Countersunk heads are recessed into wood to leave a smooth surface. Raised-head screws are occasionally used to fix fittings, such as hinges. Roundhead screws are for securing thin or very hard sheet materials.

Countersunk head　　**Raised head**　　**Roundhead**

Slotted and Phillips-head screws
Slotted screws suit traditional furniture but the screwdriver can slip as the screw is tightened. Phillips-head screws are easier to drive home as the screwdriver is less likely to slip.

Slotted screw　　**Phillips-head screw**

Knock-down fittings

Knock-down fittings enable you to join pieces of wood or man-made board together at right-angles without the need for elaborate joints. The other advantage of these fittings is that you can take them apart quickly and easily.

Use knock-down fittings where appearance is not important, for example inside a cupboard or to join a table top to a frame.

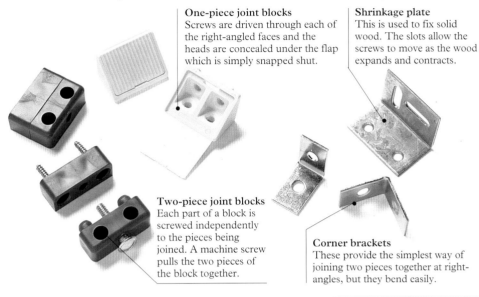

One-piece joint blocks
Screws are driven through each of the right-angled faces and the heads are concealed under the flap which is simply snapped shut.

Shrinkage plate
This is used to fix solid wood. The slots allow the screws to move as the wood expands and contracts.

Two-piece joint blocks
Each part of a block is screwed independently to the pieces being joined. A machine screw pulls the two pieces of the block together.

Corner brackets
These provide the simplest way of joining two pieces together at right-angles, but they bend easily.

Wallplugs

Woodscrews do not grip masonry or drywall, so if you have to fix a project to a wall, you must first insert wallplugs to ensure that the screws stay in the correct place. Wallplugs can be divided into two groups – those for solid, masonry walls, and those for hollow, drywall walls.

Both types are available in a range of designs. Choose a wallplug that is an appropriate size and is strong enough to support the weight of your particular project.

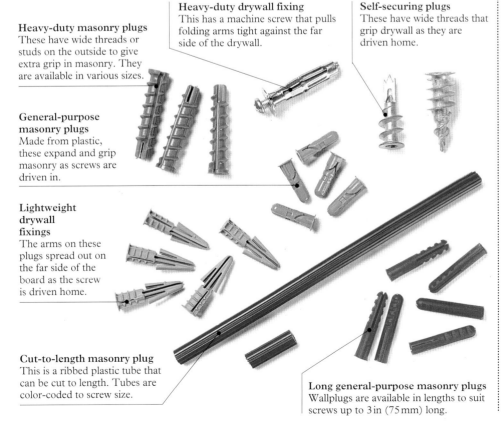

Heavy-duty masonry plugs
These have wide threads or studs on the outside to give extra grip in masonry. They are available in various sizes.

General-purpose masonry plugs
Made from plastic, these expand and grip masonry as screws are driven in.

Lightweight drywall fixings
The arms on these plugs spread out on the far side of the board as the screw is driven home.

Heavy-duty drywall fixing
This has a machine screw that pulls folding arms tight against the far side of the drywall.

Self-securing plugs
These have wide threads that grip drywall as they are driven home.

Cut-to-length masonry plug
This is a ribbed plastic tube that can be cut to length. Tubes are color-coded to screw size.

Long general-purpose masonry plugs
Wallplugs are available in lengths to suit screws up to 3 in (75 mm) long.

Hinges

The leaves of a butt hinge have to be set into recesses in order for the hinge to close properly. With flush hinges, however, there is no need to cut recesses as one leaf folds inside the other. The problem with flush hinges is that they are only strong enough to take lightweight doors. Use brass hinges where appearance is important; steel hinges are best for heavy doors and lids.

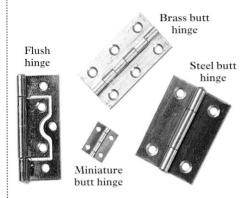

Flush hinge

Brass butt hinge

Steel butt hinge

Miniature butt hinge

Bolts and catches

Sliding bolts, which are available in many sizes, keep doors firmly closed but they are not particularly attractive. Ball catches are less obtrusive but are not so effective at keeping a door shut. Always secure bolts and catches with screws of a similar material and make sure that they don't clash with other visible metalwork, such as hinges.

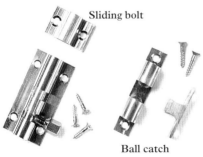

Sliding bolt

Ball catch

Mirror plates

These flat, brass plates can be used to secure not just mirrors, but a whole range of objects flush to a wall. Slotted plates enable you to lift the mirror or object off the wall without removing the central screw.

Mirror plate

FIXING TECHNIQUES

The correct method of fixing two pieces of wood together depends on how strong you want the joint to be. However, you should also consider the desired appearance of the joint.

As a general rule, always glue wood joints, even if you are fixing them with screws or nails. The exceptions to this rule are joins that are not permanent. Modern adhesives are so efficient that they can make conventional nails or screws redundant.

GOOD FIXING TECHNIQUE
Spread an even film of adhesive over one of the surfaces and reinforce joints with fixings such as screws or nails.

A general-purpose PVA adhesive is excellent for joining man-made boards as well as solid timber. Always use water-resistant adhesive on outdoor projects.

Using adhesive
Before gluing a joint, always check that the components fit neatly as there may not be time to make adjustments before the adhesive sets.

It is usually only necessary to spread adhesive on to one of the mating surfaces of a joint but it is important to make sure that you distribute an even film over the entire surface area. If only part of the joining area is glued, the joint may be substantially weakened.

Space out fixings equally and only use as many as are necessary. The main function of the nails is to secure lipping until the adhesive sets.

Make sure meeting surfaces are smooth and free from dust and grease.

Spreading the adhesive
Check that the surface is clean and free from dust before spreading on the adhesive with a spatula or length of shaped dowel. Coat all the joint surfaces with a thin film.

Joining the components
Press the parts together and make sure that the joining faces meet closely by tapping the joint with a mallet. Protect the wood from bruising with an offcut.

Cleaning up
Wipe away any adhesive that oozes out of the joint with a damp cloth. Do not allow the adhesive to set as it could then be hard to remove and could stain the wood.

Skew-nailing

Skew-nailing is a quick and simple technique to use if you are assembling a non-permanent frame.

If you fix two pieces of wood together by driving home nails at right-angles to the surface, the joint has limited strength as the nails are easily forced out. However, if you angle the nails as you hammer them in, the joint will be stronger. When you skew-nail in this way, make sure you do not position the nails along the same grain or the wood could split open.

Unless the joint is temporary, it is best to add glue before nailing the pieces together. Used by themselves, nails do not guarantee a strong joint, no matter how you hammer them in. If possible, use nails with textured shanks for a stronger grip.

Nailing in one direction
Hold the parts together and drive in a nail held at an angle of around 30°. Position the nail to one side of the joint.

Nailing in the opposite direction
Hammer in a second nail, aiming it in the opposite direction to the first. Always point the nails toward the center of the joint.

Screwing work together

After you have marked the exact position of a screw, ideally you should drill a clearance hole through the piece to be fixed and a pilot hole into the receiving piece. The bit you choose for the clearance hole should match the diameter of the screw and the bit for the pilot hole should be thinner so that the threads can bite into the wood. If you don't drill clearance and pilot holes, it is possible that the wood could split when you drive the screw home.

Although screws produce strong fixings, it is best to glue the surfaces together as well to create the strongest possible joint.

Countersinking holes
If you use countersunk screws, countersink the clearance holes so that the heads lie below the surface of the wood.

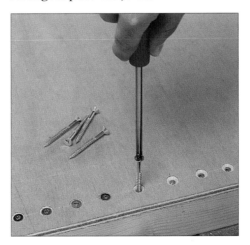

Driving the screws home
Each screw should pass cleanly through its clearance hole but bite into the pilot hole in the receiving piece.

USING CARRIAGE BOLTS

Decide to use carriage bolts where strength is important and appearance is not. They are excellent for a project such as a workbench (*see pages 112-115*).

To fit a carriage bolt, first drill a clearance hole through both pieces to be joined. The clearance hole should be marginally wider than the bolt itself. If you want the nut to lie below the surface of the wood, counterbore the exit hole. The counterbore should be wide enough to allow access to the nut with a wrench and only needs to be deep enough for the nut to be hidden from sight. Always place a washer over the end of the bolt before adding the nut.

Hammering in the bolt
Tap the bolt into the clearance hole to ensure that the square section of the bolt under the head engages the wood. This prevents the bolt turning in the hole.

Tightening the bolt
Slide a washer over the end of the bolt before tightening the nut with a ring or ratchet wrench.

HANGING AND FASTENING TECHNIQUES

Take time to learn hanging and fastening skills as they can influence the stability of a project as well as its appearance. A well fitted hinge is often seen as the mark of good woodworker.

ASSEMBLING a project or mounting it on a wall can be hugely satisfying but it is vitally important not to rush these final stages. How a hinge is fitted dictates how well the door closes, and how long a wall-mounted project stays on the wall depends on how it is fixed. If you use knock-down fittings to construct a project, they also need careful consideration as the rigidity of the structure depends on them.

Make sure you use fixings that are suitable for the job you are attempting (*see pages 52-53*).

GOOD FASTENING TECHNIQUE
Mark out the exact position of a fitting before you secure it or cut a recess for it. Always fasten a fitting with screws that are of the recommended size.

Make sure you choose fittings that are sturdy enough for the job. Lightweight fittings may bend or buckle if too much is expected of them.

Use the fitting as a template when marking out its position. With a hinge, mark its depth as well.

Cut out a shallow recess for a butt hinge to ensure a clean, tidy finish.

Fixing to solid walls

Use ordinary woodscrews driven into wallplugs to secure fittings to solid brick or block walls. A wallplug expands and grips the surrounding masonry as a screw is twisted into it; without a wallplug, a screw in a solid wall only provides a weak and insubstantial fixing.

Make sure the screws and plugs you choose are compatible with each other in terms of length and size, and drill the hole with a masonry bit to match the diameter of the plugs. If your drill has the option, it is best to switch it to a hammer action before you make the hole. It is also a good idea to tape a paper bag under the hole to catch all the brick dust as it comes out.

Drilling into the wall
Mark the position of the hole on the wall and switch your drill to hammer action. Set the drill to a slow or medium speed.

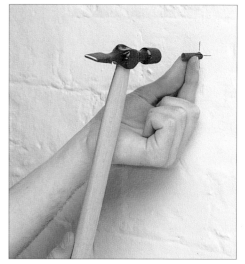

Inserting the wallplug
Blow away any dust from the hole and gently tap the wallplug in with a lightweight tack hammer.

Fixing to a hollow wall

Hollow walls are made by nailing drywall to a wooden framework. The drywall is not usually strong enough to bear a heavy weight but drywalls are nevertheless able to support picture frames and small mirrors.

If you want to secure a heavy item, such as a bookshelf, use long wood-screws and drive them directly into the wooden framework. If you want to secure light objects to the drywall, you must insert a cavity wallplug first and screw into this, otherwise the fixing will pop out.

Cavity wallplugs

Cavity wallplugs are available in various designs and sizes (*see pages 52-53*). For an expanding cavity wallplug, first drill a suitable-sized hole in the drywall with a masonry bit. Then slot in the plug and drive home the screw until it is secure.

Fitting an expanding plug
Drill a hole at your mark and gently tap home the wallplug.

Hanging the fitting
Tighten a screw into the wallplug. This should hold lightweight items.

Self-securing wallplugs

With a self-securing wallplug, you don't have to drill a hole first. Simply twist the plug into the drywall on your mark with a screwdriver – the broad threads on the plug ensure a strong fixing. Finally, insert a screw into the plug, making sure it is an appropriate size.

A self-securing wallplug
Place the tip against your mark and twist the plug in with a screwdriver.

Inserting the screw
Tighten the wallplug then drive a screw into the central hole.

Cutting a hinge recess

Clamp the door in your bench so that it does not move, then bend the hinge wide open and hold one leaf in position on the edge of the door.

Mark around the hinge leaf with a sharp pencil, making sure that you hold the lead tight against the metal to get an accurate outline. Set a marking gauge to the thickness of the hinge leaf and mark the depth of the recess on the face of the door.

Hold a sharp chisel fractionally to the waste side of the hinge outline and tap down vertically to cut the side and ends of the recess. To make the removal of the waste wood from the recess easier, use your chisel to make a series of shallow cuts inside the hinge outline. Make sure that these cuts go no deeper than the depth of the recess.

Pare away the waste wood while keeping the chisel blade horizontal (*see pages 38-39*). Keep the bevel facing upwards and at no point sink below the depth of the recess.

With all the waste wood removed, try the hinge for fit and clean up the side and ends of the recess.

Making the shallow cuts
Make the cuts about ¹/₂in (12mm) apart.

Paring in from the side
Avoid chiselling below the depth of the recess.

Screwing in the hinge
Mark through the holes in the hinge with a bradawl before inserting the screws.

SECURING KNOCK-DOWN FITTINGS

Use knock-down fittings for assembling furniture constructed from man-made boards. They are easy to fix and can be removed if you want to dismantle the joints at a later stage.

Position a fitting and mark through the screw holes with a bradawl. Then simply slot in screws of the correct size and tighten them up.

Marking the screw holes
Hold the fixing in place and mark the positions of all the screws with a bradawl.

Securing the fitting
Screw the fitting to one board before fixing it to the other. Snap down the cover flap.

SANDING AND FINISHING TOOLS

Abrasive papers are essential for successful woodworking. They wear down quickly, so always keep a good supply of various grades in your toolkit. You also need a selection of brushes with which to apply finishes.

WHEN YOU USE abrasive paper to smooth down superficial imperfections, wrap it around a sanding block to keep the paper flat. There are several types of abrasive papers that are available in grit sizes from 80 (coarse) to 220 (fine). Always start with a coarse paper and finish with a fine grade to achieve the smoothest possible finish.

In addition to abrasive papers, you may also need a filler to patch up holes and some steel wool for emphasizing the grain of the wood and for applying wax.

If the wood is to be left bare or is to be waxed, seal the surface so that it does not remain porous. To do this you need a sanding sealer or some diluted varnish.

WOOD FILLERS
A number of inexpensive wood fillers can be bought ready-mixed in a range of shades. A two-part epoxy filler is much harder and is recommended for outdoor projects. The best tool for applying filler is a purpose-made filling knife.

Ready-mixed filler
This is easy to apply and is available in a range of wood shades. It can be tinted with some dyes.

Two-part filler
With this filler, the two parts are mixed together thoroughly before application. It sets hard in about 15 minutes.

Putty knife
A putty knife has a strong flexible blade that is good for forcing filler deep into cracks and holes.

Steel wool
Graded from coarse (0) to fine (0000), steel wool is useful for emphasizing grain and forcing wax deep into wood.

Sanding block
This can be made from either cork, as here, or hardwood with a felt base, as below.

Sanding block

Flint paper
This is the cheapest type of abrasive paper. It tends to loose its 'tooth' quickly.

Aluminium-oxide paper
This is a tough, durable abrasive that can be used on wood or metal.

Garnet paper
This is made from garnet crystals and, although relatively expensive, it does maintain its 'tooth'.

Brushes

To start with, you will only need two or three brushes, including a cutting-in brush. Be wary of buying cheap brushes as the bristles fall out with alarming regularity during use. It is worth paying a little bit extra for brushes that have densely packed bristles and a well-made ferrule (the metal strap that anchors the bristles to the brush handle).

Before using a new brush, flex the bristles to weed out any loose ones – even with good-quality brushes, there are bound to be one or two loose bristles. When you have finished using a brush, wash it out thoroughly in either mineral spirits (if you have used a solvent-based finish) or water (if you have used a water-based finish). Store your brushes away from your other tools, ideally by hanging them up on a rack.

Cutting-in brush
The bristles on this brush are cut at an angle. Use a cutting-in brush when finishing mouldings and frames.

2 in (50 mm) brush
This brush is best reserved for finishing large, flat surfaces.

1 in (25 mm) brush
Use this brush when finishing small objects or details.

WOOD SEALERS

If you plan to wax the wood after you have sanded it down, or if you just want to leave it bare, you must seal the surface. If you do not seal the wood, the pores will be left open and will absorb dirt and stains. Ring marks from glasses and cups, for example, are extremely difficult to remove from a wood surface unless it has been sealed.

There are two ways you can seal the surface. Either you can use a purpose-made wood sealer or you can mix up your own sealer using clear varnish and mineral spirits.

Sanding sealer

Most sanding sealers are neutral in color so they do not tint the wood in any way. However, they help to amplify the grain of the wood, which is usually an advantage. One or two coats is normally sufficient.

Diluted varnish

Clear varnish, diluted with mineral spirits, has much the same effect as sanding sealer. Dilute the varnish (80% varnish to 20% spirits) in a clean bowl and make sure that you mix up enough to complete the job. One coat of diluted varnish is usually adequate.

Sanding sealer
This is usually alcohol-based so that the sealer can be readily absorbed by the wood. When the alcohol evaporates, the pores are sealed.

Mineral spirits

Varnish

Sanding sealer

Diluted varnish
Varnish usually coats just the surface, but when it is diluted, it is more fluid and can penetrate deep into the wood.

SANDING AND FINISHING TECHNIQUES

*The last steps toward finishing a project are often the most rewarding. Allow
yourself plenty of time to apply the final touches to ensure that you don't make
any hasty mistakes that could spoil the end result.*

YOU MAY HAVE to spend as much time on the sanding and finishing stages of a project as you have on the making of it. But you should be well rewarded as the final coating is applied and you see the beauty of the wood's color and figure emerge.

In addition to sanding down and applying a finish, you may, however, have to fill blemishes and seal resinous knots. These are vital steps that are often overlooked. If you don't do them, the end result could be a disappointment. As with any part of the construction of a project, it is the attention to detail that can make all the difference.

SOUND PREPARATION
A good end result depends on good preparation. Unfortunately, there is no substitute for hard work, but the rewards are well worth the effort.

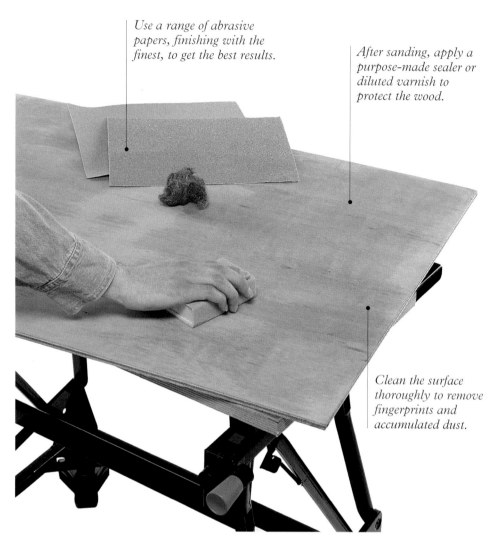

Use a range of abrasive papers, finishing with the finest, to get the best results.

After sanding, apply a purpose-made sealer or diluted varnish to protect the wood.

Clean the surface thoroughly to remove fingerprints and accumulated dust.

Applying filler

If the piece of wood you are working on is going to be painted, fill in any holes, dents or scratches in the wood with an all-purpose wood filler. If you do not intend to paint over the scars, look for a tinted filler that exactly matches your wood so that these patches are rendered almost invisible.

Use a flexible filling knife to apply the filler and squeeze it right into holes. Leave the filler slightly proud of the surface so that when it has set, you can sand it down perfectly flush with the surrounding wood.

If you have any deep holes to fill, patch them up in layers as a thick wedge of filler is likely to crack as it dries out. Allow each layer to harden before adding the next.

Applying wood filler
Force the filler into the hole or crack. Leave the surface slightly raised so that it can be sanded down flush.

Sanding down
When the filler has set hard, sand it down flush using a fine-grit abrasive paper wrapped around a sanding block.

Preparing for the finish coat

After sanding the wood down, vacuum up dust from the surface. This minimizes the amount of dust in the air that could settle on a fresh coat of varnish or paint and ruin it. Finally, wipe down the wood with a rag sprinkled with mineral spirits to remove fingerprints and oil stains that are not always easy to see with the naked eye.

Wiping down with mineral spirits
Remove stains that could impair the finish with a clean cloth or rag lightly moistened with mineral spirits.

APPLYING KNOTTING

If you plan to paint over timber, seal 'live' knots (knots that seep resin) with a shellac-based sealer called knotting. If you don't seal live knots, oozing resin could ruin the finish.

Sealing a knot
Brush on just one thin layer of knotting to seal in the resin.

Waxing

Before applying wax to bare wood, seal the surface with a coat of special sanding sealer or diluted varnish (80% varnish, 20% mineral spirits). If you don't seal the surface, the wax by itself will offer little protection to the wood and will rapidly wear off.

When the sealing coat has dried, rub the wax into the protected surface with fine grade wire wool or a clean cloth.

Applying the wax
Force the wax deep into the pores of the wood. Allow the wax to harden before polishing it with a fresh cloth.

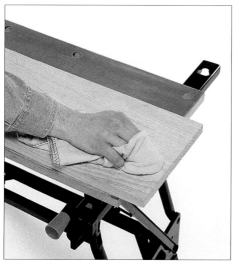

Polishing off
Use a soft cloth or duster to buff up the wax coating. Apply more wax if you want to deepen the sheen.

Brushing on stain

Test the color of the stain you intend to use on a piece of scrap wood before applying it to your project – it may turn out to be a totally different tint to what you expected. If you are happy with the color but want it darker, brush on one or two more coats.

To prevent runs and drips, lay the work horizontal, if possible. Work quickly, covering one face at a time. Keep your strokes even and try to avoid creating any puddles which could leave ugly tide marks.

When you have finished brushing, rub over the stain while it is still wet with a clean, dry cotton cloth. This helps to distribute the stain evenly over the whole surface. Finally, leave the stain to dry before adding a sealing coat of varnish or lacquer.

Staining end grain
When staining end grain, use a stipple action to ensure that the stain is deeply absorbed into the wood.

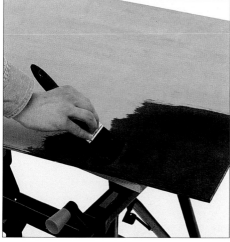

Spreading the stain evenly
Work quickly and evenly over each face, brushing out any puddles or runs as soon as they form.

WOOD FINISHES

After assembling a project, you should coat it with a finish of some kind, both to enhance the appearance of the wood and to protect it. Products range from tinted wax to colored preservatives.

THERE IS SUCH a wide variety of wood finishes available today that you should have little trouble finding something that exactly matches your needs. When making your choice, first decide on what you want the main function of the wood finish to be. Do you primarily want the finish to protect the wood, or is your main consideration the wood's appearance? If, for example, you have made an outdoor project from softwood, preserving it from rot and decay should be your chief objective. However, there is an element of choice, even when choosing a preservative. In the past, wood preservatives were a universal muddy-brown color, but you now have the option of buying tinted varieties that also improve the appearance of the wood.

If your main aim is to enrich the look of a project, the type of wood you have used should influence your choice of finish. Hardwoods generally

Solvent-based stain on redwood
Stains are made to color wood, not to protect it. They are available in a huge range of colors and shades and it is possible to buy water-based stains which are kinder to the environment. Always test a stain on an offcut to check that the color is right; if you wish, you can brush on more coats to darken the tone. After staining, coat wood with varnish.

Colored preservative on redwood
A colored preservative gives you the opportunity to stain and protect outdoor projects with just one product. Several colors are available but be sure to get a 'deep-penetrating' preservative that seeps deep into the pores of the wood. Brush on two or three coats and pay particular attention to the end grain of the wood.

Clear varnish on cherry
Varnish is one of the most durable finishes and is ideal for protecting wood from scratches, heat marks, and moisture penetration. Several thin coats are better than one thick one unless you use a 'one-coat' varnish. It is also a good idea to dilute the first coat with 20% mineral spirits to ensure that the varnish seeps deep into the pores of the wood. For outdoor projects, choose an exterior-grade varnish.

Tinted varnish on hemlock
Tinted varnish provides all the protection of a conventional clear varnish but colors the wood at the same time. Tinted varnishes are available in several natural shades as well as a few strong colors. Always test a tinted varnish on an offcut of wood first, especially if you plan to apply several coats – the more coats you apply, the darker the finish you will achieve.

have interesting and attractive grain features which should be emphasized rather than disguised. Softwoods, on the other hand, tend to be featureless and their appearance can be greatly improved by using a tinted finish.

Clear finishes

If you want to accentuate the grain of a wood while maintaining its natural color, choose a clear finish. Varnishes, available in matt, satin and gloss, effectively seal the surface and also protect it from superficial damage. Oils give a more subtle finish and you will have to apply several coats to build up a sheen. Waxes offer little protection by themselves and should be applied over a sealing coat (*see page 59*).

Tinted finishes

Stains and dyes are available in a huge range of colors, but remember that they always darken wood and never lighten it. Manufacturers now produce water-based stains and dyes which are recommended as they are kind to the environment, easy to clean from brushes, and are fast-drying. Stains or dyes by themselves give virtually no protection to wood so once you have applied the coats you require, seal the wood with a clear varnish.

Tinted varnishes and waxes provide an alternative method of coloring wood. Tinted varnishes save you having to coat stained wood with a separate coat of clear varnish, but they are only available in a limited range of colors. As with clear wax, tinted varieties should be applied on top of sealed wood.

You can, of course, paint wood. If you decide on this option, brush on a priming undercoat before applying the topcoat.

Danish oil on oak
This is just one of several oils that are used for finishing (others include teak and tung oils). It resists water and seals pores so prevents the wood from becoming dirty. Apply at least four coats to build up a deep sheen but it is important to allow each coat to dry before applying the next. You can also use Danish oil to revitalize old wood.

Wax on oak
Furniture wax is usually a mixture of beeswax and carnauba wax dissolved in turpentine. It is best to seal the pores in the wood (see page 59) before rubbing on wax with a cloth or fine wire wool. Wax gives wood a gentle sheen and is traditionally used on hardwoods such as oak. Apply two or three layers of wax and only polish once it has set hard. Add more wax polish to furniture as it is required.

Tinted wax on cherry
Conventional furniture wax is pale and barely colors timber at all. However, it is now possible to buy tinted waxes that contain stains. You can buy shades of tinted wax to suit either dark or light wood. Among the most useful tinted waxes are so-called 'antique polishes' that give the impression of an old patina and help to disguise light scratches and blemishes in the wood.

Gloss paint on redwood
When using most solvent-based paints, brush on a wood primer first otherwise the paint could peel off. Make sure the primer is dry before you apply the topcoat or the finish could be impaired. Water-based acrylic paints are an alternative to solvent paints, and dry more quickly. The example below shows raw wood (top), primer (middle), and gloss topcoat (bottom).

POWER SAWS

Power saws allow you to make accurate cuts with minimal effort. They can be guided with battens or fences to ensure that cuts are straight, even across large boards or planks.

THE TWO most frequently used types of power saw are circular saws and jigsaws. Both need to be handled with care but they slice through boards that would take a long time to cut by hand. One of the disadvantages of power saws is that they tend to leave splintered edges unless you are very cautious.

Circular saws

The blade protrudes through a slot in the bottom plate of the tool and can be raised, lowered and tilted from side to side. Depending on the type of blade fitted, you can use a circular saw for cutting man-made sheet materials as well as wood across and along the grain.

Cutting across the grain
Clamp a batten across the wood at right-angles and push the saw firmly along its edge to make the cut.

Exhaust port
Ejects sawdust and can be connected to an extractor.

Trigger
Fitted with a safety-lock button that must be pushed before the trigger will operate.

Circular saw

Tilt scale
Shows the angle of the blade for bevel cuts.

Blade guard
A spring action ensures moving teeth above the wood are always enclosed.

Riving knife
Prevents the blade jamming when ripping wood along the grain.

Blade
Size depends on the type of machine; blades are interchangeable.

Adjustable side fence
Guides the saw when making cuts parallel to a straight edge.

Blades
Most circular saws have a general-purpose blade with TCT (tungsten-carbide tipped) teeth which can cut man-made board as well as wood.

CIRCULAR SAWS: WHAT TO LOOK FOR

- Powerful motor for easy cutting.
- Thick sole plate for rigidity.
- Sole plate that can be raised and lowered to alter the depth of cut.
- TCT blade with minimum 1⅞in (46mm) depth of cut.
- Comfortable grip and good balance.
- Long guide fence.

Using the side fence
Align the blade with the marked cutting line and adjust the fence to run along the edge of the workpiece.

Jigsaws

Jigsaws have smaller motors than circular saws and the power is used to move the thin straight blades in an up-and-down motion. The blades cut on the up stroke and are small enough to be guided through curves and intricate shapes.

As with circular saws, the sole plates on most jigsaws can be tilted to vary the angle of cut. Some jigsaws also have a scrolling facility which allows the blade to be turned independently so that the whole tool does not have to be twisted. This is particularly useful if you have to cut tight curves.

JIGSAWS: WHAT TO LOOK FOR

- High-power motor.
- Variable speed so the tool can be used for cutting metals and plastics in addition to timber.
- Large depth of cut.
- Scroll action for the most effective cutting out of shapes.
- Comfortable grip.
- Dust extraction facility.

Trigger lock
Keeps the trigger depressed while the motor is running.

Trigger
Squeeze the trigger to start the motor.

Stroke-rate selector
Varies the speed of the saw blade's movement and therefore the speed of the cut.

Jigsaw

Scroll-action selector
Adjusts the forward swing of the blade which varies the cutting speed.

Exhaust port
Ejects the fine dust from the rear of the jigsaw; can be connected to a dust extractor.

Shoe (sole plate)
Can be tilted to either side of the body for miter cuts.

Blade types
These vary according to the type of cut to be made and the material to be sawn; thinner blades can make more acute angles and tighter curves.

Splinter guard
A section of clear plastic which reduces the risk of the wood surface splintering upwards as the blade cuts.

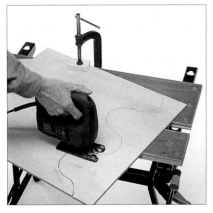

Cutting an irregular shape
Secure the board to a bench and follow the cutting line with the jigsaw.

Cutting a circle
Drill a hole on the waste side of the marked circle, insert the jigsaw blade, and cut out the shape.

POWER SANDERS

Finishing a project often takes as long as making it. Power sanders dramatically help to speed up the process and there is a huge range of models available from which you can make your choice.

SANDING can never hide defects or disguise a poorly fitting joint, but a well-sanded surface will improve the finish of any project.

A rotary or orbital sander is probably the best type of power sander to start off with. Both are versatile, give a very fine finish and are easy to control. Belt sanders are really for the more advanced woodworker who needs to remove wood rapidly from a large flat surface, such as a table top. Belt sanders can be savage and are not particularly easy to control.

Detail sanders are relatively new. They have a small triangular pad and are ideal for getting into the corners of drawers and other awkward spots. However, they are of little use when tackling large areas.

SANDERS: WHAT TO LOOK FOR

- Efficient dust extraction – models that expel dust into a bag are best.
- Variable-speed motor.
- Easy-to-fit sanding sheets.
- Power rating – the more powerful the better.
- Comfortable hand grip – particularly the front grip which is used to guide the tool.

Trigger
Can be locked in the ON position for large-scale flat sanding.

Dust bag
Collects the very fine dust produced by sanding; empty regularly.

Belt sander

Belts
Produced in most standard grades and sold individually.

Tension release
Lever is pushed forward to slacken and change the abrasive belt.

Trigger
Can be operated by the thumb for one-handed use in tight corners.

Exhaust port
Can be connected to an extractor.

Detail sander

Sanding pads
Perforated for efficient dust extraction.

Shoe release
Unclips the whole sanding plate so that it can be rotated or replaced.

Sanding into corners
The flat-iron shape of the detail-sander's shoe is perfect for sanding in tight corners.

USING A SANDER SAFELY

- Control the sander with both hands unless using a small palm sander (not illustrated).
- Ensure that the workpiece is firmly secured to a bench.
- Switch off the main power supply when changing sanding sheets and when the sander is not in use.
- Always wear a face mask to avoid inhaling dust.
- Only light pressure should be applied to the sander.

DUST BAGS

You can fit bags to the exhaust ports on most modern sanders to collect potentially harmful dust.

Using a dust bag
The collar on a disposable dust bag simply fits over the exhaust port and is clipped in place.

Changing a disk
The disks on most orbital sanders are secured with self-fastening fabric and are simple to change.

Trigger
Can be used to control the number of orbits per second on variable-speed models.

Trigger lock
Holds trigger in the ON position for larger jobs.

Orbital sander

Exhaust port
Takes fine dust particles away from the sanding plate.

Paper-clamp lever
Has a spring action to hold sanding sheets in place.

Sanding sheets
Available in a range of sizes and grades to suit different models.

Speed-control dial
Permits both controlled and fast sanding.

Trigger
Operates random-orbit action of sanding plate.

Trigger lock
Allows both hands to be used to control the sander.

Exhaust port
Can be connected to a bag or dust extractor nozzle.

Rotary sander

Adjustable handle
Can be tilted to suit the work or removed for awkward spaces.

Sanding disks
These disks have pierced holes for efficient dust removal and self-fastening fabric for easy fixing.

POWER PLANES

Power planes are powerful tools that can reduce timber very quickly. The finish
they give is less than perfect but they are excellent for preparing rough-sawn wood
to approximate shape and size.

A POWER PLANE has a revolving cutter block on the underside which is extremely efficient at shaving off layers of wood. However, even the best power planes cannot match the finish provided by a hand plane. For this reason, a power plane is best reserved for preparing rough-sawn wood – a task it will do with the minimum of effort and very quickly.

Always treat a power plane with respect and take heed of safety advice offered by the manufacturer. The cutter block turns at high speed and is potentially very dangerous. Practice handling a power plane on offcuts of wood until you get used to it.

POWER PLANES: WHAT TO LOOK FOR
• Powerful motor for fast, efficient planing.
• Variable depth of cut.
• Comfortable front grip.
• Chamfering guide set into the sole plate.
• Side fence attachment that enables rebates to be cut.

Trigger-lock button
For sustained planing, push this button in to lock the trigger in the ON position. Release the button by pressing on the trigger.

Trigger
Press the pistol trigger to switch on the motor.

Guide handle/ depth adjuster
This is a combined feature on some planes and allows the depth of cut to be altered while the plane is running. Other planes have separate depth adjusters.

Blade
A reversible and replaceable blade is clamped into the cutter block. Most power planes have two blades.

Cutter block
This is a drum which supports the blades and revolves at high speed.

Chamfer guide
This is a V-shaped groove set into the sole of the plane and is used to guide the tool when cutting chamfers.

USING A PLANE SAFELY

- When using a plane, keep your hands on the handles, never on the workpiece or body of the plane.
- Always let the cutter block come to a complete stop before resting the plane on a bench.
- Disconnect the plane from the electricity supply whenever it is not in use.
- Never allow the plane to be stationary on a workpiece; always keep it moving or it will scrape and damage the wood.
- Never force a plane to do more than it is capable of. If the motor struggles, reduce the depth of cut.

Changing blades

With most planes, each blade is clamped into the cutter block by a steel plate which is secured with screws. Always disconnect the plane from the electricity supply when swapping blades, and change both blades at the same time to ensure that the plane operates smoothly when you use it in the future.

To change a blade, use an Allen key (or special tool provided with the plane) to slacken the clamping plate. Do not completely remove the screws. Slide out the blade to one side and slot in a new one, making sure that it is the right way up. Check that the edges of the blade are correctly aligned before tightening up the clamp.

Inserting a blade
Slacken the clamping plate and pull out the old blade. Slide the replacement blade underneath the clamping plate.

Clamping down the blade
Make sure the clamping plate engages the blade along the full length of its shallow groove before tightening the screws.

Using a power plane

Take extreme care when you first use a power plane as you may find it difficult to handle. Make certain you know how to operate the tool before you switch on.

Turn the depth adjuster for the plane to make a shallow cut – this lowers the front sole plate. Place the front sole plate on one end of the secured workpiece but make sure the cutters are not touching the surface. Squeeze the trigger to start the motor and move the plane along the wood at a steady rate. At the end of the pass, release the trigger or squeeze it again to disengage the trigger lock.

Making a clean pass
Press on the front handle while planing forward. Near the workpiece edge, press on the rear handle to avoid planing too far.

Adjusting the depth
The depth of cut is governed by the alignment of the front sole plate. Raise or lower the plate by turning the adjuster knob.

POWER-PLANE BLADES

Power-plane blades are slender strips of grooved steel. As both edges are sharp, blades can be turned around when one set of edges becomes dull.

Replacement blades are available in three patterns. If you want to plane a board that is wider than the plane, you can buy round-end cutters which do not leave grooves in their wake.

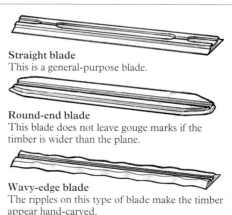

Straight blade
This is a general-purpose blade.

Round-end blade
This blade does not leave gouge marks if the timber is wider than the plane.

Wavy-edge blade
The ripples on this type of blade make the timber appear hand-carved.

POWER DRILL ATTACHMENTS

Drill attachments can often save you both time and money. For example, a sanding-disk attachment can make light work of rough timber so you don't have to invest in a power sander.

YOU CAN use your power drill for much more than just boring holes. All modern power drills can be fitted with accessories that are often well worth buying as they can take the hard work out of chores like sanding down rough boards and cutting large-diameter holes.

A further advantage of buying an attachment is cost. A sanding-disk attachment retails at a fraction of the expense of a power sander yet the results can be as good.

To get the most effective use out of attachments, you need a powerful drill that has various speed settings. You may find a single-speed drill either too fast or too slow for some cutting and sanding accessories.

Drill attachments are safe to use provided you fit them correctly and treat them with respect. Always make sure that the workpiece is firmly anchored to a workbench and always use both hands to operate and control the drill.

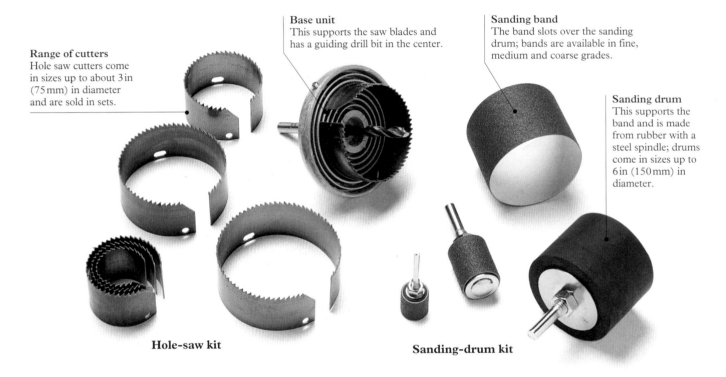

Range of cutters
Hole saw cutters come in sizes up to about 3in (75mm) in diameter and are sold in sets.

Base unit
This supports the saw blades and has a guiding drill bit in the center.

Sanding band
The band slots over the sanding drum; bands are available in fine, medium and coarse grades.

Sanding drum
This supports the band and is made from rubber with a steel spindle; drums come in sizes up to 6in (150mm) in diameter.

Hole-saw kit

Sanding-drum kit

Using a hole saw

Hole-saw attachments make neat holes up to 3in (75mm) in diameter. They can be used on wood or man-made boards up to 1in (25mm) thick and are extremely efficient.

Choose the saw blade that matches the diameter of hole you need and lock it into the base unit with the long machine screw. Fit the saw's center bit into your drill and tighten up the chuck until the bit is secure.

Set the drill to a medium speed and place the drill-bit tip on to the center mark on the workpiece. Apply gentle pressure when you switch the drill on and allow the saw to do the work. Hold the drill at right-angles to the workpiece all the time.

Securing a saw blade
Select the saw blade you need and locate it in its groove in the base unit. Lock the blade with the screw provided.

Cutting the hole
Steady the drill with two hands when making the hole but apply minimum pressure or the wood may smoulder.

Using a drum sander

Drum sanders are useful for smoothing down holes and curved edges cut out of boards or planks. It is generally best to use the largest size of drum that is feasible as small drums have a tendency to scoop out shallow dents unless you are very careful. Small drums are excellent, however, for tidying up intricate details and moldings.

When using a drum sander, do not apply too much pressure on the drum as the abrasive action works best with a light touch. Always use the sander with the drill set at a high speed and make sure the workpiece is secure.

Sanding a curved workpiece
Keep the drum moving all the time, otherwise it will form dips in the curve.

Sanding-disk attachments

Sanding disks are efficient for smoothing down rough wood, but you need to use them with care otherwise they leave unsightly, circular marks on the workpiece. Whenever you use a sanding disk, set the drill to a high speed and keep the drill moving constantly to minimize the chances of scoring the wood. It is generally best to finish off the job by hand to get a really sleek finish.

In addition to sanding disks, you can add buffing mops to a backing disk. These make light work of polishing waxed surfaces. You can also buy clamps designed to secure a drill to a workbench so that when you fit it with a sanding disk, you can use it as a stationary bench sander.

SCREWDRIVER BITS

Provided you have a drill with variable speeds, you can use it as a power screwdriver which can save you time and energy. Screwdriver bits for a power drill are usually sold as kits that contain everything you need, including a chuck attachment and a range of screwdriver tips.

To use a power drill as a screwdriver, switch to a slow speed, slot a drill tip into the end of the attachment and tighten the attachment in the drill's chuck.

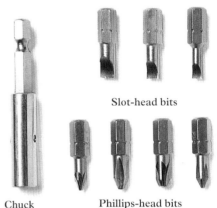

Slot-head bits

Phillips-head bits

Chuck attachment

Screwdriver-bit kit
A kit contains slot-head and Phillips-head bits made from hardened steel.

Backing disk
The backing disk is made from rubber with a steel spindle that fits into the drill's chuck. Sizes range up to 8 in (200 mm).

Buffing mop
A lambswool buffing mop is tied around the backing disk and can give waxed surfaces a magnificent sheen.

Sanding disks
These are circular abrasive disks that are available in a variety of grit sizes. They are secured to the backing disk with a metal boss.

71

SIMPLE JOINT TECHNIQUES

Once you have mastered the woodworking joints illustrated on the next eight pages, you will be able to take on almost any furniture project. You will also be able to select joints when planning your own designs.

LEARNING TO MAKE strong, tight-fitting joints is central to the art of woodworking as the strength and stability of most items of furniture depend on them. There are many different types of joint and they all have advantages and disadvantages. Some types of joint are easy to make but relatively weak, while others are difficult to construct but are exceptionally sturdy. Succesful joint-making relies on precise marking and measuring (*see pages 24-27*) as well as accurate sawing (*see pages 30-31*) and cutting (*see pages 38-39*).

BUTT JOINTS

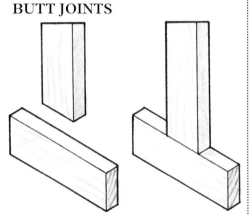

The simplest of all methods of joining two pieces of wood together is to butt them against each other. The strength of the joint relies entirely on glue and any additional fixings such as nails or screws. Butt joints are not strong but you can use them in basic frames that are unlikely to be put under stress.

When you make a butt joint, plane the two meeting surfaces perfectly flat and smooth and check that they are square to each other. Spread a film of adhesive over one of the surfaces and clamp them together.

Checking the pieces are square
Use a try square to ensure that the pieces meet at a perfect right-angle. The meeting surfaces should be flat so that the joint has no gaps when you assemble it.

MITERED BUTT JOINT

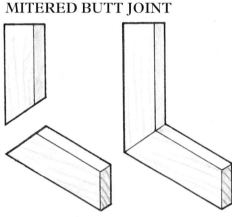

This is a variation on the simple butt joint and is often selected for picture frames and small boxes. Again, the joint derives what strength it has from the adhesive and fixings you use. If you decide to reinforce the joint with nails or screws, try to avoid driving them straight down the end grain of one of the pieces as they will not grip well. If you can, nail or screw at right-angles across the joint.

Marking the components
Use a combination square and pencil to mark the 45° miters. Crosshatch the waste to clarify the cutting angle.

Accurate sawing is particularly important when making mitered-butt joints. If the 45° cuts are inaccurate,
the joint will be lopsided. It is best to mark out the components using a combination square before you cut the angles in a miter box. This enables you to check the saw cuts for accuracy as you make them.

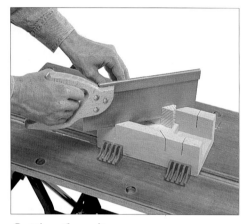

Cutting the miters
Align your marks with appropriate slots in your miter box and saw off the waste.

Adhesive tends to be readily absorbed by end-grain faces so seal them first with a thin coating of adhesive. When this is dry, add more adhesive before assembling and clamping the joint.

Test fitting
Check that the mating faces form a neat joint before assembling and gluing.

SIMPLE CORNER LAP JOINT

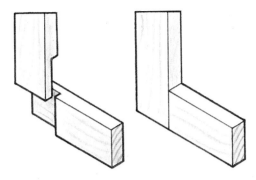

This joint is considerably stronger than a butt joint because the two pieces actually interlock with each other. In addition to gluing the meeting faces and edges, you can also screw through the joint for extra strength. Corner lap joints are commonly used in the construction of basic frames where all the components have the same thickness.

Start by checking that all the edges of the pieces you are joining are square and flat. Mark out the width of the joint on one component by placing one piece across the other. Make sure that the edge is flush with the end of the piece you are marking. Mark a cutting line across the first piece and then double-check that it is accurate with a try square. Use your pencil and try square again to mark the width of the joint down the sides of the piece.

To mark the depth of the joint, use a marking gauge (*see pages 24-27*). Set the gauge to half the thickness of the piece and score a cutting line along the two sides and the end of the wood.

Cut the shoulder of the joint to the depth line with a back saw before cutting down the grain to remove the waste wood. Tidy up the joint with a chisel and then repeat the process with the second piece of wood.

Marking the depth of the joint
Mark a cutting line to exactly half the thickness of the wood down both sides and along the end.

Sawing the shoulder
Cut down to the depth line with a back saw. If possible, use the right-angled slots in a miter box to guide the saw.

Checking for fit
When you have cut out both pieces, check that they join together neatly to form an exact right-angle.

CROSS LAP JOINT

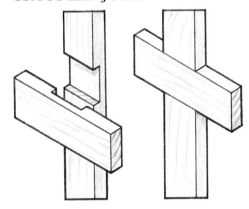

You can use a half-lap joint to secure sections that cross along their length. As the pieces are locked together, they cannot twist out of alignment.

Mark out the width of the joint by laying one piece on top of the other and scribing down the sides. If the pieces cross at a right-angle, check for accuracy with a try square. Score the depth of the joint – which should be exactly half the thickness of the wood – with a marking gauge.

Cut down to the depth lines with a back saw and use a sharp bevel-edge chisel to remove the waste and to create a flat surface (*see pages 38-39*).

Then cut out the joint in the second piece of wood and try the two for fit. If necessary, use your chisel to pare away slivers until the two pieces join together neatly with the top and bottom surfaces perfectly flush.

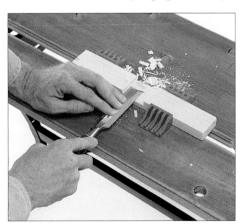

Cleaning out the joint
Once you have removed the bulk of the waste wood, pare away slivers to smooth the bottom and sides of the joint.

Checking for fit
Test the joint before gluing up and clamping. The joint should be tight and the top and bottom faces flush.

T-LAP JOINT

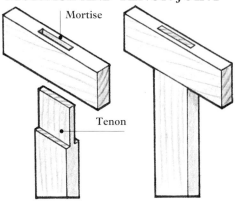

You can use this variation of the half-lap joint to attach the end of one piece of wood to the middle of another. This joint is commonly used to fix bearers to supports, for example in garden furniture. You can strengthen the joint by adding screws but make sure that the screws are not long enough to pass right through.

Mark out the width of the joint by placing one piece over the other and score the depth of the joint with a marking gauge set to half the thickness of the piece. One simple way of checking that your marking gauge is set to the correct depth is to score a line running the stock against one side of the wood and then to run the stock along the opposite side. If you have set the gauge to exactly half the thickness of the wood, the pin in the gauge should score the same line both times.

Cut out the waste wood in both halves of the joint using a back saw and chisel. Then check that they fit before gluing up and clamping the pieces together.

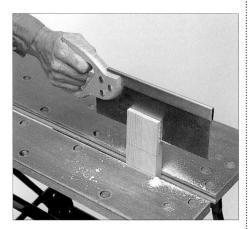

Sawing out the waste
Always saw to the waste side of the cutting line and then clean up the joint with a sharp bevel-edge chisel.

MORTISE AND TENON JOINT

Mortise

Tenon

The mortise and tenon joint is one of the most widely used of all wood-working joints. The reason for its popularity is that it combines mechanical strength with a large surface area for gluing. The tenon is secured on all four sides and, if it fits securely in its mortise, it cannot wobble and is difficult to pull out.

Measuring the mortise
As a general rule, the width of the mortise should be approximately one-third of the thickness of the wood. If it is wider, it is possible that the sides could split open when pressure is put on the tenon. Conversely, if the mortise is too narrow, the tenon could be made weak.

As a convention, it is usual to cut the mortise first and to make the tenon fit the mortise exactly. So you

need to mark the length and width of the mortise first.

Decide on the width of the tenon (this is often the width of the piece of wood from which the tenon is cut) and transfer the measurement to the mortise piece. Check that the lines you mark are at right-angles using a try square. If you are making a through tenon – that is, the tenon is going to go right through the piece – mark the width of the tenon on the underside of the mortise piece as well.

Marking the mortise width
Measure the exact thickness of the mortise piece and divide the figure by three to determine the approximate width of the mortise. Select a chisel that is close to a third of the thickness of the piece and set the gap between the two pins on your mortise gauge to the precise span of the chisel blade.

Adjust the stock of the mortise gauge so that when it is held against the face of the mortise piece, the two pins score parallel lines in the middle of the edge. You can check that you have centered the lines accurately by running the stock against the opposite face. If it is correct, the pins should scribe identical lines. For a through tenon, it is recommended that you also mark the width of the mortise on the other edge.

Marking out the mortise
Mark the length of the mortise first, then set the pins of a mortise gauge to the span of a chisel that is about one-third of the width of the wood. Score parallel lines between the breadth marks. Mark the mortise on both sides of the wood.

Drilling out the waste
Remove the bulk of the waste with a drill. Hold the drill vertically and improvise a depth stop by wrapping a piece of tape around the bit.

To remove the bulk of the waste use a drill fitted with a bit slightly smaller in diameter than the width of the mortise. Hold the drill vertically and fit a depth gauge so that you do not drill right through the piece.

Cleaning out the mortise
Hold your chisel vertically and push down to clean up the mortise. Guide the blade between your finger and thumb.

When making a through tenon, drill from both edges. When you have removed most of the waste, clean the

mortise with your chisel, making sure that the surfaces are vertical as well as flat and smooth.

When you have made the mortise, carefully measure it up and transfer the measurements to the tenon piece. The easiest, and most accurate, way of doing this is with a marking gauge.

Cutting out the tenon
Saw down one face of the tenon at an angle of around 45°, then turn the wood around and cut down the other face.

Cut the tenon shoulders before sawing down the grain to remove the waste. Saw down the grain in stages. To remove the waste, clamp the piece in your workbench and saw down at an angle of around 45°.

Sawing down to the shoulder
Finish by sawing horizontally down to the shoulder of the tenon. This is easiest if you mount the piece upright.

Turn the piece around and saw down the other side at a similar angle. Finally, mount the piece vertically and saw horizontally down to the shoulder.

Checking for fit
Dry-assemble the components before clamping and gluing. Pare away shavings from the tenon if the joint is too tight.

When you have cut out the tenon, try it in the mortise. If necessary, pare away thin slices of wood from the mortise with a chisel until the joint slots together neatly.

EDGE-TO-EDGE JOINT

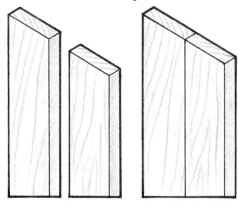

As very wide boards of solid wood tend to warp and split, it is sometimes better to join several narrower pieces together edge-to-edge to achieve the same width. This technique is often used to make table tops and other broad surfaces. However, edge-to-edge joints are not mechanically strong as they do not interlock in any way; they rely entirely on the strength of the glue.

Rubbing the boards together
After you have smeared glue along the edges, firmly rub the boards together while keeping the faces flush.

Plane the edges of the boards until they are perfectly flat and smooth (*see pages 42-45*). Any undulations will make the joint weak. Once you have levelled the edges, spread an even layer of adhesive over both the meeting surfaces. Press the two edges together and, while the glue is still wet, slide them up and down against each other. This rubbing action (the joint is sometimes called a rub joint) sucks the boards together as the glue is squeezed out. With short boards, clamping is not necessary, but it is best to clamp long boards (*see pages 48-49*).

THROUGH DADO JOINT

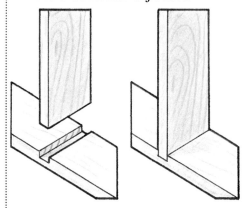

Through dado joints are simple but strong. They are ideal for bookcases or storage units where load-bearing boards have to be joined at right-angles to uprights. In the basic form of the joint (as illustrated), only one component has to be shaped. In more complex versions, the horizontal boards are notched.

Marking up

Draw the position and width of the horizontal board with a pencil on to the piece that is to have a dado (housing) cut into it. Check that your marks are exactly at right angles to the edges with a try square and continue the lines across the sides of the wood. To prevent the wood from splintering later on when you saw it, carefully run along the cutting lines with a sharp craft knife held against a steel straightedge.

Next, set your marking gauge to approximately one-third of the thickness of the wood and draw depth lines for the dado along both edges of the wood between the width lines.

Sawing down the sides
Cut down the sides (known as the cheeks) of the dado, as far as the depth lines, with a back saw. Check your progress regularly.

Anchor the piece of wood horizontally to your workbench and cut down the sides of the dado as far as the depth marks with a back saw. Take your time while doing this, making sure that you push your saw horizontally and keeping it on the waste side of the cutting lines. Check your progress at regular intervals.

Cleaning out the dado
Use a mallet and chisel to remove most of the waste from the dado. Chisel from both sides and clean up by hand.

After cutting down the sides, chisel out the waste in between the saw cuts. Work carefully from both edges of the wood (*see pages 38-39*) and finish by paring the bottom of the dado flat. If the sides of the dado are not perpendicular, straighten them up by paring down vertically.

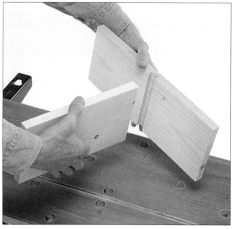

Checking for fit
The joint should be a tight fit. If necessary, pare fine shavings away from the sides of the dado.

Test the fit of the joint and take off shavings from the dado until the board fits tightly. Glue the joint and weight it if clamping is awkward.

INTERLOCKING JOINT

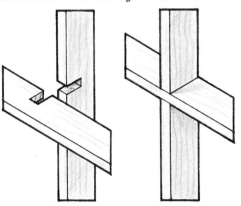

This is essentially a cross lap joint in which the pieces are joined edge on to each other. One interlocking joint by itself is not particularly strong because, if more stress is applied to one side of the joint than to the other, the wood could split. However, if several pieces of wood are joined together using tight interlocking joints to form a grid, the whole structure should be stable.

Use the two pieces to be joined as templates when you mark out the

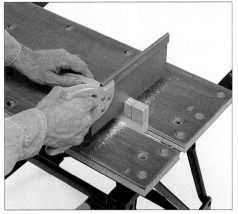

Cutting down to the line
Saw down the sides of each cut-out to the halfway line. Chop out the waste using a chisel and mallet.

positions and widths of the cut-outs. Check that the lines lie at right-angles to the edges of the wood with a try square and score cutting lines against a steel straightedge to prevent splintering when you start sawing. Score the depth of the cut-outs with a marking gauge set to half the width of the pieces.

Clamp the wood firmly before you cut down to the depth lines with a back saw. Keep an eye on the guide lines as you make each cut, as it is easy to let the saw wander. After you have sawn down the sides, chip out the waste wood with a chisel and clean up the sides. When you have cut out both parts, assemble the joint.

Fitting the joint together
Lock the two sections together in a dry run before adding adhesive to make the joint permanent.

RABBET JOINT

The rabbet joint is not particularly strong but it is more stable than a butt joint and has the advantage of hiding the end grain of the horizontal piece in a rabbet. Rabbet joints are frequently used in shelves and boxes.

The first thing to do is to check that the piece that is going to fit into the rabbet is cut square. The easiest way of doing this is to hold a try square across the top.

To score the depth of the rabbet on the upright piece, set your marking gauge to about a quarter of the thickness of the wood. Run the gauge up both edges and across the end of the wood. Scoring a clean

line across end grain can be difficult as the pin tends to get snagged. If you find this to be the case, reinforce the line with pencil. Finish the marking stage by setting your marking gauge to the exact thickness of the other piece of wood and transfer this measurement to the inside face of the upright.

Cutting the rabbet
Cut the shoulder first, then down the grain, to release the waste. If necessary, tidy up the joint with a sharp chisel.

When you cut out the rabbet, saw across the grain first. Clamp the piece firmly so that it cannot slip

and keep the blade of the saw horizontal all through the cut. When you reach the depth line, mount the piece upright and cut down the end grain to release the waste.

Assemble the joint in a dry run before adding glue. If clamping the joint together proves awkward, tap in two or three small nails to hold the pieces together until the glue sets. If you want to remove the nails later, leave their heads slightly above the surface so you can lever them out.

Fitting the joint together
Try the joint first before adding glue. The pieces should meet neatly at right-angles with no gaps.

DOWEL JOINTS

Dowels provide an inexpensive way of fixing pieces of wood together, in almost any configuration, without having to cut a joint. You can use either dowelling pins or a jig to make sure the holes line up perfectly every time.

YOU CAN USE dowels to join boards edge-to-edge or at right-angles to each other. They provide a relatively strong joint – provided you use a good glue – and the only difficulty in using them lies in drilling accurate holes.

Dowels come in various diameters, the most common being $^{1}/_{4}$in (6mm), $^{3}/_{8}$in (10mm) and $^{1}/_{2}$in (12mm). Dowels should ideally have shallow grooves or flutes down their sides so that excess glue can escape when they are tapped home.

SIMPLE DOWEL JOINT

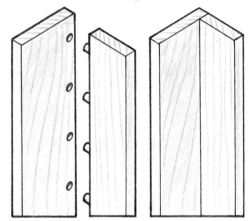

Using dowelling pins

You can use dowelling pins to align holes in edge-to-edge boards (as shown) as well as to match up holes in boards that you want to join at right-angles. Pins are available in sizes to match the diameters of most dowels.

To use dowelling pins, first use your marking gauge to score a line down the middle of the edge of a board. Then mark the positions of the dowels along this line. In most instances, you need to space dowels about 150mm (6in) apart.

Secure a dowelling bit that matches the diameter of your dowels into your drill and make holes at each of the dowel positions. Fit a depth gauge to the bit so that you do not drill more than half the length of a dowel, and make sure that each hole is drilled vertically.

Tap along the length of the joint to make sure the edges meet and that the dowels are driven into their holes.

Squirt glue into each hole before inserting the dowels. Also smear adhesive along one mating edge.

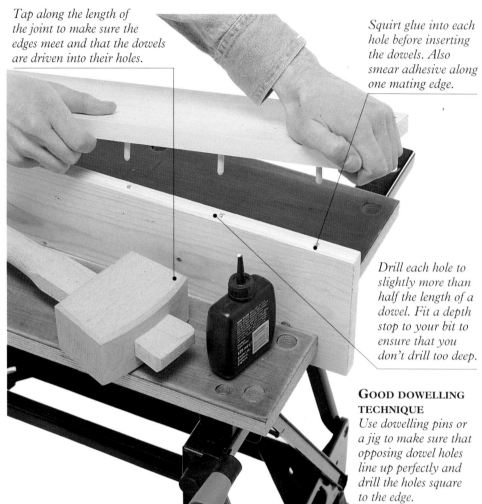

Drill each hole to slightly more than half the length of a dowel. Fit a depth stop to your bit to ensure that you don't drill too deep.

GOOD DOWELLING TECHNIQUE
Use dowelling pins or a jig to make sure that opposing dowel holes line up perfectly and drill the holes square to the edge.

Drilling the dowel holes
Use a depth stop or piece of tape to judge the depth of each hole accurately. Hold the drill square to the edge.

Inserting the pins
Drop a dowelling pin of the right size into each hole. Make sure that each pin fits snugly in its hole.

When you have drilled out all the holes, drop a dowelling pin into each one. Then align the second piece on top of the pins, making certain that the faces of the pieces are parallel and flush with each other. Tap down on the second piece of wood so that each pin makes a mark along its edge. Remove the second piece of wood and drill holes at each pinprick.

Force glue and then dowels into each hole in the first row and smear a film of adhesive all along the edge. Put glue into the second row of holes and position them over the dowels. Tap the wood on to the dowels with a mallet and wipe away any excess glue with a damp cloth.

Positioning the second board
Place the second board over the pins, making sure that the faces of the two boards are perfectly aligned.

Checking the pin marks
Press or tap the two boards together, then lift off the second board which should have marks along its edge.

Driving the joint together
Drill holes at each mark in the second edge, then insert glue and dowels and tap the pieces together with a mallet.

Using a dowelling jig

A dowelling jig is a particularly useful tool to use when you want to join boards together at right-angles. There are many different designs and you can improvise your own jig to suit special projects (*see page 96*).

First you need to mark up your boards. Take the board that is going to have dowels inserted into its edge and score a line precisely down the middle of the edge with a marking gauge (*see pages 24-27*). Without adjusting your marking gauge, score a line on the face of the second board, parallel to its edge. The depth of this second line should be exactly half the thickness of the first board. Clamp the two boards together, the second board on top of the first. The marked edge should be visible and the marked face should be uppermost. Pencil in the spacings of the dowels along the top board.

Position your jig on top of the boards and decide which of the guide holes you are going to use. With most jigs, there are four diameter options in each plate of the jig to suit most dowel sizes. Adjust your jig so that the guide holes of your choice are positioned exactly over your scribed lines. Site the top guide hole over the mark for the first dowel and drill down vertically, using a bit of the correct diameter. Be sure to fit a depth stop, not forgetting to take into account the thickness of the plate. After drilling the first hole, keep the jig stationary and drill horizontally into the edge of the bottom board. Move the jig along and drill all the holes in this way. Insert glue and dowels, and assemble the boards, using a mallet to seat the joint.

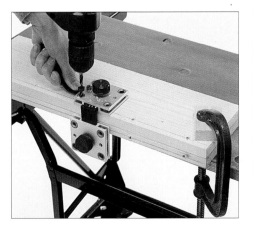

Setting up the jig
Adjust the plates of the jig so that corresponding holes are positioned exactly over your guide lines.

Drilling through the jig
Slide the jig to each dowel position and drill into the face first, then into the edge. Be sure to fit a depth stop.

Gluing up the dowels
Force adhesive into each hole before tapping in a dowel. Glue the meeting surfaces as well for a strong joint.

THE PROJECTS

The best way to master woodworking skills is to make projects that involve using them. In this section, there are 22 project designs that range from the simple to the slightly more challenging. In making these projects, you will use a whole range of techniques and skills, and the more you practice, the more proficient you will become. All of the designs are for practical items or pieces of furniture.

BIRD BOX

*This nesting box will encourage birds to move into even the smallest
urban garden. It can be made from almost any type of wood, as the
assembly is simple and no jointing is required.*

THE SPECIFICATIONS for the box
are suitable for small birds, but
you can check and adapt the
entrance size for specific species.
A thin sheet of metal protects the
entrance hole from predators. As
far as possible, use weatherproof
materials such as galvanized tacks.

PROJECT PLANNER

- Mark out and prepare wooden
  components
- Work components to shape and drill
  holes
- Assemble box and fit top
- Clean up and apply finish

WHAT YOU NEED

CUTTING LIST
- Back: one 16 x 7 x ¾in
  (405 x 178 x 19mm) length of softwood
- Sides: two 10 x 6 x ¾in (255 x 150 x
  19mm) lengths of softwood
- Front: one 8 x 6 x ¾in
  (200 x 150 x 19mm) length of softwood
- Bottom: one 5¼ x 4½ x ¾in
  (131 x 112 x 19mm) length of softwood
- Top: one 7¾ x 6¾ x ¼in
  (195 x 170 x 6mm) length of plywood
- Hinge: one 7¾ x 2in (195 x 50mm)
  strip of tough leather or webbing
- Entrance hole protector: one
  2½ x 2½in (63 x 63mm) piece of thin
  sheet metal
- 1½in (38mm) pins or small nails
- ½in (12mm) galvanized tacks
- Screws: ten 1¼in (32mm) No.8
  countersunk

TOOLS REQUIRED
- Straightedge, try square and sliding
  bevel
- Panel saw
- Block plane
- Hammer, bradawl and screwdriver
- Power drill and bits

SEE ALSO

SKILLS
- Measuring and marking techniques
  (*see pages 24–27*)
- Sawing techniques (*see pages 30–31*)
- Drilling techniques (*see pages 34–35*)
- Planing techniques (*see pages 42–45*)
- Sanding and finishing techniques
  (*see pages 60–61*)

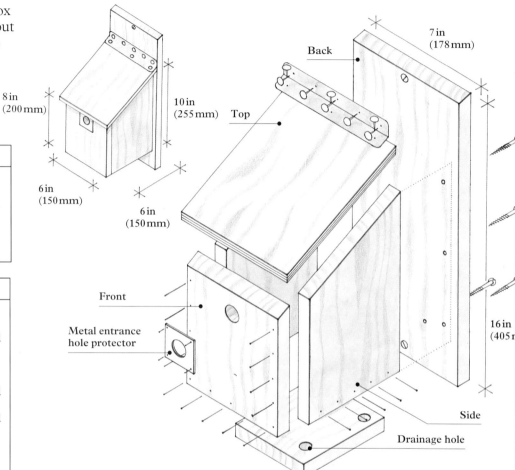

8in
(200mm)

6in
(150mm)

10in
(255mm)   Top

6in
(150mm)

Back

7in
(178mm)

Front

Metal entrance
hole protector

Drainage hole

Side

16in
(405mm)

Preparing the wood

1 Mark out the components and
cut them to length and width
(*see pages 24–27 and 30–31*).

2 Mark the sloping ends of the
sides, using a sliding bevel set to
60°, and cut off the waste with a panel
saw. Plane the top ends straight and
square to the faces (*see pages 42–45*).

Marking out with a sliding bevel

Shaping and drilling

1 Hold the front piece firmly in
your workbench and mark the
bevel on the top end to match the
slope of the sides. Use a block plane
to shape the bevel, working from
both edges so that the plane does
not split the grain as it would if you
planed across in only one direction
(*see pages 42–45*).

Shaping the bevel with a block plane

2 Drill the entrance hole in the front piece to 1 in (25 mm) in diameter, with the center 1½ in (38 mm) from the top end (*see pages 34–35*). Cut the same size hole from the piece of sheet metal and pin the metal around the entrance.

Pinning metal strip to entrance hole

3 Drill at least four ½ in (12 mm) holes in the base for ventilation.

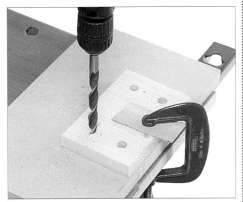

Drilling ventilation holes in base

Assembling the box

1 Glue and pin the front piece over the edges of the sides. Carefully position the base and, when it fits correctly, glue and pin it into place through the front and sides. Make sure that the three back edges are flush, and plane them if necessary.

2 Lay the assembly in place on the back piece, with equal lengths of the back piece above and below the box. Mark the inside and outside edges with a pencil.

3 Drill three clearance holes for screws between the pencil lines on each side and two between the base lines. Mark through the clearance holes onto the sides and base of the box.

4 Drill pilot holes at your marks, apply glue on the back edges of the sides and base, and screw the back piece into place.

Fitting the top and finishing

1 Plane a bevel on the back end of the top in the same way as you did for the front end.

2 Cut a strip of material for the hinge, mark a line down the middle and line this up with the back end of the top. Tack the hinge to the top, using galvanized tacks. Where the tacks come through the back of the plywood, knock the points over to give a secure fixing.

3 Lay the box on its back, carefully position the top, and tack the hinge to the back piece, ensuring that the top overlaps by at least ¼ in (6 mm) all round.

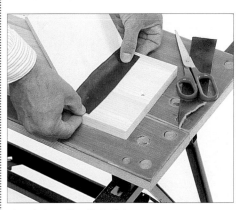

Applying flexible hinge to top

4 Clean up the box, and apply a non-toxic, weatherproof finish. Fix the box to a tree with screws.

BULLETIN BOARD

*Bulletin boards are useful features, both at home and in public places such as
offices, clubs and schools. This design uses mitered softwood mouldings
glued and screwed to a MDF base and packing strips.*

THIS BULLETIN BOARD is designed
around six 12in (305mm) cork tiles,
but can be made to any size using a
different number of tiles, or by cutting them
to suit the dimensions of an available space.
Any moulding with a flat back is suitable as a
surround. The final size of the base is
determined by the size and number of cork
tiles used and the width of the moulding; it is
trimmed to size after the surround is fixed.

PROJECT PLANNER

- Mark and cut out components
- Fit first two packing strips to base
- Glue on cork tiles
- Fit remaining packing strips
- Cut miters on mouldings and fit to
  board
- Trim finished assembly
- Apply finish and fit mirror plates

WHAT YOU NEED

CUTTING LIST
- Tiles: six 12in (305mm) square cork
  flooring tiles plus tile adhesive
- Moulding: two 40in (1015mm) and
  two 28in (710mm) lengths of
  pre-moulded softwood
- Base: one 40 x 28 x ³⁄₈in
  (1015 x 710 x 10mm) MDF board
- Packing strips: two 39in (990mm) and
  two 27in (685mm) lengths of MDF, the
  same thickness as the cork tiles and
  ¹⁄₄in (6mm) narrower than the moulding
- Screws: ³⁄₄in (19mm) No.8 countersunk

TOOLS REQUIRED
- Straightedge and try square
- Jigsaw and back saw
- Block plane
- C-clamps
- Miter box
- Power drill, bits, bradawl and screwdriver

SEE ALSO

SKILLS
- Measuring and marking techniques
  (*see pages 24–27*)
- Sawing techniques (*see pages 30–31*)
- Drilling techniques (*see pages 34–35*)
- Planing techniques (*see pages 42–45*)
- Clamping techniques (*see pages 48–49*)
- Fixing techniques (*see pages 54–55*)
- Sanding and finishing techniques
  (*see pages 60–61*)

Cork tile

Mirror plate

Dimension to suit

MDF base board

Dimension
to suit

Softwood
front
moulding

Countersunk
clearance hole
through base

MDF packing
strip

Dimension
to suit

Marking and preparation

1 Make a simple scale drawing of
the board, based on the number
and size of cork tiles to be used and
the moulding selected. Calculate the
finished size of the various
components from the drawing.

2 Cut strips of MDF ¹⁄₄in (6mm)
narrower than the moulding for
the packing strips, either sawing them
off a larger sheet or from off-cuts.
Plane the edges straight and parallel.

3 Cut the MDF base slightly oversize, ensuring that all the corners
are square.

4 Lay the packing strips and tiles
on the base board to check how
they fit, and make any necessary
adjustments.

Marking the width of the packing

Laying out tiles and packing

Laying the tiles

1 Glue packing pieces along one long edge and one adjacent end of the baseboard, butting them up to each other at the corner.

2 Cramp the packing pieces in place so that their edges are flush with the baseboard (*see pages 48–49*).

Gluing and clamping packing to base

3 When the glue is dry, stick the cork tiles to the base with tile adhesive, using the two packing strips as guides. Because tile adhesive sets quickly, push the tiles up tight to one another immediately.

Laying cork tiles onto base

4 When the tiles are securely fixed, fit and glue the last two packing strips on the baseboard and clamp them in place.

Fitting the face mouldings

1 Mark off the four lengths of face moulding from the outer edges of the packing strips, and cut miters at each end to your marks (*see pages 30–31*). Check the fit on the board and, if necessary, make very fine adjustments to the joints with a block plane. With miters, it is better to err on the side of overlength; if a piece is too short, it is useless.

2 Drill clearance holes through the base and packing pieces at 9 in (230 mm) intervals (*see pages 34–35*).

3 Spread glue thinly on one of the packing pieces that is flush with the baseboard. Place the matching moulding on and clamp it securely, ensuring it is positioned accurately.

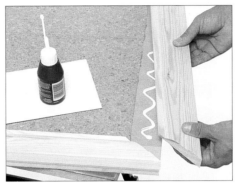

Gluing the moulding

4 Next, turn the board over and drill short pilot holes through the clearance holes into the moulding. Screw through to the moulding and remove the clamps. Repeat with each moulding in turn.

5 Using a block plane, level the last two edges of the base so that they are flush with the packing pieces and the mouldings (*see pages 42–45*).

Finishing and hanging

1 Mask off the cork tiles with tape and paper, and apply paint or clear varnish to the face mouldings and edges (*see pages 60–61*).

2 Screw a pair of brass mirror plates to the top of the back and fix the board to the wall.

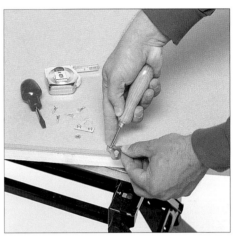

Fitting mirror plates to the back

SHOE STORAGE RACK

*This useful rack is made from dowelling and softwood, using
simple rabbet joints..The rack is designed to hold two pairs of adult
shoes on each pair of shoe rails.*

Most shoe racks are kept in the bottom of a closet and the dimensions for this one enable it to fit inside a standard 24 in (610 mm) deep closet. However, it is possible to adjust both the width and depth of the rack to suit a closet of a different size. If you want, you can make the shoe rails from 1 in (25 mm) diameter brass rods, in which case drill the sides as instructed and cut the rods to size with a hacksaw.

PROJECT PLANNER

- Make the components
- Cut the joints
- Assemble the frame
- Clean up and finish

WHAT YOU NEED

CUTTING LIST
- Sides: two $21^5/8$ x 9 x 1 in (550 x 230 x 25 mm) lengths of softwood, made by joining together two narrower strips
- Front rail: one $25^1/2$ x $2^3/4$ x 1 in (648 x 70 x 25 mm) length of softwood
- Back rails: two $25^1/2$ x 2 x 1 in (648 x 50 x 25 mm) lengths of softwood
- Shoe rails: four $23^1/2$ x 1 in (598 x 25 mm) lengths of dowelling
- Screws: eight $1^1/2$ in (38 mm) No. 8 countersunk

TOOLS REQUIRED
- Straightedge and try square
- Bench plane and block plane
- C-clamps and bar clamps
- Back saw and panel saw
- Power drill and bits
- 1 in (25 mm) chisel
- Bradawl and screwdriver

SEE ALSO

SKILLS
- Measuring and marking techniques (*see pages 24–27*)
- Sawing techniques (*see pages 30–31*)
- Drilling techniques (*see pages 34–35*)
- Cutting and shaping techniques (*see pages 38–39*)
- Planing techniques (*see pages 42–45*)
- Clamping techniques (*see pages 48–49*)
- Sanding and finishing techniques (*see pages 60–61*)
- Simple joint techniques (*see pages 72–77*)

Preparing the sides

1 Join together two narrow strips of softwood to make up the side pieces. Plane the edges to be joined straight and square with a bench plane (*see pages 42–45*).

2 Spread glue thinly on the meeting edges of the strips and clamp them together (*see pages 48–49*). Make sure that the pieces are perfectly aligned, then wipe away any excess glue.

3 When the glue has dried, use a bench plane to level the faces until they are flush.

Cutting the sides

1 Mark up outlines of the two side pieces for the rack on the pieces you have joined together (*see pages 24–27*). Use a try square and straightedge to keep the lines clean and accurate. Saw off the waste, keeping your saw to the waste side of the cutting lines (*see pages 30–31*).

Shaping the side pieces

2 Saw the side pieces to length and clean up the end grain with a block plane. Clean up long edges down to the pencil line with a bench plane.

Drilling the sides

1 Mark the centers for the shoe rails on the two side pieces. The sides should be mirror images of each other.

Marking the rail centers

2 Select a drill bit to match the size of the dowelling for the shoe rails. Drill the holes in both side pieces ½in (12mm) deep.

Drilling the rail holes

3 Mark and cut each of the four shoe rails. All the rails must be equal in length.

Cutting the rabbet joints

1 Cut the front and back rails ¾in (19mm) overlength. Use a bench plane to square up the sides.

2 Mark the notches for the back rails by holding the rails in position and scribing round them (*see pages 72–77*). Use a back saw to cut away the waste.

Scribing a housing for a back rail

Assembling the shoe rails

1 Smear glue over the ends of the shoe rails and slot them into the holes in the side pieces.

Fitting a shoe rail

2 Check that the rails are square to the side pieces and then use bar clamps to hold the assembly rigid.

Fitting the front and back rails

1 Hold each overlength rail in place and mark where to drill countersunk clearance holes.

2 After drilling the countersunk clearance holes, reposition the rails. Push a bradawl through the clearance holes to mark pilot holes.

3 Drill the pilot holes in the side pieces before gluing and screwing the rails in place.

4 When the glue is dry, saw off ends of the rails at each side and plane them flush with a block plane.

5 Bevel the top edge of the front rail to the same angle as the side pieces, using a bench plane.

Cleaning up and finishing

1 Carefully clean up the rack with abrasive paper and finish it off by applying at least two or three coats of clear varnish.

PICTURE FRAME

*Using a miter box and the wide range of ready-made mouldings available
at lumber yards, it is a simple job to create a hand-made
frame of virtually any size.*

THE DIMENSIONS of this project depend on the size of the picture or mirror you want to frame. If you are framing a picture, make allowances for a mounting mat, assuming you want to use one. The thickness of the backing frame must be sufficient to allow for the glass, mounting mat, picture and backing panel, plus a little extra so that the retaining pins are easy to tap in. You can also use the frame for a mirror, in which case only the glass and backing panel need be catered for. Buy a generous amount of moulding as it is only too easy to cut miters the wrong way by mistake.

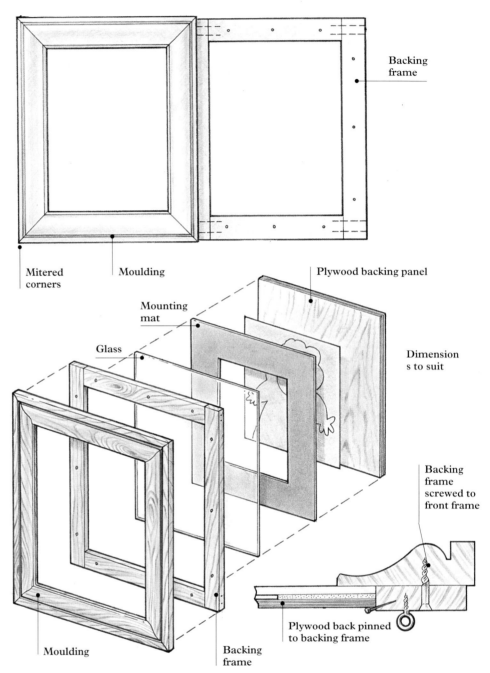

Backing frame

Mitered corners

Moulding

Mounting mat

Glass

Plywood backing panel

Dimensions to suit

Backing frame screwed to front frame

Plywood back pinned to backing frame

Moulding

Backing frame

PROJECT PLANNER

- Mark out and prepare wood for backing frame
- Assemble backing frame
- Cut miters on face moulding
- Fit mouldings to backing frame
- Clean up and apply finish
- Mount picture/mirror

WHAT YOU NEED

CUTTING LIST
- Moulding: Ogee or any flat-backed moulding
- Backing frame: planed softwood, such as 2 x 1 in (50 x 25 mm)
- Backing panel: $^3/_{16}$ or $^1/_4$ in (5 or 6 mm) plywood or MDF
- Clear glass: usually $^1/_8$ in (3 mm) thick, cut to size
- Mirror glass: usually $^3/_{16}$ in (5 mm) thick, cut to size
- Mounting mat: usually $^3/_{32}$ in (2 mm) thick
- Countersunk screws and finish nails
- Picture wire and screw eyes

TOOLS REQUIRED
- Straightedge, try square and sliding bevel
- Panel and back saws
- Block plane
- Miter box
- Tack hammer
- Power drill and bits
- Screwdriver
- Craft knife or scalpel

SEE ALSO

SKILLS
- Measuring and marking techniques *(see pages 24–27)*
- Sawing techniques *(see pages 30–31)*
- Drilling techniques *(see pages 34–35)*
- Planing techniques *(see pages 42–45)*
- Clamping techniques *(see pages 48–49)*
- Fixing techniques *(see pages 52–53)*
- Sanding and finishing techniques *(see pages 60–61)*

Cutting the backing frame

1 Calculate the dimensions of the backing frame after choosing the moulding. The width of the pieces should allow for a rabbet of approximately $^1/_2$ in (12 mm) for the glass, mounting mat and backing panel.

2 Mark out the four pieces of softwood for the backing frame, saw them to length, and plane the ends square *(see pages 24–27)*.

3 Nail and glue the backing frame sections together. This is made easier if you drill small clearance holes for the nails first. Make sure that the pieces being nailed together meet at right-angles and that the outer edges of the frame are flush. Sink the heads of the nails into the wood using a nail set.

Pinning backing frame sections

Cutting the mouldings

1 Mark out the miters on the moulding with a sliding bevel, making sure that the 45° cut is angled the correct way. Cut the miters in a miter box, using a back saw (*see pages 30–31*).

Cutting the moulding in a miter box

Assembling the picture frame

1 Use the backing frame to mark out a backing panel from a piece of thin plywood or MDF. Saw the panel to size and check for fit inside the backing frame.

Marking out the backing panel

2 Drill three clearance holes through each piece of the backing frame and countersink them so that the screw heads will lie below the surface.

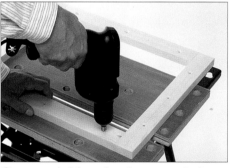
Countersinking the clearance holes

3 Position the mouldings on the backing frame to make sure the miters fit neatly. Clamp the mouldings lightly to the frame, to keep the mitered joints as tight together as possible. A thin piece of scrap wood will prevent the C-clamps from damaging the moulding (*see pages 48–49*).

4 Drill pilot holes through the clearance holes in the backing frame into the back of the moulding pieces. Secure the mouldings with screws driven through the holes in the backing frame.

Finishing and hanging the frame

1 Clean up the face of the frame and apply your chosen finish. This could be varnish, stain or paint.

2 If using a mounting mat, cut it to size and cut out the aperture for the picture, using a craft knife.

3 When the finish is dry, carefully place the various parts into the rabbet behind the moulding. The order should be: glass, mounting mat (if used), picture and backing panel.

4 Secure the backing panel by driving small nails at an angle into the inside edge of the backing frame. Hang the picture on wire stretched between two screw eyes fixed to the sides of the frame.

Securing the backing panel

BIRD FEEDER

*This project uses straight and angled half-lap joints in solid wood to
make a simple but sturdy structure that can be erected anywhere in
the garden to attract birds.*

YOU CAN MAKE this bird feeder from softwood but it must
be treated with a non-toxic preservative to help it withstand
outdoor conditions. Use an exterior grade plywood to make
the roof, upstands and table, and choose a waterproof glue to join
the components. You can adapt the dimensions of the design but
the basic features should remain the same. The upstands around
the sides prevent too much food from being swept off the table and
the roof offers protection from weather.

PROJECT PLANNER

- Mark out components
- Cut roof post joints
- Make gables and cross beam
- Prepare the plywood
- Assemble the table
- Make the main post
- Treat and install the feeder

WHAT YOU NEED

CUTTING LIST
- Main post: one length of 2 x 2 in
  (50 x 50 mm) softwood approximately
  6 ft (1.8 m) long; allow at least 12 in
  (305 mm) to be buried in the ground
- Support blocks: four 2 x 2 in
  (50 x 50 mm) pieces of softwood with a
  total length of 12 in (305 mm)
- Cross beam: one 15 x 2 x 2 in
  (380 x 50 x 50 mm) length of softwood
- Roof posts: two 16 x 3 x 1 in
  (405 x 75 x 25 mm) lengths of softwood
- Gables: two 12 x 3½ x 1 in
  (305 x 90 x 25 mm) lengths of softwood
- Feed table: one 15½ x 15½ x ¾ in
  (394 x 394 x 19 mm) length of
  exterior-grade plywood
- Upstands: two 24 x 1⅝ x ¼ in
  (610 x 40 x 6 mm) lengths of exterior-
  grade plywood
- Roof: two 17½ x 8 x ¼ in
  (444 x 200 x 6 mm) lengths of
  exterior-grade plywood
- Screws: eight 1¼ in (32 mm) No. 8 and
  ten 3 in (75 mm) No. 10 countersunk
- Small nails

TOOLS REQUIRED
- Try square and straightedge
- Marking gauge and sliding
  bevel
- Bench plane and block plane
- Panel and back saws
- 1 in (25 mm) chisel
- Jigsaw
- Bradawl
- Power drill and bits
- Tack hammer
- C-clamps

SEE ALSO

SKILLS
- Measuring and marking techniques
  (*see pages 24–27*)
- Sawing techniques (*see pages 30–31*)
- Drilling techniques (*see pages 34–35*)
- Cutting and shaping techniques
  (*see pages 38–39*)
- Planing techniques (*see pages 42–45*)
- Clamping techniques (*see pages 48–49*)
- Sanding and finishing techniques
  (*see pages 60–61*)
- Power saws (*see pages 64–65*)
- Simple joint techniques
  (*see pages 72–77*)

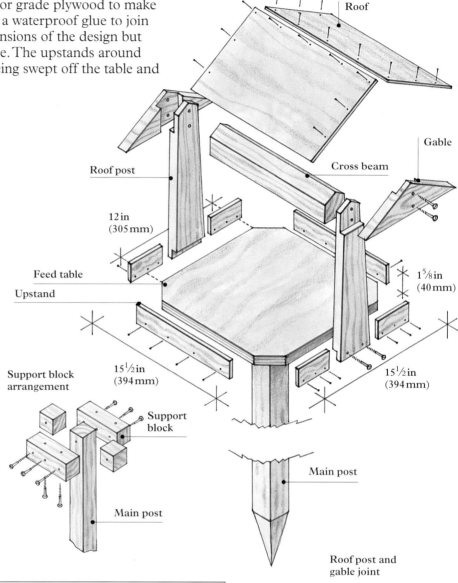

Roof

Gable

Cross beam

Roof post

12 in
(305 mm)

Feed table

Upstand

1⅝ in
(40 mm)

Support block
arrangement

Support
block

15½ in
(394 mm)

15½ in
(394 mm)

Main post

Main post

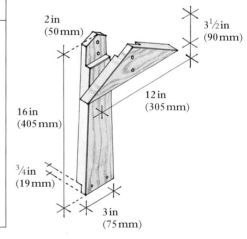

Roof post and
gable joint

2 in
(50 mm)

3½ in
(90 mm)

16 in
(405 mm)

12 in
(305 mm)

¾ in
(19 mm)

3 in
(75 mm)

Preparing the wood

1 Mark the roof posts and gables, leaving the ends of the roof posts without bevels and slightly overlength (*see pages 24–27*).

Marking the taper on a roof post

2 Cut the waste from the gables close to your pencil lines, then plane the edges (*see pages 42–45*).

3 Cut the tapers on the roof posts with a panel saw, and plane the edges smooth.

4 Mark and cut the half-lap joints and rabbets on the roof posts (*see pages 72–77*).

Cutting the gable housings

1 Position the half-lap joints cut in the roof posts on top of the gables. Mark the outlines of the housings on the gables.

2 Use a marking gauge to scribe the depth of the housings on the the gables and cut out the waste.

3 Dry assemble the posts to the gables and plane the ends of the posts down so that they lie flush.

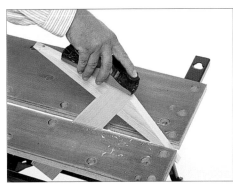

Planing the top of a roof post

Making the cross beam

1 Cut the cross beam to length and transfer the angle of the gables to the beam ends. Plane down to the lines.

Planing the bevels

Preparing the plywood

1 Cut the plywood components to size, using a jigsaw or panel saw. Cut the corners off the feed table piece and plane bevels along one long edge of both the roof pieces.

Sawing the plywood

Assembling the joints

1 Drill countersunk clearance holes through the joints (*see pages 34–35*). Mark and drill the pilot holes, then glue and screw the posts, gables and cross beam together.

2 Mark the feed-table edge for pilot holes by pushing a bradawl through clearance holes in the roof-post rabbets. Drill the pilot holes.

3 Glue and nail the roof pieces to the cross beam and gables, then fix the upstands to the feed table and screw the roof posts to the table.

Making the main post

1 Saw the main post to length. Cut and drill the support blocks and screw them to the post.

Cleaning and installing

1 Clean up the feeder and treat it with preservative. Drive the post into the ground and screw the table in place through the support blocks.

KNIFE BLOCK

This safe and convenient way of storing sharp kitchen knives is made from three lengths of fine hardwood and looks good in any kitchen. The knife slots are chiselled out before the wood pieces are glued together.

CHOOSE A hardwood that does not stain when used in the kitchen: ash, maple or beech are suitable, but oak is prone to discolouring in a hot and steamy kitchen environment. This project is easy to make if certain operations are not done until the end. Leave the components oversize until after they have been glued together so that you can mark out and chisel the slots confidently and accurately. The meeting surfaces of the three pieces need to be perfectly smooth and flat before they are glued together. This means that you have to plane the faces very accurately.

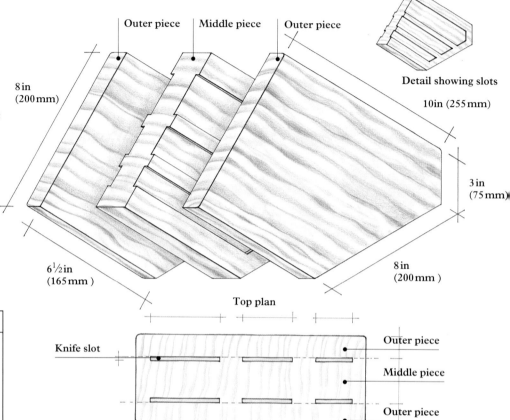

Detail showing slots

Top plan

Knife slot

Outer piece
Middle piece
Outer piece

PROJECT PLANNER

- Mark out and prepare wood
- Plane the three components flat
- Mark out and cut slots for knives
- Glue block together
- Mark and shape block to finished size
- Clean up and apply finish

WHAT YOU NEED

CUTTING LIST
- Outer pieces: two 12 x 8½ x 1 in (305 x 215 x 25 mm) lengths of hardwood
- Middle piece: one 12 x 8½ x 1½ in (305 x 215 x 38 mm) length of hardwood

TOOLS REQUIRED
- Try square, straightedge and marking gauge
- Panel saw
- Bench plane
- Mallet
- 1 in (25 mm) chisel
- C-clamps

SEE ALSO

SKILLS
- Measuring and marking techniques (*see pages 24–27*)
- Cutting and shaping techniques (*see pages 38–39*)
- Planing techniques (*see pages 42–45*)
- Clamping techniques (*see pages 48–49*)
- Fixing techniques (*see pages 54–55*)
- Sanding and finishing techniques (*see pages 60–61*)

Preparing the lumber

1 Hold each outer piece firmly in your workbench and use a bench plane to level the inside faces (*see pages 42–45*). Check that they are flat with a straightedge or try square (*see pages 24–27*), then plane the outside faces of the outer pieces until the blocks are ¾ in (19 mm) thick.

Testing for flatness

2 Plane one face of the middle piece flat and test it. Use a marking gauge to mark the thickness from the flat face and then plane the other face carefully to the lines. Check that all three pieces fit together perfectly.

Marking and cutting the slots

1 Mark the three slots on both faces of the middle piece. To ensure that the slots appear in the right place, make a template of the block, and use this as a guide.

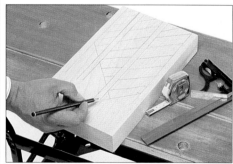

Marking out the knife slots

2 Using a 1 in (25 mm) chisel and mallet, chop out slots deep enough to accommodate the thickness of a knife blade, keeping closely to the pencilled outlines (*see pages 38–39*). It does not matter if the slots are a little rough, as they will not be seen.

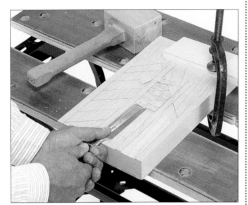

Chopping out the slots

Gluing and clamping

1 Spread waterproof glue on the raised parts of one face of the middle piece (*see pages 54–55*). Place this on one of the outer pieces, then spread glue on the opposite face and place the remaining outer piece on it. Do not use so much glue that the slots become blocked up.

2 Because glue will make the whole assembly slippery and difficult to cramp, secure the three pieces between blocks fixed to your bench before applying full pressure across the joins with C-clamps (*see pages 48–49*).

Clamping the block

Trimming and finishing

1 When the glue has dried, use your template to mark the finished outline on the assembled block (*see pages 24–27*). Make sure that the outlines on both faces are square across the top and bottom.

Marking out the final shape

2 Saw off the waste pieces close to the pencil lines, and then plane the whole block to the finished size, making sure that the edges and ends are square to the two faces. Use a bench plane to soften the long edges to a radius of about $\frac{1}{16}$ in (1.5mm),

then clean up the whole block with abrasive paper.

Planing the edges

3 Apply a light vegetable oil, such as sunflower or soya oil, to finish (*see pages 60–61*). Do not use olive or corn oil, as these will stain the wood.

SPICE RACK

*This adaptable project uses half lap joints to make a strong frame. The
top shelf is drilled to make holes for storing eggs, but it can be left whole
to provide an extra surface for keeping herb and spice jars.*

HALVING JOINTS are comparatively simple to make but
only work well if they are cut accurately. This means
careful marking out with a sharp pencil, accurate sawing,
and fine paring with a chisel. Scribing with a craft knife before
cutting joints and cross-cutting plywood also helps achieve good
results. The dimensions given here are for standard commercial
spice jars, but you can alter the height and width of the
components to suit your needs. Again, you can shape the top
edge of the back to any design, but always use a half-
template to get the symmetry correct.

PROJECT PLANNER

- Mark out and prepare timber and
  plywood
- Shape and drill shelves
- Cut joints for end frames
- Assemble frames and shelves
- Make and fit back
- Clean up and apply finish

WHAT YOU NEED

CUTTING LIST
- Back: one 18 x 12¾in (460 x 325mm)
  length of ¼in (6mm) plywood
- Shelves: two 20⅝ x 3⅛in (524 x 80mm)
  lengths of ⅜in (9mm) plywood
- Frames: one 79 x ⅞ x ⅞in (2m x 22 x
  22mm) length from 1 x 1in
  (25 x 25mm) softwood
- Screws: eight ⅝in (16mm) No.4
  countersunk

TOOLS REQUIRED
- Try square, straightedge and craft knife
- Jigsaw and back saw
- Bench plane
- ¾in (19mm) chisel
- Power drill and bits
- C-clamps, bradawl and screwdriver

SEE ALSO

SKILLS
- Measuring and marking techniques
  (*see pages 24–27*)
- Sawing techniques (*see pages 30–31*)
- Drilling techniques (*see pages 34–35*)
- Cutting and shaping techniques
  (*see pages 38–39*)
- Planing techniques (*see pages 42–45*)
- Clamping techniques (*see pages 48–49*)
- Fixing techniques (*see pages 54–55*)
- Sanding and finishing techniques
  (*see pages 60–61*)
- Simple joint techniques (*see pages 72–77*)

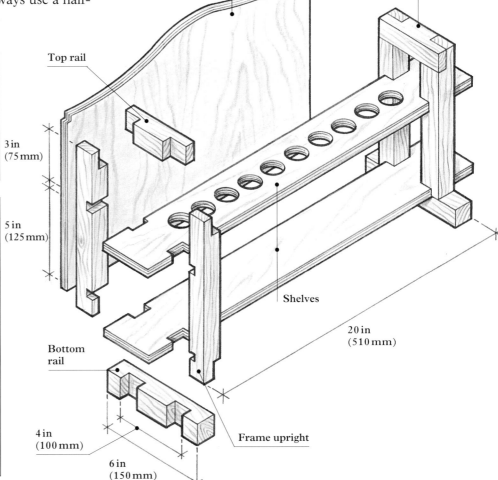

Back

End frame

Top rail

3 in
(75 mm)

5 in
(125 mm)

Shelves

20 in
(510 mm)

Bottom
rail

4 in
(100 mm)

6 in
(150 mm)

Frame upright

Preparing the components

1 Mark out the shelves, using a craft
knife to scribe the upper surface
of the ends (*see pages 24–27*).

2 Cut the shelves to size with a
jigsaw. Position the blade on the
waste sides of the lines to prevent
splintering the wood (*see pages 30–31*).

3 Plane the wood for the end
frames ⅞in (22mm) square,

checking the finished piece for
accuracy (*see pages 42–45*).

Making the shelves

1 Draw a center line down both
faces of the top shelf. Mark
equally spaced centers for the egg
holes with a bradawl.

2 Using a 1in (25mm) spade bit,
drill out the holes from both faces
at slow speed (*see pages 34–35*).

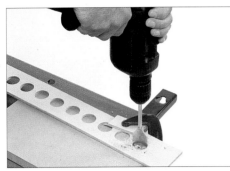

Drilling the holes

3 Mark the rabbets for the frame uprights in the shelf pieces. They should be ¼in (6mm) deep and allow the uprights to fit snugly.

4 Cut the shelves to the lines, saw out the waste, and clean up with a chisel (*see pages 38–39*).

Cutting the rabbets

Making the end frames

1 Cut the uprights and top and bottom rails to length. Mark the half-lap joints with a pencil. Take care to produce right- and left-handed components (*see pages 72–77*).

2 Saw the waste out, and use a chisel to perfect the joints (*see pages 38–39*).

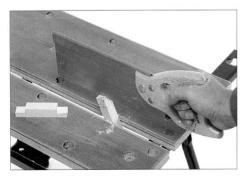

Cutting the half-lap joints

3 Clamp the four uprights together. Mark the shelf rabbets, drawing across all four uprights at once so that the shelves will be level with each other. The rabbets should

be ¼in (6mm) deep, and just wide enough to take the shelves.

4 Cut the rabbets in the uprights and check the shelves for fit.

Assembling the frames and shelves

1 Apply glue to all of the joint surfaces and clamp the end frame components together with the shelves in place, using offcuts to protect the wood (*see pages 48–49*). Check that the joints are correctly positioned and that the frame is square.

Gluing up the frames

Making and fitting the back

1 Mark out and cut from thin MDF or plywood a template for one half of the back panel. Mark this half and the vertical center line on the back panel piece, then turn the template over and mark the full shape.

Marking with a template

2 Scribe one face of the back panel piece and cut out the profile with a jigsaw. Clean up the edge with abrasive paper.

3 Trim the panel so that it fits correctly between the two uprights of the frames.

4 Mark lines to correspond with the mid-point of the thickness of the two shelves, and drill four counter-sunk clearance holes along each line.

5 Use a bradawl to mark pilot holes through the back into the back edges of the shelves. Drill the holes, and screw the back into place.

6 Use abrasive paper to finish the rack and lightly soften the sharp edges. Apply your selected finish (*see pages 60–61*).

SHELVING UNIT

This project uses simple dowel joints to make an eye-catching shelving unit that can be used to display ornaments or books. Finish the unit with either varnish or paint.

YOU NEED TO make a simple jig (guide) for this project so that you can accurately locate the drilling centers for the dowel joints. The dowels themselves are not particularly strong but the backing strips on the shelves provide rigidity. You can adapt the width of the shelves to suit a specific space but, for shelves longer than 39 in (990 mm), you should make them from thicker boards. Most lumber yards supply S4S softwood in 8 in (200 mm) widths (*see pages 10–13*), so you do not have to join boards edge to edge to make the shelves and uprights.

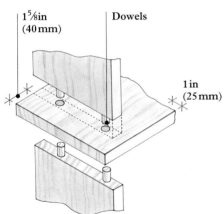

Detail of dowel joints

PROJECT PLANNER

- Prepare components
- Make dowelling jig
- Fit dowels
- Assemble components
- Clean up and finish

SEE ALSO

SKILLS
- Measuring and marking techniques (*see pages 24–27*)
- Sawing techniques (*see pages 30–31*)
- Drilling techniques (*see pages 34–35*)
- Planing techniques (*see pages 42–45*)
- Clamping techniques (*see pages 48–49*)
- Fixing techniques (*see pages 54–55*)
- Sanding and finishing techniques (*see pages 60–61*)
- Dowel joints (*See pages 78–79*)

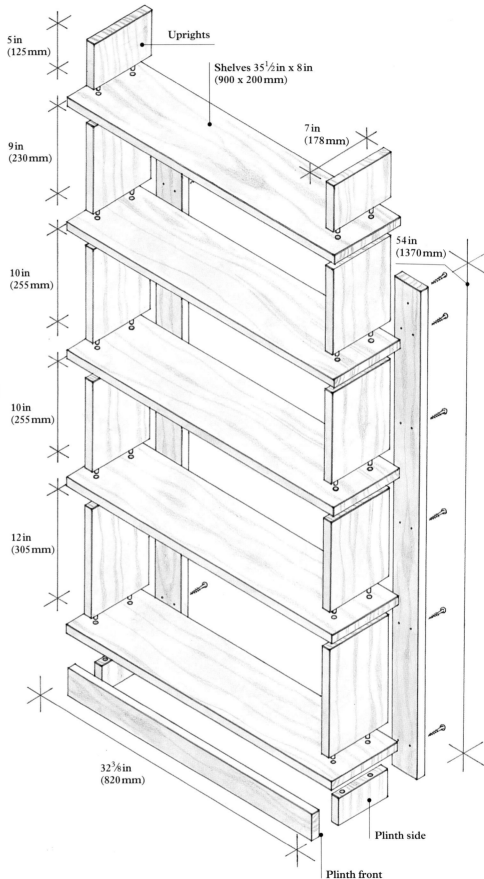

WHAT YOU NEED

CUTTING LIST
- Back strips: two 54 x 2⅝ x 1 in (1370 x 65 x 25mm) lengths of softwood
- Uprights: two 5 x 7 x 1 in (125 x 178 x 25mm), two 9 x 7 x 1 in (230 x 178 x 25mm), four 10 x 7 x 1 in (255 x 178 x 25mm) and two 12 x 7 x 1 in (305 x 178 x 25mm) lengths of softwood
- Plinth front: one 32⅜ x 3 x 1 in (820 x 75 x 25mm) length of softwood
- Plinth side pieces: two 6 x 3 x 1 in (150 x 75 x 25mm) lengths of softwood
- Shelves: five 36 x 8 x 1¼ in (915 x 200 x 32mm) lengths of softwood
- Dowels: twenty-four 2 x ⅜ in (50 x 10mm)
- Screws: twenty-two 1½ in (38mm) No. 8 countersunk

TOOLS REQUIRED
- Straightedge and try square
- Panel saw
- Block plane and bench plane
- Power drill and bits
- Screwdriver
- Hammer and mallet
- Pincers
- C-clamps and bar clamps
- Bradawl and dowelling pins

Preparing the lumber

1 Mark all the shelves and verticals to length and cut them to size with a panel saw (*see pages 24–27 and 30–31*).

2 Trim the ends of the shelves and uprights with a block plane and smooth the long edges with a bench plane (*see pages 42–45*). Make sure that all the pieces have an even width and that all of their edges and ends are flat and square.

3 Mark, cut and finish the plinth components and the backing strips. As for the shelves and the uprights, plane down all the edges until the boards are the correct width and length.

Making the jig

1 This jig will help you to position the dowel holes accurately in the shelves and uprights. First, shape a piece of waste board or MDF, approximately 5 in (125mm) long, to the exact width of the shelves.

2 Toward one end of the offcut, draw a pencil line across one face. Make absolutely sure that the line is at right-angles to the edge. On the reverse face, draw a similar line across the middle of the offcut.

3 Mark centers 2 in (50mm) in from each end of the first line. Tap a finish nail about halfway into the offcut at each center. Snip off the heads of the nails with pincers, leaving just ¹⁄₁₆ in (1.5mm) projecting.

4 Mark a parallel line ½ in (12mm) to the side of the first line. Cut a batten to length and glue and screw it accurately to the new line (*see pages 54–55*). Plane the offcut flush to the edge of the batten.

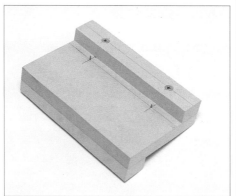

The finished jig showing the position of the pins for marking the verticals

5 On the reverse face of the offcut, tap in nails as described above and fix a batten 2⅛ in (53mm) to the side of the line.

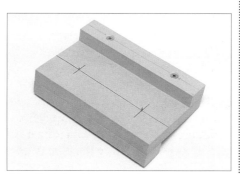

The finished jig showing the position of the nails for marking the shelves

6 Mark one edge of the jig with a pencil or crayon so that you can be sure of using it the right way round each time.

Marking for the dowels

1 Mark the back edges of all the shelves so that you know which way they are going to face. Place the jig against one end of the first shelf with the batten tight against the edge. Make sure that the marked edge of the jig is on the same side as the marked edge of the shelf and check that the jig is the right way up.

2 Align the edges of the jig with the edges of the shelf, then press down hard on the jig so that the pins leave two clear marks on the wood underneath. Mark the drilling centers on the other end of the shelf in a similar way and then repeat the process with all the other shelves.

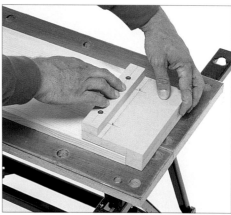

Marking the shelves

3 Use your jig to mark the top and bottom ends of the uprights in the same way. The only ends that do not need marking are the top ends of the top verticals and the bottom ends of the plinth sides.

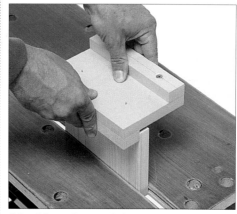

Marking the uprights

Drilling the dowel holes

1 Select a drill bit for the dowels. It is a good idea to check that the bit is the correct size by drilling a hole in a scrap piece of wood and tapping in a dowel. The dowel should be a tight fit.

2 Once you have found a bit of the right size, drill holes through all the shelves at the marks left by your jig. When you drill the holes in the boards, make sure that you place an offcut underneath the wood (*see pages 34-35*).

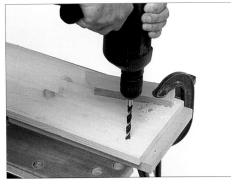
Drilling dowel holes in a shelf

3 Once you have drilled all the holes in the shelves, wrap tape around the bit as a depth gauge – the distance from the bottom of the tape to the tip of the bit should be approximately ⅝in (16mm).

4 Clamp the first upright in your workbench and drill the end at the two pin marks to the correct depth. Repeat at the other end, and then drill the other uprights and the plinth side pieces.

Assembling the shelves
1 Apply a little glue to each hole in each shelf and knock in dowels. The dowels should project the same amount on each face of the shelf.

2 Glue and fit a pair of the longest uprights to each end of one of the shelves, tapping the components together with a mallet.

Fitting the first shelf

3 Smear glue over the protruding dowels and into the holes before slotting on the next pair of uprights.

Fitting the next pair of uprights

4 Continue to build up the shelves and uprights, from the bottom to the top. However, do not fit the plinth side pieces at this stage. As you fit each upright, lay a scrap of wood over the top and tap it with your mallet to close the joint.

Tapping home an upright

5 When you have fitted all the uprights, lay the assembly on its back and use bar clamps to pull all the joints tight (*see pages 48–49*). Turn the assembly over and apply clamps to the back as well so that equal pressure is applied to the joints all round. Check that all the uprights are square to the shelves and adjust them if necessary before the glue dries.

Fitting the plinth
1 Mark centers for a pair of dowels in both of the front edges of the plinth side pieces. Drill holes to a depth of ½in (12mm) at each mark and then slot in dowelling pins (*see pages 78–79*).

2 Use the dowelling pins to transfer drilling centers onto the back face of the plinth front. Drill holes ½in (12mm) deep at each mark.

3 Cut four dowels to ¾in (19mm) length and glue them into the edges of the plinth side pieces.

4 Glue and fit the front of the plinth to the side pieces. Clamp the assembly until the glue is dry.

Final assembly
1 Apply glue to the top surfaces of the plinth and fit it to the dowels projecting from the bottom shelf. Fit bar clamps to hold the plinth in place.

2 Lay the shelf unit on its back over the two back strips. Check that the outer edges of the back strips are flush with the ends of the shelves and that the top and bottom ends are in line.

3 Carefully mark the back strips to show the positions of the shelves and all the uprights.

Marking the back strips

4 Remove back strips. Mark and drill two countersunk clearance holes at each shelf position. Drill single holes to secure top verticals.

5 Turn the unit over and reposition the back strips. Use a bradawl to mark through the clearance holes.

6 Remove back strips and drill pilot holes in the shelf backs. Glue and screw the back strips into place.

Cleaning up and finishing
1 Clean up the whole unit with abrasive paper and smooth down any uneven edges (*see pages 60-61*).

2 Finish by applying several coats of clear varnish or alternatively, paint in a color of your choice.

GARDEN PLANTER

This versatile plant box can be made rectangular or square and its dimensions
can be adapted to suit your requirements. It uses tongue-and-groove strips
held together in a mortise-and-tenoned frame.

THIS PROJECT needs careful planning before you start making it. Tongue-and-groove strips with a V-joint (TG&V) are readily available, but they may vary in size. The width of the strips determine the overall dimensions of the planter as the side panels are made with whole strips. Cut all of the frame components oversize to start with and trim them down to exact size when you assemble the frame.

PROJECT PLANNER

- Make posts
- Mark up tenons and mortises
- Cut mortises and tenons
- Assemble frame
- Fit TG&V strips
- Make and fit capping pieces
- Make and fit base
- Clean up and finish

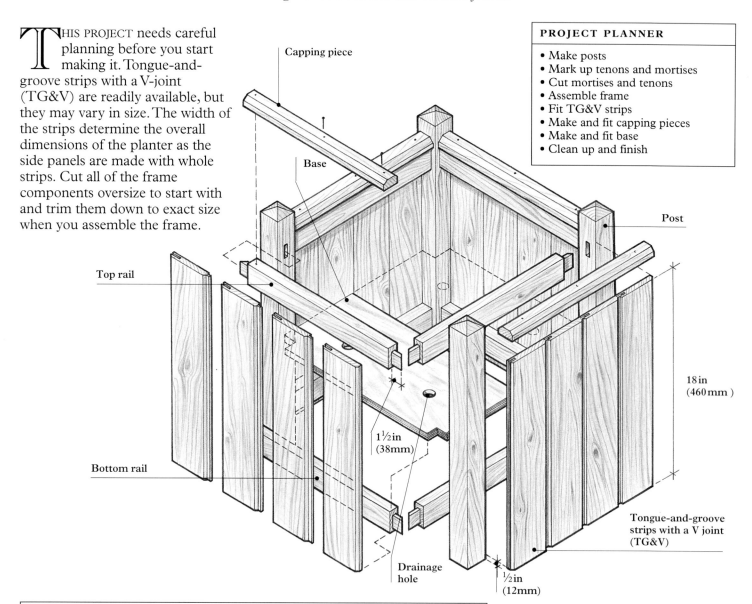

Capping piece

Base

Top rail

Bottom rail

Post

18 in (460 mm)

1½ in (38 mm)

Drainage hole

½ in (12 mm)

Tongue-and-groove strips with a V joint (TG&V)

WHAT YOU NEED

CUTTING LIST

- TG&V strips: calculate the number of 4 x ⅜ in (100 x 10 mm) softwood strips needed for each side; each strip should be 18 in (460 mm) long
- Posts: four 20 in (510 mm) lengths of 2 x 2 in (50 x 50 mm) S4S softwood
- Rails: eight lengths of 2 x 1 in (50 x 25 mm) S4S softwood; the rail lengths are determined by the number of TG&V strips used. Allow 1½ in (38 mm) at end of each rail for tenons
- Capping strips: four lengths of 2 x 1 in (50 x 25 mm) S4S softwood; the lengths of the capping strips are determined by the lengths of the rails
- Base: one sheet of ⅜ in (10 mm)

plywood, determined by the dimensions of the finished frame
- TG&V pins: ¾ in (19 mm) finish nails
- Capping strip pins: 1½ in (38 mm) finish nails
- Wood filler

TOOLS REQUIRED

- Straightedge, try square, marking gauge
- Back saw
- Block and bench planes
- Bar clamps
- Mortise gauge
- Mallet and ½ in (12 mm) chisel
- Tack hammer
- Power drill and bits
- Jigsaw

SEE ALSO

SKILLS
- Measuring and marking techniques (*see pages 24–27*)
- Sawing techniques (*see pages 30–31*)
- Drilling techniques (*see pages 34–35*)
- Cutting and shaping techniques (*see pages 38–39*)
- Planing techniques (*see pages 42–45*)
- Clamping techniques (*see pages 48–49*)
- Fixing techniques (*see pages 54–55*)
- Sanding and finishing techniques (*see pages 60–61*)
- Simple joint techniques (*see pages 72–77*)

Making the posts

1 Mark the shallow bevels on the top of each post and cut off the waste with a back saw. Clean up the end grain with a sharp block plane (*see pages 30–31 and 42–45*).

Sawing a bevel

2 Cut the four posts to length and check that they are identical.

Marking the tenons

1 Cut the eight rails to approximate length. At this stage the rails need to be 2 in (50 mm) or so overlength.

2 Dry assemble the required number of TG&V strips for one side. This is made easier if you saw the strips to roughly the right length. Plane off the tongue of the last strip.

3 Use the assembled strips to mark the tenon shoulders at each end of one of the rails (*see pages 72–77*). Leave about 1½ in (38 mm) at each end of the rail for the tenons.

Marking the tenon shoulders

4 If you are making a square box, line all the rails up and lightly clamp them together (*see pages 48–49*). Mark shoulders across all of them using the first rail as a guide. The best tool to use for this is a try square. If you are making a rectangular box, you should mark the rails in pairs.

5 Remove the clamps and mark the shoulders all around each rail individually at both ends.

6 Use a marking gauge to outline the tenons with equal shoulders on either side. The tenons should be two-thirds the thickness of the rails – this means that for 1 in (25 mm) thick wood, the tenons should be approximately ⅝ in (16 mm) wide. The top and bottom shoulders should be ¼ in (6 mm) deep.

Marking the mortises

1 Mark each post across two adjacent faces 1⅝ in (40 mm) from the top, to give the line of the top edge of the top rails. Similarly, mark for the bottom rail ¼ in (6 mm) from the bottom of the posts on the same two adjacent faces.

2 Position a rail against each mark, making sure that it is at right-angles to the post, and scribe lines on either face. To mark the length of each mortise, draw a guideline ¼ in (6 mm) in from each line top and bottom.

3 Taking each post in turn, mark the thickness of the TG&V strips against one face. This will give you the exact positions of the outer faces of the rails.

4 Use a marking gauge to scribe the width of the mortise at each joint. Each mortise should be two-thirds of the thickness of a rail – approximately ⅝ in (16 mm). Crosshatch the area that is to be cut away to avoid mistakes later on.

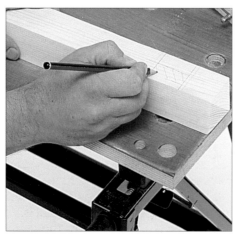
Marking the position of a mortise

Chopping out the mortises

1 Use a ½ in (12 mm) chisel and mallet to chop out the mortises (*see pages 72–77*). The mortises do not go right the way through the wood but stop in the center of the posts where two adjacent mortises meet. Clean up the mortises after removing the bulk of the waste and check that all its surfaces are square and parallel.

Chopping out mortises

Cutting the tenons

1 Measure the depth of the mortises and mark each tenon to suit. Cut the ends of the tenons in a miter box. If you want to cut the tenons square, which is easier, reduce their length by ½ in (12 mm).

2 Use a back saw to cut off the waste from the top, bottom and sides of the tenons.

Cutting the top and bottom shoulders

3 Slot each tenon into a mortise and check it for size. If it is necessary, pare down a tenon with a sharp chisel until it fits snugly. Mark each set of joints so that they are easy to identify.

Assembling the frame

1 Dry assemble the frame and check that it is square by comparing diagonal measurements. When you are satisfied, take the pieces apart again and start gluing up the joints. Spread waterproof adhesive over the tenons and slot them into the mortises.

Gluing mortise and tenon joints

2 Hold the joints secure with bar clamps until the adhesive sets hard (*see pages 48–49*).

Fitting the TG&V strips

1 Cut strips of TG&V to fit between the top of the top rail and the bottom of the bottom rail. Carefully plane the tongues off four of the strips.

2 Lay the frame on its side and nail the first strip in place on the outside of the frame, with the groove against a post. Fix the strip to the rail with four nails. Tap the first pair of nails through the strip, just to the side of the groove; tap the second pair of nails through the tongue. Use a nail punch and hammer to sink the nail heads into the surface of the wood.

Nailing the first strip

3 Slide the groove of the next strip on to the exposed tongue and nail it in place through its tongue only. Add all the strips along one side in this fashion until you reach the last one.

4 As the last strip in the row has no tongue, fix it through the face with a pair of nails positioned near the post.

Fitting the last strip in a row

5 After completing one row, fit strips to the remaining three sides, making sure that the tops are all level.

Fitting the capping strips

1 Measure the distance between the posts and cut capping strips to fit exactly.

2 Plane the strips to a width of 1⅝in (40mm) and chamfer the two top edges with a bench plane.

3 Spread a little waterproof adhesive on the top edges of the rails and nail the capping strips in place. The capping strips must cover the end grain of the TG&V panels. Punch the nail heads below the surface of the wood.

Nailing a capping strip

Fitting the base panel

1 Take the inside measurements of the box, between the TG&V panels, and cut the plywood sheet to these dimensions, less ³⁄₃₂in (2mm) all around.

2 Saw cutouts at each corner of the base panel to allow clearance for the posts.

3 Use a power drill and a ½in (12mm) bit to make four drainage holes in the base panel.

Drilling the drainage holes

4 The whole base will not fit in the frame, so cut it in half with a jigsaw or panel saw.

5 Drop the two panel pieces in place on to the top edges of the bottom rails.

6 To provide extra stability for the base panel, you can nail and glue blocks to the bottom rails.

Finishing

1 Cover the heads of all the nails with exterior-grade wood filler, using a flexible filling knife.

2 Clean up the whole project with abrasive paper and apply exterior-quality paint or varnish (*see pages 60–61*).

OCCASIONAL TABLE

This adaptable little table looks good in either a living room or bedroom. The support rails are fixed to the legs with mortises and 'haunched' tenon joints, and are locked with a cross-lap joint in the middle.

YOU CAN adapt the size of this table by cutting the top to a bigger size and extending the length of the rails. The simple haunched tenons are a variation on those described on pages 72–77 and are there to stop the rails from twisting. Any wood can be used, but softwood is easier to work and matches well with plywood. You can finish the table by staining and varnishing, or by painting.

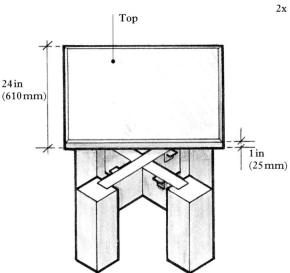

Top

24 in
(610 mm)

1 in
(25 mm)

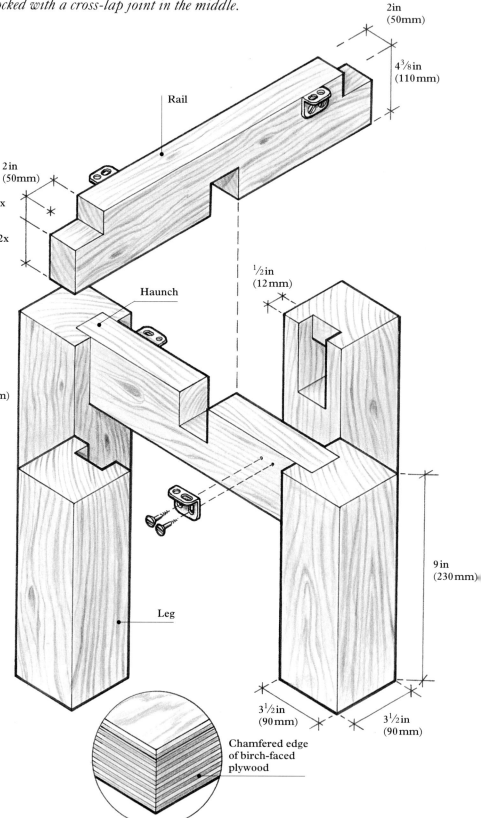

Rail

2 in
(50mm)

x

2x

2 in
(50mm)

4³⁄₈ in
(110 mm)

Haunch

¹⁄₂ in
(12 mm)

9 in
(230 mm)

Leg

3¹⁄₂ in
(90 mm)

3¹⁄₂ in
(90 mm)

Chamfered edge of birch-faced plywood

PROJECT PLANNER

- Prepare the components
- Mark out the joints
- Cut the joints
- Assemble the frame
- Clean up and assemble the table
- Apply a finish

SEE ALSO

SKILLS

- Measuring and marking techniques (*see pages 24–27*)
- Sawing techniques (*see pages 30–31*)
- Drilling techniques (*see pages 34–35*)
- Cutting and shaping techniques (*see pages 38–39*)
- Planing techniques (*see pages 42–45*)
- Clamping techniques (*see pages 48–49*)
- Fixing techniques (*see pages 54–55*)
- Sanding and finishing techniques (*see pages 60–61*)
- Simple joint techniques (*see pages 72–77*)

WHAT YOU NEED

CUTTING LIST
- Top: one 24 x 24 in (610 x 610 mm) length of 1 in (25 mm) birch plywood
- Frame rails: two 24⅜ x 4⅜ x 2 in (620 x 110 x 50 mm) lengths of softwood
- Legs: four 9 x 3½ x 3½ in (230 x 90 x 90 mm) lengths of softwood
- Shrinkage plates: four
- Screws: sixteen ⅝ in (16 mm) No. 6 roundhead

TOOLS REQUIRED
- Straightedge, try square and craft knife
- Jigsaw
- Bench plane and block plane
- Power drill and bits
- Back saw
- Tape measure
- Mortise gauge
- Mallet and ¾ in (19 mm) chisel
- Bar clamps
- Screwdriver

Preparing the top

1 Mark out the top using a pencil, then score cutting lines against a steel straightedge with a craft knife so that the plywood will not splinter when it is sawn (*see pages 24–27*).

2 Cut the shape out to the waste side of the scored lines with a jigsaw (*see pages 30–31*).

3 Plane the edges to the finished size and lightly chamfer the edges (*see pages 42–45*).

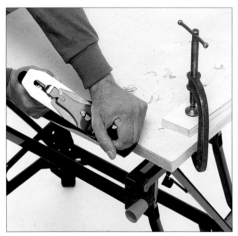

Chamfering the edges

Preparing the table base

1 Plane down the wood for the rails and the legs until it is smooth and perfectly flat. Saw the two rails to length, not forgetting that each rail will have a 2 in (50 mm) tenon at each end.

2 Cut one leg to size and use it as a template for marking the others. This will ensure that all the legs are the same length.

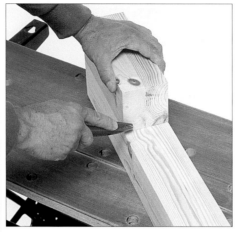

Using one leg as a template

Marking the mortises and tenons

1 Mark out the mortises in the legs (*see pages 72–77*). As the tenons are stopped tenons (they don't go all the way through the legs), each mortise should be only marginally deeper than 2½ in (63 mm). This depth allows for the depth of the tenon – 2 in (50 mm) – plus the depth of the haunch recess – ½ in (12 mm). Make the length of each mortise two-thirds of the width of a rail; the haunch recess takes up the remaining third.

2 Carefully mark the width of each mortise to match the thickness of a rail, using a mortise gauge.

3 Mark the haunched tenons on the ends of the rails. Each tenon should be 2 in (50 mm) long.

Marking a tenon

Cutting the mortises and tenons

1 Always cut the mortises first and shape the tenons to fit. Drill out the bulk of the waste with a bit that is slightly smaller in diameter than the width of the mortises (*see pages 34–35*).

Drilling out waste from a mortise

2 Remove the rest of the waste from the mortises and haunch recesses with a mallet and chisel. Take care to keep the surfaces of the mortises straight and parallel (*see pages 38–39*).

Chiselling the mortise to size

3 Finish off the mortises by paring down the surfaces with a sharp chisel. Make sure the bottom of each mortise is square and clean so that there is nothing to prevent the tenon from fitting properly.

4 Saw off the waste from each rail to create the haunched tenons.

Cutting a tenon

5 Dry fit the tenons individually to the mortises, and mark each pair. They should slot together with hand pressure only.

Making the cross-lap joint

1 The two halves of the joint are identical, except that one has the cut in its top edge and the other in the bottom. Mark them out exactly at the halfway point on each rail, making them half the depth of the rails and the same width (*see pages 72–77*).

2 Cut most of the waste away with a tenon saw and chisel, leaving the openings slightly too tight to fit.

Sawing the cross-lap joint

3 Pare each joint lightly with a chisel until the two pieces slide together snugly. Check that the edges

of each piece are flush top and bottom, and that they are square to each other.

Assembling the frame

1 First, carefully slot the two rails together – the lap joint does not require any glue.

2 Apply glue sparingly to each mortise and tenon, one at a time. After you have assembled the mortise and tenon joints, put bar clamps across each pair of legs to hold them square to the rails (*see pages 48–49*). Remember to put packing at the ends of the clamps to protect the wood.

Gluing up the joints

3 When the glue has dried, clean up the rails and legs, and soften all the edges with sandpaper.

4 Lightly chamfer the bottoms of the legs with a block plane to prevent them from splintering when the table is in use.

Assembling the table

1 Lay the table top upside down and position the frame, also upside down, on top. Make sure that the legs are accurately positioned with equal spaces to each side. To help you locate the frame, draw diagonal lines across the bottom of the table and a line down the middle of each outside face of a leg. Match up the lines on the legs with the lines on the table to place the frame.

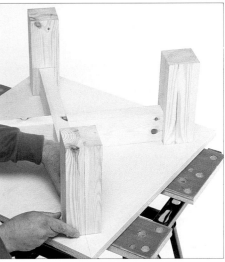

Aligning the base on the top

2 Fix the frame to the top with four shrinkage plates. It is best to position each plate just behind a leg so that it cannot be seen. Use roundhead woodscrews to secure the plates.

Fixing the frame to the top

Applying a finish

1 Clean up the whole table, softening the edges on the top with sandpaper (*see pages 60–61*). If you want to disguise the laminated edges of the plywood top, nail and glue moulding strips to the sides. Cut the ends of the mouldings in a miter box so that they meet neatly and sink the heads of the nails below the surface of the wood so that they are not visible. Patch the holes with filler before finishing.

2 Apply your chosen finish, either staining and varnishing the table, or painting it.

TOWEL RACK

This project uses simple dowel and half-lap joints. You can change the dimensions to suit your needs, but those given here make a lightweight towel rack that can be used in most rooms.

THIS TOWEL RACK consists of a pair of end frames joined together by rails. It does not have to be very robust, so dowel joints are strong enough for the end frames. As long as you take care when you mark out the positions of the joints and dowels, the components should fit together easily. You can make the towel rack from S4S softwood or from hardwood (*see pages 12–15*). However, avoid using oak as any dampness in the towels will stain the wood black and this could mark the towels themselves.

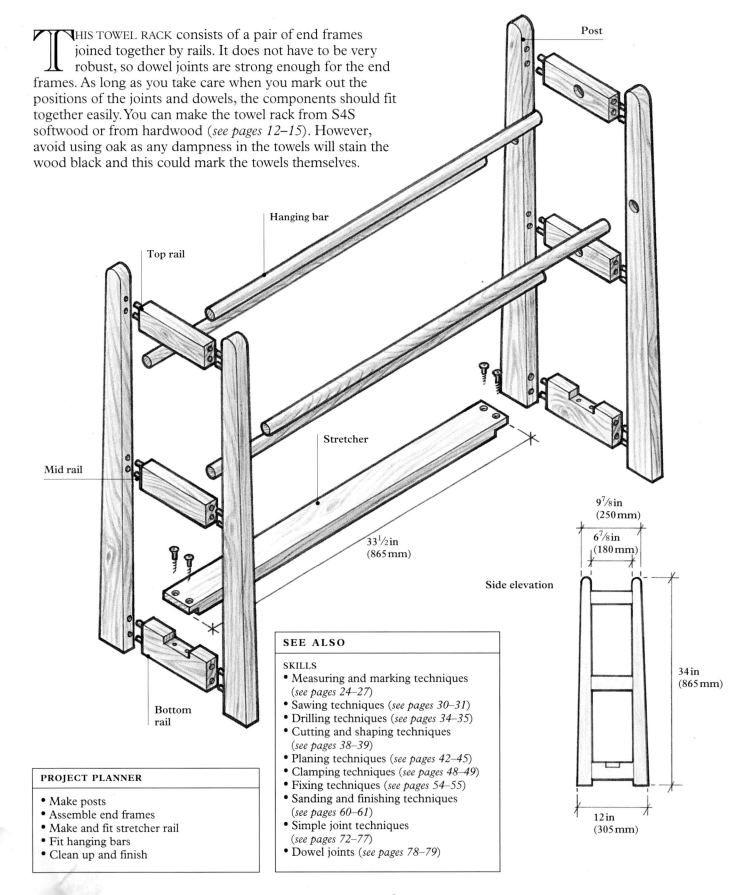

Post

Hanging bar

Top rail

Mid rail

Stretcher

33¹⁄₂ in
(865 mm)

9⁷⁄₈ in
(250 mm)

6⁷⁄₈ in
(180 mm)

Side elevation

34 in
(865 mm)

12 in
(305 mm)

Bottom rail

SEE ALSO

SKILLS
- Measuring and marking techniques
  (*see pages 24–27*)
- Sawing techniques (*see pages 30–31*)
- Drilling techniques (*see pages 34–35*)
- Cutting and shaping techniques
  (*see pages 38–39*)
- Planing techniques (*see pages 42–45*)
- Clamping techniques (*see pages 48–49*)
- Fixing techniques (*see pages 54–55*)
- Sanding and finishing techniques
  (*see pages 60–61*)
- Simple joint techniques
  (*see pages 72–77*)
- Dowel joints (*see pages 78–79*)

PROJECT PLANNER

- Make posts
- Assemble end frames
- Make and fit stretcher rail
- Fit hanging bars
- Clean up and finish

WHAT YOU NEED

CUTTING LIST

- Posts: four 34 x 3 x 1 in
  (865 x 75 x 25 mm) lengths of softwood
  or hardwood
- Bottom rails: two 7 x 3 x 1 in
  (178 x 75 x 25 mm) lengths of softwood
  or hardwood
- Rails: four 7 x 2 x 1 in
  (178 x 50 x 25 mm) lengths of softwood
  or hardwood
- Connecting rail: one 34 x 2 x 1 in
  (865 x 50 x 25 mm) length of softwood
  or hardwood

- Hanging rails: four 33 in (840 mm)
  lengths of 1 in (25 mm) dowelling
- Dowels: twenty-four 2 in (50 mm)
  lengths of $\frac{3}{8}$ in (10 mm) dowelling
- Screws: four 1$\frac{1}{4}$ in (32 mm)
  No.8 brass countersunk

TOOLS REQUIRED
- Straightedge and try square
- Ripsaw or panel saw
- Back saw

- Bench plane and block plane
- Bar clamp
- Dowel pins
- Power drill and bits
- $\frac{3}{4}$ in (19 mm) chisel
- Bradawl
- Screwdriver

Making the posts

1 To ensure the posts are identical, make a template for them from spare sheet material – ³⁄₁₆ or ¼in (5 or 6mm) MDF is ideal.

2 Draw up the template full size and cut it out. When you make the template, remember that the inside edge should be cut at right-angles to the bottom end and that the outside edge should slope towards the top. The angle of the slope is determined by the width of the posts at the top and bottom.

3 Round off the top of the template and then use it to mark out wood for the four posts.

Marking the posts

4 Cut the waste from the posts (*see pages 30–31*) and then plane down until the edges are smooth and the posts are the correct width at the top and bottom (*see pages 42–45*).

Sawing out the posts

5 Clean up the end grain at the bottom end of each post with a block plane and check that the ends are flat and square.

6 Shape the rounded tops of the posts with your block plane and finish with abrasive wrapped round a flat block (*see pages 60–61*).

Rounding off the top of a post

Making the end frames

1 Lightly clamp the posts together in line (*see pages 48–49*) and mark the positions of the three end frame rails across all of them.

2 Mark and cut the rails to length with a back saw, and plane them to their finished sizes. Check that the ends of the rails are square to the sides and edges.

3 Mark the end of each rail for a pair of dowels (*see pages 78–79*) and mark the drilling centers with a sharp bradawl.

4 Drill the holes, which should be slightly deeper than half the length of a dowel. It is easier to judge the depth of the holes required if you fit a depth stop to the drill bit or mark the bit by wrapping tape around it (*see pages 34–35*).

5 Slot dowelling pins into the holes in the ends of the rails and position the rails against their marks on the posts. Push the rails hard against the posts so that the pins mark the drilling centers.

6 Drill out the dowel holes in the posts, making sure that they are only slightly deeper than half the length of a dowel.

7 Apply waterproof adhesive to the dowels and their holes and then assemble the posts and all three rails to complete the construction of the two end frames.

Assembling the dowel joints

8 Use bar clamps to hold the frames together until the glue dries (*see pages 48–49*). If necessary, smooth down both sides of each joint with a bench plane.

Making the stretcher

1 Mark the stretcher slightly overlength and shape it to the correct width and thickness with a bench plane.

2 Mark the shoulder lines for the halving joints on the stretcher. The distance between the shoulder lines should equal the overall length of the towel rack minus the thicknesses of the two end frames (*see pages 72–77*).

3 Mark out the half-lap joints at both ends of the stretcher rail and at the two mid-points of the bottom rails on the end frames (*see pages 72–77*).

4 Cut the waste from the joints with a back saw. Clean up the joints with a ¾in (19mm) chisel, (*see pages 38–39*) and make sure the joint surfaces are flat and square.

Cutting a half-lap joint

5 Next, drill two countersunk clearance holes at each end of the stretcher (*see pages 34–35*) and dry assemble the joint. Make sure the two parts fit together tightly and then mark the bottom rails through the clearance holes with a bradawl.

6 Remove the connecting rail and drill small pilot holes in the bottom rails at all the marks made by your bradawl.

Assembling the towel rack

1 Mark the positions of the hanging bars on the inside faces of the two end frames.

Marking centers for the hanging bars

2 It is important that the hanging bars fit tightly into their holes. You may find that your dowelling is actually slightly less than 1 in (25 mm) in diameter, in which case it will be loose in holes made by a 1 in (25 mm) drill bit. Drill test holes in scrap timber and check that the dowelling fits firmly into them.

3 The depth of the holes for the hanging bars should be just over half the thickness of the frames, so make sure that the center point of your bit does not break through the opposite face of the wood. Tape the drill bit to indicate the correct depth before drilling the holes.

Drilling holes for the hanging bars

4 Mark and cut the dowelling for the hanging bars to length with a back saw. Cut one dowel first and then use it as a gauge for marking the length of the others.

Marking the hanging bars

5 Fix the stretcher to the bottom rail of one of the end frames using screws.

Fixing the stretcher

6 Smear waterproof adhesive over the ends of the hanging bars and push them into their holes.

Gluing a hanging bar

7 When you have glued all the hanging bars to the frames, screw the stretcher to the second end frame. Use bar clamps to hold the assembly together until the glue sets.

Cleaning and finishing

1 When the glue has dried, plane any unevenness in the joints flush and round off remaining sharp edges with abrasive paper.

2 Before you use the towel rack, you should apply several coats of varnish to seal the wood or, alternatively, paint it in a color of your choice.

WORKBENCH

This project uses both standard and 'stub' mortise and tenon joints to make a strong workbench that should give many years of service. It is made from softwood and plywood.

A WELL DESIGNED workbench, such as this one, is an invaluable asset in any workshop or studio. It can take considerable weight and is sturdy enough to withstand rough treatment. You can adapt the dimensions of the workbench to fit a specific space, and you can also fit it with a vise if you need one. The tenons that are used to join the long rails to the legs are called 'stub' tenons because they are just ⅜in (10mm) long.

Front elevation

Work top

Long rail

68in (1725mm)

71in (1800mm)

Side elevation

35½in (900mm)

End frame

26in (660mm)

29½in (750mm)

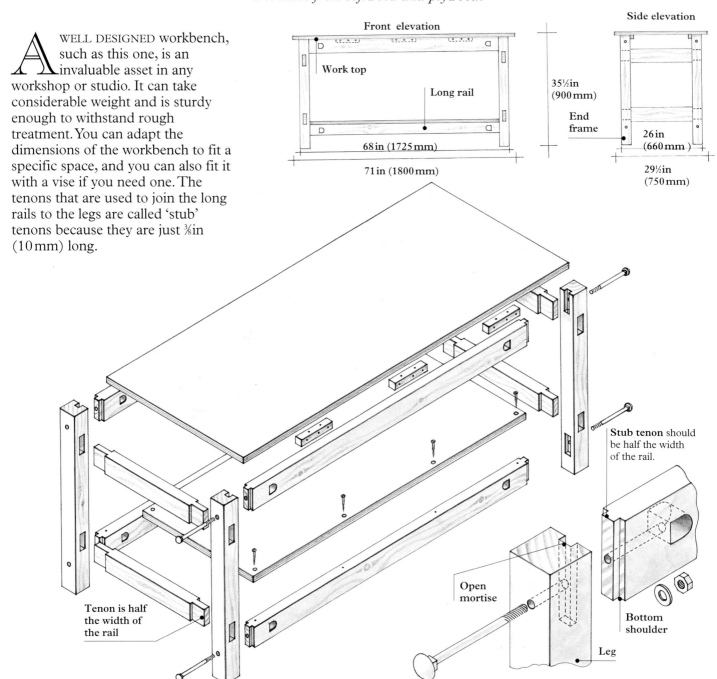

Stub tenon should be half the width of the rail.

Open mortise

Bottom shoulder

Leg

Tenon is half the width of the rail

PROJECT PLANNER
• Prepare and make mortises   • Prepare and cut tenons   • Assemble end frames   • Drill for carriage bolts   • Assemble frame   • Fit shelf and work top   • Clean up

SEE ALSO

SKILLS
• Measuring and marking techniques (*see pages 24–27*)
• Sawing techniques (*see pages 30–31*)
• Drilling techniques (*see pages 34–35*)
• Cutting and shaping techniques (*see pages 38–39*)
• Planing techniques (*see pages 42–45*)

• Clamping techniques (*see pages 48–49*)
• Sanding and finishing techniques (*see pages 60–61*)
• Power saws (*see pages 64–65*)
• Simple joint techniques (*see pages 72–77*)

WHAT YOU NEED

CUTTING LIST
- Legs: four 34$\frac{1}{2}$ x 3 x 3 in
  (876 x 75 x 75 mm) lengths of softwood
- Top rails: two 62$\frac{3}{4}$ x 5 x 1 in
  (1595 x 125 x 25 mm) lengths of
  softwood
- Bottom rails: two 62$\frac{3}{4}$ x 4 x 1$\frac{1}{2}$ in
  (1595 x 100 x 38 mm) lengths of
  softwood
- End rails: four 26 x 4 x 1$\frac{1}{2}$ in
  (660 x 100 x 38 mm) lengths of
  softwood
- Top: one 71 x 29$\frac{1}{2}$ x 1 in
  (1800 x 750 x 25 mm) length of
  plywood

- Shelf: one 63$\frac{1}{2}$ x 25$\frac{1}{2}$ x 1 in
  (1615 x 648 x 25 mm) length of
  plywood
- Fixing blocks: six 5 x 1 x 1 in
  (125 x 25 x 25 mm) lengths of softwood
- Carriage bolts: eight
  7 x $\frac{3}{8}$ in (178 x 10 mm) bolts with
  washers and nuts
- Screws for fixing blocks: thirty 1$\frac{1}{2}$ in
  (38 mm) No. 8 countersunk
- Screws for shelf: eight 1$\frac{1}{2}$ in (38 mm)
  No. 8 countersunk

TOOLS REQUIRED
- Straightedge, try square and
  mortise gauge
- Bench plane
- Back saw
- Bar clamps
- Power drill and bits
- $\frac{3}{4}$ in (19 mm) chisel and mallet
- Ring spanner
- Jigsaw
- Screwdriver
- Bradawl

Preparing the legs

1 Cut the legs to length, making sure the ends are flat and square to the faces (*see pages 24–27 and 30–31*). If necessary, smooth down the faces of the legs with a bench plane (*see pages 42–45*).

2 Mark the positions of all the rails on one leg (*see pages 72–77*). Transfer the rail positions to all the other legs by clamping them together and marking across using a try square or combination square.

3 Release the legs from your clamps and mark the rail positions on adjacent sides.

4 Use a mortise or marking gauge to mark out where to cut the mortises for each joint in each leg (*see pages 72-77*).

Cutting the mortises

1 Cut the shallow mortises for the stub tenons using a chisel and mallet. When you have removed most of the wood, clean up each mortise to your lines.

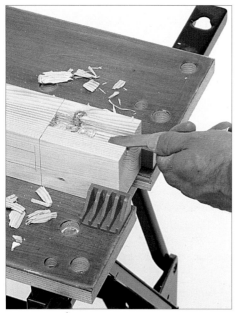

Shaping a shallow mortise to receive a stub tenon

2 When you cut the through mortises for the long tenons on the end rails, drill out the bulk of the waste with a bit slightly smaller than the width of the mortises. Carefully chop out the remaining wood with a chisel and mallet.

Chopping out a through mortise

3 Clean up the surfaces of the through mortises by paring down with a sharp chisel. It is best to work from both faces of the leg to obtain the neatest possible finish.

Marking the tenons

1 Cut the rails slightly overlength and check that the edges and faces on each one are square to each other. If necessary, work them with a bench plane.

2 Measure and mark the shoulders for the through tenons on the end rails. Add ¼ in (6 mm) onto the end of each tenon – so that the ends of the tenons can be planed flush with the legs later – and then cut the end rails to length.

3 Mark the shoulders for the stub tenons on the long rails and add on the depth of the shallow mortises. Saw the long rails to length.

4 Mark the thickness and length of each tenon with a marking gauge. The stub tenons on the long rails do not have shoulders along their top edges; shoulders all around are optional on the other tenons.

Cutting the tenons

1 Saw out the stub tenons, making sure that you hold the blade of the saw parallel to the face of the rail. Keep the saw just to the waste side of the cutting lines.

Cutting the waste from a stub tenon

2 The through tenons on the end rails are long, so take your time when cutting them, especially when sawing down the grain of the wood. If you rush the job, you may cut the tenons inaccurately which will result in weak joints.

Cutting a tenon on an end rail

3 After sawing the waste from the tenons, hold each one in turn against its mortise and trim it with a sharp chisel until it is a tight fit.

Assembling the end frames

1 To assemble the end frames, simply glue the through tenons on the end rails into their mortises. Use long bar clamps to hold the two frames rigid and square until the glue dries (*see pages 48–49*).

2 When the glue has dried, remove the clamps and saw off the ends of the tenons that protrude through the legs. Use a block plane to finish off the tenons flush to the legs.

Drilling the stub tenons

1 Drill the bolt holes in the shallow mortises first. To find the center of a mortise, draw diagonal lines across the mortise bottom. Drill holes through each mortise where the diagonals cross, using a ⅜ in (10 mm) bit. To get the neatest finish, drill the

holes from both sides using a spade bit. Drill gently so that the wood does not splinter.

2 The next step is to mark the drilling center on the end of each tenon. The easiest way to mark a tenon is to assemble a joint and to slot the ⅜in (10mm) drill bit through the hole in the mortise. Lightly tap the drill bit to leave a center mark on the end of the tenon. Mark the ends of all the tenons in this way.

3 Mark a 1¼in (32mm) access hole for the washer and nut on one face of each rail. The access hole should be centered 3¾in (95mm) from the shoulder of each joint. When making the access holes, drill through the rail into an offcut to prevent splintering.

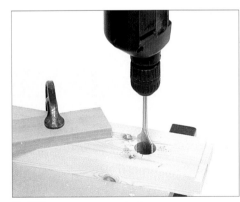

Drilling an access hole

4 Drilling the clearance holes for the bolts requires care as it is easy to let the bit stray while drilling down the grain. Before you drill a clearance hole, clamp the rail to your work-bench and hold the drill so that the bit is parallel to both the faces and edges of the rail. Drill all the holes from the center marks in the ends of the stub tenons right through to the access holes.

Drilling a clearance hole

Assembling the workbench base

1 You can use a chisel to cut flat faces on the sides of the access holes nearest to the tenons. This makes it easier to tighten the nuts.

2 To assemble the frame, fit each stub tenon into its mortise. Tap bolts through the clearance holes and thread on washers and nuts through the access holes.

3 Tighten the nuts with a wrench of the correct size. When you tighten the nuts, the bolts should bring the joints firmly together.

Assembling the top rails

Fitting the shelf and top

1 Use a jigsaw to cut the plywood for the shelf. The shelf lies between the lower end rails and rests on top of the long rails.

2 Draw lines parallel to the long edges of the plywood to correspond with the center lines of the top edges of the rails. Mark equally spaced drilling centers for four clearance holes along each line.

3 Drill and countersink clearance holes in the top face of the shelf. Slide the shelf into place and then drill pilot holes into the rails through the clearance holes. Screw the shelf into place.

Fitting the shelf

4 Cut the plywood for the top of the workbench to size with a jigsaw. Place it face down on the floor and lay the base on it.

5 Cut the fixing blocks to length and mark them for clearance holes – there should be three clearance holes in one face of each block and two clearance holes in an adjacent face. Drill countersunk clearance holes at each mark.

6 Position three blocks against each rail, one in the center and one toward each end. Mark through the clearance holes to make centers for the pilot holes.

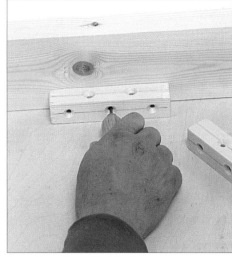

Locating the pilot holes

7 Drill pilot holes in the inside face of each rail and then glue and screw the blocks to them.

8 Fix the blocks to the top in a similar way, making sure the pilot holes do not break the top face.

Cleaning and finishing

1 Clean up the faces and edges with abrasive paper, and round off all sharp edges so that there is no danger of splinters breaking off when the bench is in use (*see pages 60–61*). Chamfer the edges of the plywood with a block plane.

2 If you wish, you can leave the workbench untreated. However, one or two coats of a clear varnish will help to slow down the build-up of dirt and stains and keep your workbench in good condition.

CHILDREN'S TOY CHEST

Constructed from MDF with butt joints, this sturdy chest is ideal for storing toys and playthings. The panels can be painted in bright, cheerful colors to make it even more appealing.

MEDIUM-DENSITY fiberboard (MDF) is an excellent material to use when constructing boxes. Unlike timber, it moves uniformly when it expands and contracts. This means that it does not warp like wood, and panels can be butted up to each other and fixed without you having to worry about them losing shape. MDF also takes paint well, which makes it ideal for the kind of knocks children's furniture has to put up with. The lid can be lifted off, so there is no danger of trapped fingers.

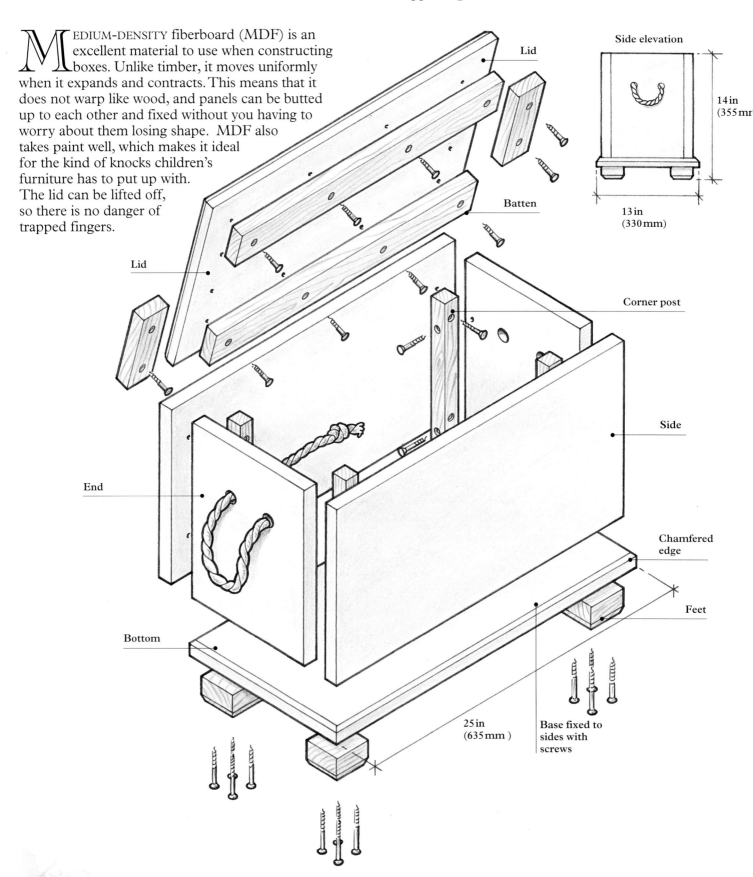

Lid

Batten

Side elevation

14 in
(355 mr)

13 in
(330 mm)

Lid

Corner post

Side

End

Chamfered edge

Feet

Bottom

25 in
(635 mm)

Base fixed to sides with screws

PROJECT PLANNER

- Mark out and cut MDF panels to size
- Mark out and cut solid wood to size
- Mark out and drill handle holes
- Mark and drill clearance holes in corner posts
- Assemble sides to ends
- Chamfer base and lid
- Fit base to sides
- Fit battens to lid
- Fit feet to base
- Clean up and apply paint finish

WHAT YOU NEED

CUTTING LIST
- Lid and bottom: two 25 x 13 x 1 in (635 x 330 x 25mm) lengths of MDF
- Sides: two 24 x 12 x 1 in (610 x 305 x 25mm) lengths of MDF
- Ends: two 14 x 10 x 1 in (355 x 255 x 25mm) lengths of MDF
- Corner posts: four 10½ x ⅞ x ⅞in (268 x 22 x 22mm) lengths of softwood
- Battens: two 21¾ x 1½ x ⅞in (553 x 38 x 22mm) and two 6¾ x 1½ x ⅞in (170 x 38 x 22mm) lengths of softwood or MDF
- Feet: four 3 x 3 x 1½in

(75 x 75 x 38mm) lengths of softwood
- Screws: thirty-eight 1½in (38mm) No. 8 countersunk and sixteen 2 in (50mm) No. 8 countersunk
- Thick rope

TOOLS REQUIRED
- Straightedge and try square
- Circular or rip saw and back saw
- Bench plane and block plane
- Bradawl and screwdriver
- Power drill and bits
- C-clamps

SEE ALSO

SKILLS
- Measuring and marking techniques
  (*see pages 24–27*)
- Sawing techniques (*see pages 30–31*)
- Drilling techniques (*see pages 34–35*)
- Planing techniques (*see pages 42–45*)
- Clamping techniques (*see pages 48–49*)
- Fixing techniques (*see pages 54–55*)
- Sanding and finishing techniques
  (*see pages 60–61*)

Preparing the carcass

1 Mark out the side and end panels on a sheet of MDF. Before you cut them, check that the marked panels are square (*see pages 24–27*).

Marking out the panels

2 Cut close to the outside of the marked lines, using a circular saw or ripsaw, and plane the edges with a bench plane (*see pages 30–31 and 42–45*).

Cutting out the panels

3 In the two end panels mark the centers of the holes for the rope handles. Clamp each panel flat on an offcut of wood before you drill the holes (*see pages 34–35*).

Drilling holes for the handles

Preparing the corner posts

1 Plane the faces of 1 x 1in (25 x 25mm) softwood square to each other before sawing the posts to length. Check that the finished posts are truly square all along their lengths.

2 Mark the centers of the three clearance holes along two adjacent faces of the posts, setting the top and bottom holes approximately 1 in (25mm) from each end. Off-set the holes along one face, to allow the screws to pass each other.

3 Drill through the marks using a drill bit that allows the screws to pass through without binding. Countersink the holes along two adjacent faces.

Assembling the carcass

1 First, clamp the corner posts to each of the end panels. Clamp carefully to make sure that the outer face and bottom end of each of the posts is flush with the edge and bottom end of the end panel.

2 Use a bradawl to mark the centers of the pilot holes in the end panels; make the marks through the clearance holes in the posts.

3 Drill pilot holes ½in (12mm) into the panels, using a drill bit smaller than the thread of the screws. Apply glue sparingly and screw the corner posts in place.

4 To fix a side panel to an end panel, first lay the end panel flat. Stand a side panel against the end panel, making sure that the top and bottom edges are aligned, and make marks for pilot holes through the clearance holes in the corner post. Drill pilot holes and then glue and screw the side panel to the end panel.

Assembling the sides

5 Glue and screw the whole carcass together in this way. If any of the panels are out of alignment, plane them flush when the glue has dried.

Making the lid and base

1 Place the carcass on a sheet of MDF. Use a piece of waste MDF ½in (12mm) wide as a scribing block to create the overhang, and mark all round the carcass sides to give the correct sizes of the lid and base. Cut the lid and base slightly oversize and plane them down to your pencil lines.

Marking out the base and top

2 If you want to chamfer the edges of the lid and base, you should do so with a block plane.

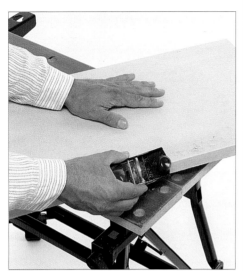

Planing the chamfers

Fitting the base

1 Place the carcass over the base with a ½in (12mm) overhang all round and mark the inside and outside faces with a pencil. Mark centers at 6in (150mm) intervals between the lines and drill out countersunk clearance holes. Stand the carcass on the lid, check the overlap is equal, and pencil lines around the inside and outside.

2 Place the base the correct way up over the bottom of the carcass, and mark the carcass for pilot holes. Drill the pilot holes and glue and screw the base to the carcass.

Fitting the base to the carcass

Preparing and fitting the battens

1 Before cutting all the locating battens to length, plane the edges of the lumber smooth and straight, using a bench plane.

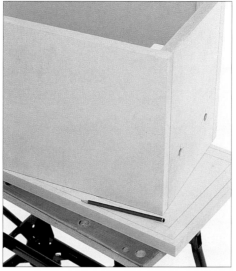

The position of the carcass marked on the lid before fitting the base

2 The battens are positioned against the inner lines on the lid, so mark and cut them to length.

3 Drill countersunk clearance holes in the battens, then position them on the underside of the lid and mark it for pilot holes. Drill the pilot holes, apply glue sparingly, and screw the battens in place. Check that the lid sits correctly on the carcass.

Fitting the battens

Preparing and fitting the feet

1 Measure and cut four 3 x 3in (75 x 75mm) feet from 1½in (38mm) thick softwood. Mark and drill countersunk clearance holes in the corner of each foot to take 2in (50mm) No. 8 screws.

2 Position each foot ½in (12mm) in from each corner of the base,

using a ½in (12mm) thick scribing block as a guide. Mark pilot holes in the base through the feet with a bradawl, then drill pilot holes and glue and screw the feet in place.

Fitting the feet

Cleaning and finishing

1 Lightly clean up the whole project with abrasive paper and soften the sharp edges.

2 Feed rope through the holes to create handles. Tie the knots before you cut the rope to length. It is best to remove the rope before you start painting the box.

Fitting the handles

3 MDF edges are very absorbent, so prime or seal them before applying normal undercoats and topcoats. Rub the box down with fine abrasive paper between coats of paint to remove dust particles and small blemishes.

TRELLIS

This attractive project uses mortise and tenon, and cross-lap joints.
The completed trellis makes a focal point within a garden, and can
provide support for a variety of climbing plants.

THE WOOD for this project must be weatherproof. You can use pressure-treated softwood available at building-supply stores, or cedar, redwood, or cypress, woods that are naturally resistant to decay. Pressure-treated and naturally resistant woods are sold in nominal sizes that are smaller than the stated sizes. Take care to select straight pieces, as this saves having to plane them by hand before you make the joints. Parts of this project can be vulnerable until the whole trellis is assembled, so clamp strips of waste wood in place to support free ends where necessary.

Joint at
top of post

Crosspiece

Top
bearer

Post

84 in
(2140 mm)

Brace

12 in
(305 mm)

Rail

23⅝ in
(600 mm)

48 in
(1220 mm)

Ground
level

Tenon on
cross rail

PROJECT PLANNER

- Mark out joints on lumber
- Cut joints and dry fit
- Assemble top frame
- Assemble post frames
- Install trellis in place

WHAT YOU NEED

CUTTING LIST
- Posts: four 96 x 2¼ x 2¼in
  (2440 x 56 x 56mm) lengths from 2½ x
  2½in (63 x 63mm) S4S softwood
- Cross rails: two 27 x 3¾ x 1¼in
  (685 x 95 x 32mm) lengths from 4 x
  1½in (100 x 38mm) S4S softwood
- Top bearers: two 53 x 3¾ x 1¼in
  (1345 x 95 x 32mm) lengths from
  4 x 1½in (100 x 38mm) S4S softwood
- Crosspieces: three 66 x 3¾ x 1¼in
  (1675 x 95 x 32mm) lengths from
  4 x 1½in (100 x 38mm) S4S softwood
- Braces: six 34 x 1¾ x ¾in
  (865 x 45 x 19mm) lengths from
  2 x 1in (50 x 25mm) S4S softwood
- Screws: six 3in (75mm) brass
  No. 10 countersunk
- Nails: 2in (50mm) galvanized
- Optional: four metal fence post spikes
  or materials for concrete: sand, cement
  and gravel

TOOLS REQUIRED
- Straightedge, try square and sliding bevel
- Mortise gauge
- Panel saw and back saw
- Mallet and 1in (25mm) chisel
- Bradawl, drill and screwdriver
- Hammer
- C-clamps

SEE ALSO

SKILLS
- Marking and measuring techniques
  (see pages 24–27)
- Drilling techniques
  (see pages 34–35)
- Cutting and shaping techniques
  (see pages 38–39)
- Planing techniques (see pages 42–45)
- Clamping techniques (see pages 48–49)
- Fixing techniques (see pages 54–55)
- Simple joint techniques (see pages 72–77)

Marking out

1 Mark out the finished lengths and
joints on the various components
except the braces (see pages 24–27).

2 Use C-clamps to clamp together
the components that are the same
– posts together, top bearers together
and so on. Mark across them while
they are clamped so that you know
that the joints will all be at the same
location when they are assembled.

3 Mark 30° bevels on the top
bearers and crosspieces. Then
use a mortise gauge to mark the
mortise positions for the rails on the
posts. It is always best to mark

everything at the same time, even if it
takes longer, as this removes any
confusion at a later stage.

Marking the bevels

Cutting the joints

1 Cut the mortises in the posts with
a chisel and mallet and make sure
they are square and clean (see pages
72–77). If necessary, pare down the
surfaces of the mortises.

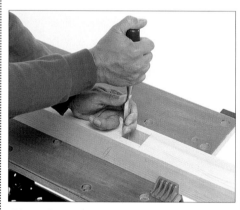

Chopping out a mortise

2 Cut the tenons on each end of
the cross rails with a back saw
(see pages 72–77).

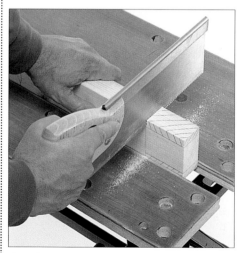

Cutting a tenon shoulder

3 Use a hand saw to cut slots
in the tops of the four posts and
clean them out with a chisel.

4 Dry assemble the four mortise-
-and-tenon joints, make any
adjustments, and clamp strips of
waste across the tops of each pair of
posts to keep them parallel.

5 Check that the distance between
the marked cross-lap joints on the
top bearers corresponds to
the distance between the posts.
Saw out and clean up the notches
in the undersides of the top bearers,
using a chisel (see pages 72–77).
The cross-laps in the top
bearers must be no more than
1in (25mm) deep.

Finishing a cross-lap joint

6 Cut the six cross-lap joints
that take the crosspieces in the
upper sides of the top bearers, and
check for fit.

Assembling the top frame

1 Saw the 30° bevels on the ends
of the top components and
clean them up with a plane (see
pages 42–45).

2 Drill countersunk clearance holes
in the undersides of the two top
bearers for the brass screws that will
hold the cross-lap joints together (see
pages 34–35).

3 First, knock the joints together
with a mallet and then use a
bradawl to mark the pilot holes in
the crosspieces.

Knocking home the joint

4 Dismantle the frame and drill the pilot holes in the crosspieces. Spread waterproof glue lightly over each half of each cross-lap joint, then knock the joints back together and secure them with the screws.

Screwing a cross-lap joint

Assembling the posts

1 Dismantle the dry-assembled posts, spread glue on the tenons, and then reassemble the joints again.

Assembling a mortise and tenon joint

2 Having glued all the mortise and tenon joints, clamp waste strips across the tops of the posts to hold them parallel.

3 Mark the positions of the six braces on the assembled posts and cut the mitered ends of the braces in a miter box. Make sure that you secure the miter box firmly to your workbench before you start sawing or else it will move about.

Sawing the braces

4 Drill clearance holes for nails in the braces so that the wood does not split open, and then nail the braces in place.

Installing the trellis

1 Remove the strips of waste wood that are clamped across the tops of the posts.

2 If you are intending to paint or stain the trellis, you should do so at this stage (*see pages 60–63*). Allow the finish to dry completely before continuing.

3 Use the top frame to mark out the location of the four posts in the ground. You can either set the bottom of the posts in concrete or fit them into metal fence post spikes (see panel below).

4 To set the posts in concrete, dig out a hole for each post. Each hole should be approximately 18 in (460 mm) deep and 12 in (305 mm) square at the top.

5 Pack down a layer of small stones or crushed bricks in the bottom of each hole. This helps to improve drainage.

6 Next, mix up concrete in the proportions: one part cement; two parts sand; three parts aggregate (gravel). Add a little water to the ingredients and mix them up – the concrete should have a firm, not runny, consistency.

7 With the help of an assistant, place the four posts upright in their holes and pour concrete around them.

8 After filling all the holes, check that the posts are vertical and leave the concrete to set hard.

9 When the concrete is hard, drop the top frame over the notches in the top of the posts and secure it by skew-nailing through the joints.

USING A METAL FENCE POST SPIKE

1 A fence post spike has a long tapering shaft with a square cup on the top. The shaft is driven into the ground and the post is slotted into the cup. Depending on the design of the spike, the post is secured in the cup by nails or by tightening up bolts that clamp the post rigid. Choose spikes with cups that match the size of the trellis posts.

2 Use a heavy hammer to knock each spike into the ground at its mark. As you hammer each spike, check regularly that is going into the ground vertically. Continue to hammer in the spikes until only the cups are visible above the ground.

3 Insert the posts into the cups of the spikes. If necessary, tap them in with a mallet.

4 Secure the posts by hammering nails through the slots in the cups or by tightening up the bolts.

5 Check that the posts are vertical before positioning the top frame and skew-nailing it in place.

A fence post spike

DISH RACK

This project uses half-lap and dowel joints. Dowels are also used to make the slats. The finished rack can be either freestanding or hung from a wall over a draining board.

THE END FRAMES of the rack are constructed from 1 in (25 mm) S4S softwood. The half-lap joints look simple but they must be made carefully so that all the components fit together neatly. The first task is to make a full-size drawing of an end frame as the angles are determined by the dimensions of the components. Once you have made the drawing, you can use it as a template.

Moisture from wet plates will tend to spoil any finish applied to the rack, so it is best to leave the wood bare.

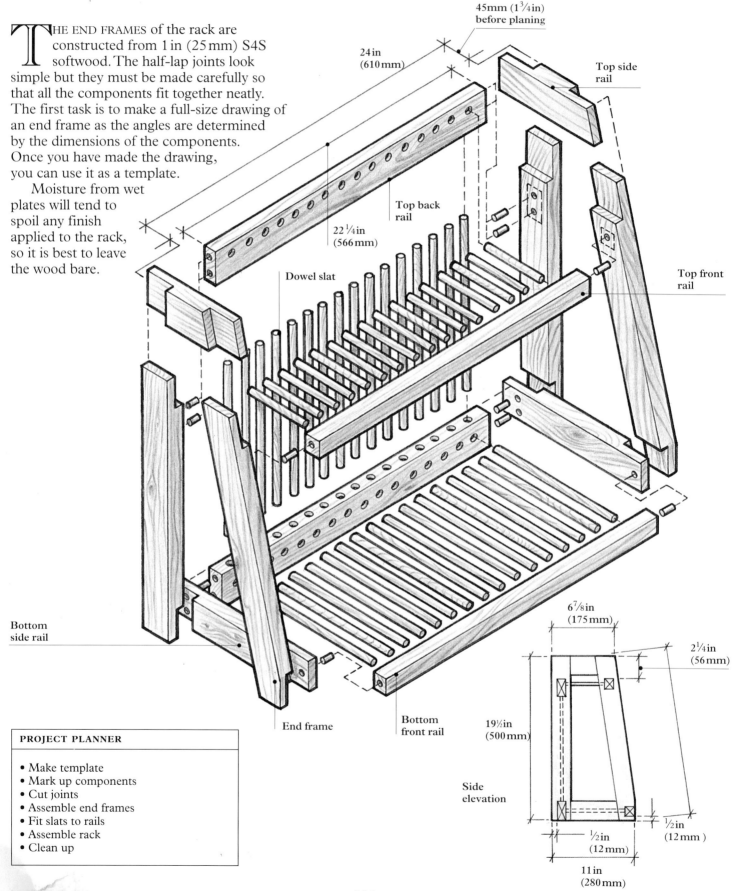

45mm (1¾in) before planing

24in (610mm)

Top side rail

Top back rail

22¼in (566mm)

Dowel slat

Top front rail

Bottom side rail

End frame

Bottom front rail

6⅞in (175mm)

2¼in (56mm)

19½in (500mm)

Side elevation

½in (12mm)

½in (12mm)

11in (280mm)

PROJECT PLANNER

- Make template
- Mark up components
- Cut joints
- Assemble end frames
- Fit slats to rails
- Assemble rack
- Clean up

SEE ALSO

SKILLS

- Measuring and marking techniques (*see pages 24–27*)
- Sawing techniques (*see pages 30–31*)
- Drilling techniques (*see pages 34–35*)
- Cutting and shaping techniques (*see pages 38–39*)
- Planing techniques (*see pages 42–45*)
- Clamping techniques (*see pages 48–49*)
- Hanging and fastening techniques (*see pages 56–57*)
- Sanding and finishing techniques (*see pages 60–61*)
- Simple joint techniques (*see pages 72–77*)
- Dowel joints (*see pages 78–79*)

WHAT YOU NEED

CUTTING LIST

- End frame verticals: four $19\frac{1}{2}$ x $1\frac{3}{4}$ x $\frac{7}{8}$in (500 x 45 x 22mm) lengths of softwood
- End frame horizontals: two 11 x $1\frac{3}{4}$ x $\frac{7}{8}$in (280 x 45 x 22mm) and two $6\frac{7}{8}$ x $1\frac{3}{4}$ x $\frac{7}{8}$in (175 x 45 x 22mm) lengths of softwood
- Back rails: two $22\frac{1}{4}$ x $1\frac{3}{4}$ x $\frac{7}{8}$in (566 x 45 x 22mm) lengths of softwood
- Front rails: two $22\frac{1}{4}$ x $\frac{7}{8}$ x $\frac{7}{8}$in (566 x 22 x 22mm) lengths of softwood
- Bottom slats: sixteen $9\frac{5}{8}$in (245mm) lengths of $\frac{3}{8}$in (10mm) dowel
- Back slats: sixteen $13\frac{1}{8}$in (334mm)

lengths of $\frac{3}{8}$in (10mm) dowel.
- Top slats: sixteen $5\frac{1}{2}$in (140mm) lengths of $\frac{3}{8}$in (10mm) dowel
- Dowel joints: twelve $1\frac{3}{8}$in (35mm) lengths of $\frac{3}{8}$in (10mm) dowel

TOOLS REQUIRED

- Straightedge and try square
- Back saw
- Sliding bevel and marking gauge
- 1in (25mm) chisel
- C-clamps and bar clamps
- Block plane and bench plane
- Power drill and bits
- Dowel pins

Marking the end frames

1 Draw a full-size template of the end frames on a sheet of spare hardboard. Use a try square or combination square and steel rule to make the drawing, taking the dimensions for the components directly from the wood you are going to use. Include on the drawing the positions of the rails.

Drawing up the template

2 Mark the components for the end frames directly from the template.

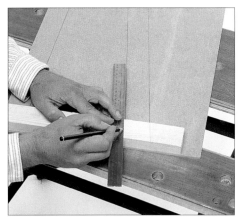

Marking up an end frame component

3 Saw the components to length and then mark the half-lap joints at the end of each piece with a marking gauge (*see pages 72-77*). Remember that the two end frames are mirror images of each other so make sure that you mark the joints the right way around.

Cutting the half-lap joints

1 Cut out the half-lap joints with a tenon saw, making sure that you hold the saw to the waste side of the cutting lines.

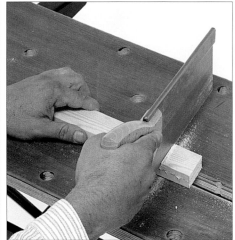

Cutting a half-lap joint

2 Use a sharp chisel to clean up the faces of the joints, making sure that they are flat and square to the edges (*see pages 38–39*). It is best to work on pairs of joints at the same time so that you can check them for fit as you progress. This can take time, but it is important that each joint fits together precisely.

Assembling the end frames

1 Use a waterproof glue to join the components of each end frame together. Make sure that the shoulders of each joint are closed up tight and secure them with C-clamps until the glue dries hard (*see pages 48–49*).

Clamping an end frame

2 When the glue is dry, use a block plane to shave down any wood that protrudes beyond a joint (*see pages 42–45*).

3 If necessary, smooth the faces of the two frames flush, using a bench plane.

Marking the rails

1 Cut the four rails to length with a tenon saw, making sure they have square ends and are all exactly the same length.

2 Clamp the rails together and mark out the positions of the slats at 1in (25mm) intervals with a try square or combination square.

Marking the slat positions

3 Release the clamp and mark the slat positions around two adjacent faces on the back rails.

4 Taking each front rail in turn, score a center line along the length of the back edge with a marking gauge. This line should cross all the marks for the positions of the slats to give you the centers where the holes should be drilled.

5 Mark a central line along the top edge of the bottom back rail and a similar line along the bottom edge of the top back rail.

6 The centers for the horizontal slats on the top back rail are set ¾in (19mm) below the top edge. Set your marking gauge to this measurement and score a line along the face of the rail. The horizontal slats on the bottom back rail are set along a central line, so adjust your marking gauge to half the width of the rail before scoring a line along the face.

Fitting the slats

1 Mark each slat center with a bradawl. These marks will prevent the bit from skidding when you start drilling the holes for the slats.

2 All the slats are housed ⅜in (10mm) into the rails. Select a ⅜in (10mm) bit, to match the diameter of the dowelling, and fit it with a depth stop. If you do not have a suitable depth stop, wrap a piece of colored tape around the bit, ⅜in (10mm) from the end, to act as a depth gauge (*see pages 34–35*).

3 Drill ⅜in (10mm) deep holes at each center, making sure that you hold the drill square to the lumber every time. Remember that it is better to drill the holes a little too deep, rather than too shallow. However do not set your drill to a high speed or the bit may go right through the wood.

Drilling the slat holes

Fitting the rails

1 Mark each end of the front rails with diagonals. This will give you precise centers for the dowels that are used to secure the rails to the two end frames.

2 Drill the centers in the ends of the front rails to a depth of ¾in (19mm).

3 Mark for two dowels in the ends of both back rails and again drill holes to a depth of ¾in (19mm).

Drilling dowel holes

4 Outline the positions of the rails on the two end frames and then use dowelling pins to mark the drilling centers on the inside faces of the frames.

Transferring the dowel centers

5 Very carefully drill all the holes in the end frames to a depth of ¾in (19mm).

Assembling and finishing

1 Measure up and then cut the dowelling for the slats to length with a tenon saw.

2 Smear a little glue over the ends of the slats when you fit them into their appropriate holes in the frames. Assemble one row of slats at a time and when you have fitted a complete row, clamp the rails together until the glue dries.

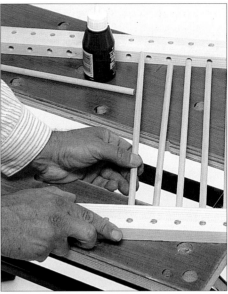

Fitting the slats

3 Tap glued dowels into the holes in the ends of the rails and then add the end frames.

4 Hold the entire assembly together with bar clamps until the glue is dry (*see pages 48–49*).

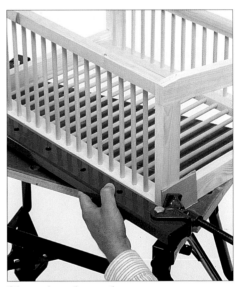

Clamping the rack

5 When the glue has set, remove all the clamps and clean up the whole rack with fine abrasive paper (*see pages 60–61*).

6 If you want to hang the rack on a wall, screw a support batten to the wall to fit underneath the bottom rail at the back and attach mirror plates to the tops of the end frames. Check that the support batten is horizontal before you screw it in place (*see pages 56–57*).

BLANKET CHEST

This handsome box, made from solid wood, has no cut joints, but is glued and screwed together. The box is strong and can be used for storing all sorts of items as well as blankets and linen.

A S SOLID WOOD expands or contracts according to the moisture content in the atmosphere, you have to take into account the potential for movement across the width of the wood when constructing a project like this. Much of the skill in making the box lies in allowing for shrinkage and expansion in components such as the lid and base. S4S softwood with a clear finish is used in the example, but you could paint the box or apply stencils.

PROJECT PLANNER

- Prepare the components
- Make the carcass
- Make and fit the lid and base
- Clean up and finish

SEE ALSO

SKILLS
- Measuring and marking techniques (*see pages 24–27*)
- Sawing techniques (*see pages 30–31*)
- Drilling techniques (*see pages 34–35*)
- Cutting and shaping techniques (*see pages 38–39*)
- Planing techniques (*see pages 42–45*)
- Clamping techniques (*see pages 48–49*)
- Fixing techniques (*see pages 54–55*)
- Sanding and finishing techniques (*see pages 60–61*)

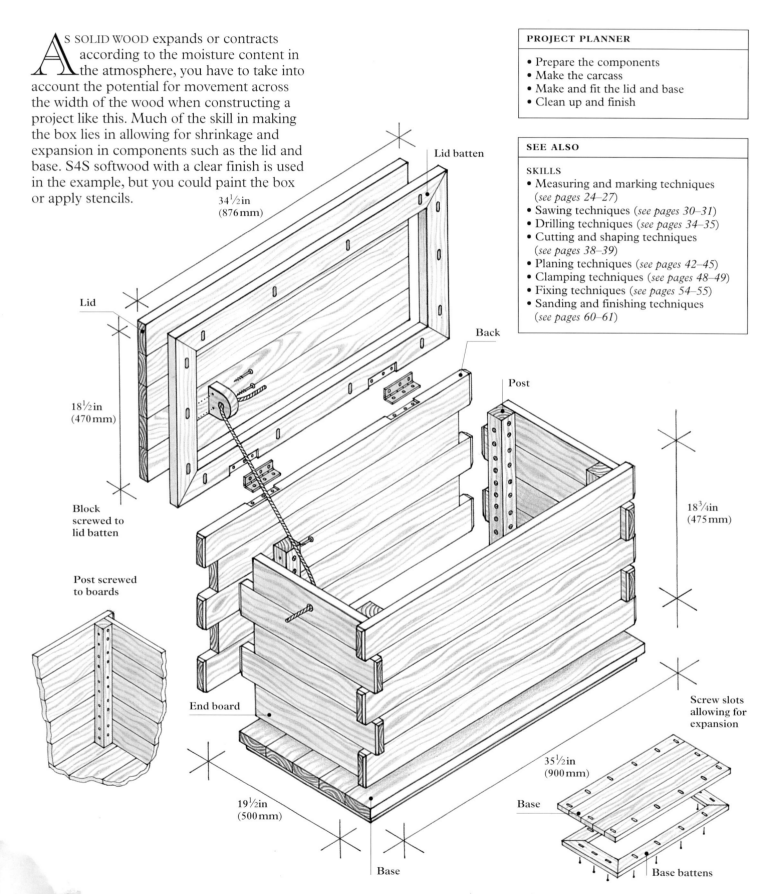

Lid batten

34½in (876mm)

Lid

Back

Post

18½in (470mm)

18¾in (475mm)

Block screwed to lid batten

Post screwed to boards

End board

Screw slots allowing for expansion

35½in (900mm)

Base

19½in (500mm)

Base

Base battens

WHAT YOU NEED

CUTTING LIST
- Base: softwood boards to make a panel measuring $35\frac{1}{2}$ x $19\frac{1}{2}$ x 1 in (900 x 500 x 25 mm)
- Lid: softwood boards to make a panel measuring $34\frac{1}{2}$ x $18\frac{1}{2}$ x 1 in (876 x 470 x 25 mm)
- Front and back boards: six $35\frac{1}{2}$ x $3\frac{3}{4}$ x 1 in (900 x 95 x 25 mm) and four $32\frac{5}{8}$ x $3\frac{3}{4}$ x 1 in (830 x 95 x 25 mm) lengths of softwood
- End boards: four $19\frac{1}{2}$ x $3\frac{3}{4}$ x 1 in (500 x 95 x 25 mm) and six 17 x $3\frac{3}{4}$ x 1 in (430 x 95 x 25 mm) lengths of softwood
- Lid battens: two $35\frac{1}{2}$ x $2\frac{5}{8}$ x 1 in (900 x 65 x 25 mm) and two $19\frac{1}{2}$ x $2\frac{5}{8}$ x 1 in (500 x 65 x 25 mm) lengths of softwood

- Base battens: two $34\frac{1}{2}$ x $2\frac{5}{8}$ x 1 in (876 x 65 x 25 mm) and two $18\frac{1}{2}$ x $2\frac{5}{8}$ x 1 in (476 x 65 x 25 mm) lengths of softwood
- Posts: four 20 x $1\frac{1}{4}$ x $1\frac{1}{4}$ in (510 x 32 x 32 mm) lengths of softwood
- Hinges: one pair $2\frac{1}{2}$ in (63 mm) brass butt, with screws to fit
- Screws for posts: eighty $1\frac{3}{4}$ in (45 mm) No. 8 countersunk
- Screws for lid battens: fourteen $1\frac{1}{2}$ in (38 mm) roundhead with washers
- Screws for base battens: fourteen $1\frac{1}{2}$ in (38 mm) No. 8 steel countersunk
- Screws for base and stay block: sixteen $1\frac{1}{2}$ in (38 mm) No. 8 countersunk
- Stays: one length of cord

TOOLS REQUIRED
- Straightedge, try square and sliding bevel
- Bench plane and block plane
- Back saw and miter box
- Power drill and bits
- Bar clamps
- $\frac{3}{4}$ in and $\frac{1}{8}$ in (19 mm and 3 mm) chisels
- Screwdriver

Preparing the wood

1 Mark out the boards to make the lid, the base and the sides (*see pages 24–27*). Cut the boards slightly overlength at this stage – they can be trimmed to exact sizes later on (*see pages 30–31*). As you cut the boards, mark them so that they are easy to identify.

2 Use a bench plane to trim the edges of the boards for the lid and base. The edges must be perfectly smooth and square (*see pages 42–45*). It is worth taking time over this, as any gaps between boards will show up when the chest is finished.

Marking up for the carcass

1 Cut the four corner posts to their finished length, which is equal to the total of five widths of the boards for the sides and ends. Check that the posts are straight and square.

2 Clamp the long boards for the front and back panels together and mark their finished lengths.

Marking a set of long boards

3 Saw the long boards to size and then scribe a line 1½in (38mm) in from each end. The corner posts will be lined up with these marks when you assemble the carcass.

4 Cut and mark the four long boards for the end panels in exactly the same way.

5 Mark the lengths of the short boards from the pencil lines on the long boards. Cut them to length.

Assembling the carcass

1 Mark all around the four posts to show the positions of the five boards.

2 Each board is fixed to a corner post with two screws. Mark the clearance holes on the posts, making sure that you stagger the holes slightly so that screws driven into adjacent faces will not collide.

3 Drill the clearance holes in the posts and countersink them (*see pages 34–35*).

4 Arrange a panel of boards to make the front, making sure that the short boards align with the marks on the long boards. Smear some glue along the side of the post and then screw it to the boards.

Screwing a post to the boards

5 After fitting two posts to the front panel, construct the back panel in a similar way.

6 Having constructed the front and back panels, add boards to the posts to make up the end panels.

Making the lid and base

1 Apply glue to the sides of the boards for the lid and base and clamp them together, making sure they stay flat and that any steps between them are kept to a minimum (*see pages 48–49*).

2 When the glue is dry, plane the surfaces flat (*see pages 42–45*). Mark out the finished sizes and saw the lid and the top to size. Clean up the end grain with a block plane and use a bench plane to make the long edges straight and square.

Cutting the battens

1 Cut the eight pieces of batten to length. The batten frame to the lid is larger than the panel, while that for the base is smaller. Mark the miters at the ends of the battens.

2 The battens on the lid overlap the edges by approximately ½in (12mm). Mark this overlap on each batten, making sure that you align the miter mark with a corner of the lid first.

Marking the overlap

3 With the base, the battens are inset by ½in (12mm). Mark the positions of the battens on the base.

4 Cut miters at the end of the battens in a miter box using a back saw.

Cutting a miter at the end of a batten

5 Having cut the miters, position the battens on the lid and base and check that they fit neatly.

6 Mark the position of the clearance slots for screws in the long battens; space the slots out at approximately 10 in (255 mm) intervals.

7 The slots in the short battens need to be spaced out roughly 6 in (150 mm) apart. Make sure that the slots are evenly spaced out before you drill and cut them all.

8 To make a slot, first mark its position and then drill out three holes in line with each other. Aim to make each slot no longer than ½ in (12 mm).

Drilling the holes for a slot

9 After you have drilled the holes for a slot, remove the waste in between them with a chisel.

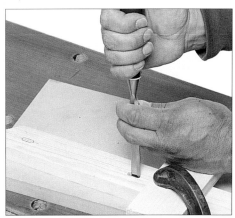

Clearing out the waste

Fitting the base
1 Place the carcass over the base, making sure that there is an equal overlap all the way round. Mark the position of the carcass on both the inside and outside.

2 Remove the carcass and then mark the screw positions in the base. Make sure the nails do not align with the batten screws.

3 At each mark, drill out and cut clearance slots as described above, running across the grain of the base. Countersink the clearance slots so that the screw heads do not interfere when the battens are fitted.

4 Turn the carcass upside down and screw the base in place. Make sure that the base is accurately positioned and that there is an equal overlap all the way round.

5 Lay the base battens against their marks and countersink the holes and slots. Mark pilot holes through the clearance holes and slots with a bradawl before screwing the battens to the base. Make sure that the heads of the screws are recessed sufficiently not to scratch the floor.

Assembling the lid
1 The lid battens are fixed in much the same way as the base battens, except that roundhead screws with washers are used. When you add the screws, ensure their positions do not interfere with the top edges of the carcass when the lid is closed.

Screwing the battens to the lid

Fitting the lid
1 Mark the positions of the hinges on the lid and on the top edge of the back panel.

2 Use a sharp ¾ in (19 mm) chisel to cut the hinge recesses in the lid (*see pages 54–55*), and fit the hinges with screws.

3 Cut the hinge recesses in the back panel and carefully screw the lid in place.

Cutting a hinge recess in the back panel

4 To prevent the lid tearing off the hinges, thread knotted cord through a small hole drilled in an end panel. Thread the other end of the rope through a block screwed to the inside of the lid batten.

Fitting the rope stay

Cleaning and finishing
1 Clean up the whole chest with abrasive paper and smooth down rough edges.

2 Apply a finish of your choice. If you varnish the chest, brush on at least three coats.

CHILD'S DESK

*The construction of this desk involves no traditional jointing. It can be made
from a single 8 x 4ft (2440 x 1220mm) sheet of 1in (25mm) MDF, with
softwood battens to provide rigidity and strength.*

THIS PROJECT exploits the versatility of
MDF. Once all the components have
been cut out, they are simply glued and
screwed together. When you saw out or sand
down the components, be sure to wear a face
mask, as MDF creates a very fine dust.

The small metal feet that protect the bottom
edges of the desk are sometimes called 'domes
of silence'. They are readily available from
hardware stores but you could fit screw-in
rubber feet as an alternative.

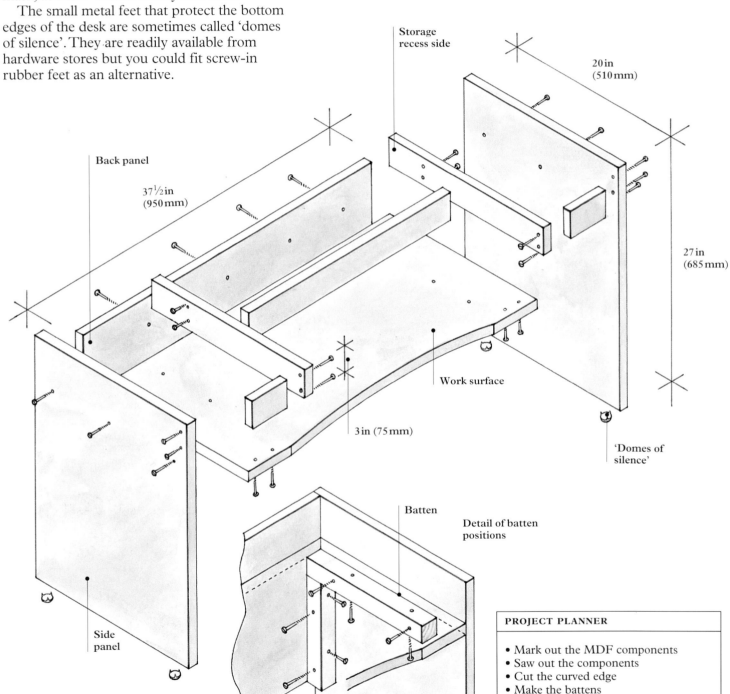

Storage
recess side

20 in
(510 mm)

Back panel

37½ in
(950 mm)

27 in
(685 mm)

Work surface

3 in (75 mm)

'Domes of
silence'

Batten

Detail of batten
positions

Side
panel

PROJECT PLANNER

- Mark out the MDF components
- Saw out the components
- Cut the curved edge
- Make the battens
- Drill the screw holes
- Assemble the desk
- Clean up and finish

SEE ALSO

SKILLS
- Measuring and marking techniques (*see pages 24–27*)
- Sawing techniques (*see pages 30–31*)
- Drilling techniques (*see pages 34–35*)
- Planing techniques (*see pages 42–45*)
- Clamping techniques (*see pages 48–49*)
- Fixing techniques (*see pages 54–55*)
- Sanding and finishing techniques (*see pages 60–61*)
- Power saws (*see pages 64–65*)

WHAT YOU NEED

CUTTING LIST
- Work surface: one $37\frac{1}{2}$ x $18\frac{1}{2}$ x 1 in (950 x 470 x 25 mm) sheet of MDF
- Back panel: one $37\frac{1}{2}$ x $11\frac{3}{4}$ x 1 in (950 x 300 x 25 mm) length of MDF
- Side panels: two 27 x 20 x 1 in (685 x 510 x 25 mm) lengths of MDF
- Storage recess dividers: one $27\frac{1}{2}$ x 3 x 1 in (700 x 75 x 25 mm), two $18\frac{1}{2}$ x 3 x 1 in (470 x 75 x 25 mm) and two 4 x 3 x 1 in (100 x 75 x 25 mm) lengths of MDF
- Battens: four $11\frac{3}{4}$ x $1\frac{1}{4}$ x $1\frac{1}{4}$ in (300 x 32 x 32 mm) lengths of softwood
- Screws for battens: sixteen 2 in (50 mm) No. 8 countersunk

- Screws for desk: at least fifty $1\frac{1}{2}$ in (38 mm) No. 8 countersunk
- Feet: four 'domes of silence'

TOOLS REQUIRED
- Straightedge, try square and thin, flexible stick
- Jigsaw and power saw
- Bench plane and block plane
- Bradawl and hammer
- Back saw
- Power drill and bits
- Screwdriver
- Bar clamps

Marking out the MDF

1 Using a sharp pencil and a steel straightedge, draw out the cutting list of all the components on a sheet of MDF (*see pages 24–27*). Work as accurately as you can and allow at least ¼in (6mm) between adjacent pieces for cutting out.

Marking out the MDF components

2 Before cutting them out, check that the components are exactly the right size by comparing diagonal measurements. This is an important step, as any inaccuracies at this stage will slow you up when you assemble the components.

Cutting out the components

1 Cut out all the components slightly oversize with a power saw (*see pages 64–65*). Be sure to wear a face mask when you do this so that you do not inhale dust.

2 Carefully trim down all the edges with a bench plane until all the components are the exact size you want them to be (*see pages 42–45*). Compare components that should be the same size to check that they are in fact identical.

Marking the component positions

1 Mark up the side panels, back panel and work surface to show where all the divider components fit. The most accurate way to do this is to use the actual components as guides. For example, position a divider against the top edge of the back panel and mark a line against it.

Using a storage divider to mark the back panel

2 Mark the centers of the screw clearance holes on the side and back panels, as well as on the underside of the work surface.

Making the curved edge

1 Mark the curved front end of the work surface with a thin stick or length of dowel. The easiest way to do this is to ask an assistant to bend the stick to the desired curve while you mark round it with a pencil. The curve only needs to be approximately 1 in (25 mm) deep at the center of the work surface.

Bending the flexible stick to the curve

2 Cut to the waste side of your curved line with a jigsaw (*see pages 64–65*), and smooth the end down with abrasive paper.

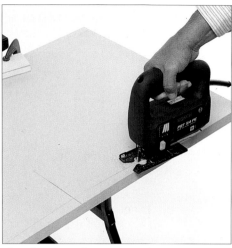

Cutting out the curve with a jigsaw

Making the battens

1 Mark and cut the softwood support battens to length with a back saw (*see pages 30–31*).

2 Drill and countersink clearance holes in the battens, making sure that holes in adjacent sides are offset slightly so that the screws do not collide. The holes should be no closer than 1in (25 mm) to each end.

Drilling the clearance holes

1 Drill out all the clearance holes in the side and back panels, as well as in the work surface. Countersink the holes so that the heads of the screws lie below the surface of the MDF once they are in place.

2 Clean the exit holes on the reverse sides of the panels so that no waste can interfere when you start assembling them.

Assembling the desk

1 It is important to drill pilot holes for all screws driven into MDF. This is particularly true when fixing into the edge of MDF to prevent the material from splitting. As a general rule, use a drill bit that is only just smaller in diameter than the diameter of the screw. For example, for a screw ³⁄₁₆in (5mm) in diameter, use a ⅛in (3mm) drill bit.

2 Start assembling the desk by laying the back panel flat. Position the two battens that anchor it to the side panels and mark through the clearance holes with a sharp bradawl.

3 Drill pilot holes in the MDF to accommodate the screws. Make sure that you do not drill right through the MDF.

4 Glue and screw the battens to the ends of the back panel, making sure that they surfaces are flush. Wipe off excess glue while it is still wet.

5 Taking each in turn, position the side panels against the back panel and its battens. Mark through the clearance holes in the battens and drill out all the pilot holes in the side panels.

6 Glue and screw the side panels to the back panel. Use bar clamps to hold the assembly rigid until the glue sets.

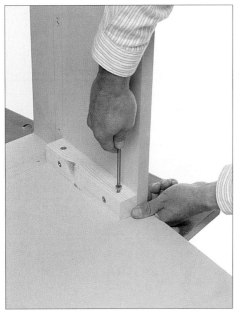

Fixing the back panel to a side panel with a batten

7 Glue and screw the battens that support the work surface to the two side panels. Make sure that the battens are parallel with the ends of the panels.

8 Apply glue to the edges of the work surface and then lay it on top of the support battens. Drill pilot holes through the clearance holes in the side panels into the ends of the work surface. Secure the work surface with screws driven up through the support battens and also through the side panels.

Drilling pilot holes through an end panel into the work surface

9 The next step is to position the dividers on the work surface and to glue and screw them into place. First, fix the dividers with screws driven into the ends of the components through countersunk clearance holes. This includes the long divider at the back of the work surface, which is anchored by screws driven through the two side dividers.

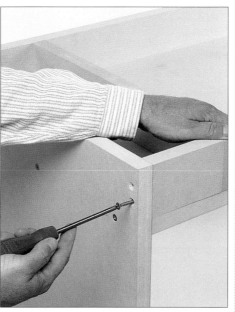

Fixing a divider through holes drilled in an end panel

10 The dividers also need to be secured from underneath, so fix them with screws driven up through the work surface. The back divider requires three screws.

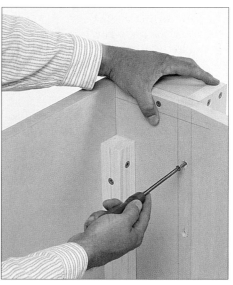

Securing the dividers from underneath (side removed for clarity)

11 Finish the construction by hammering a pair of 'domes of silence' to the bottom edge of each side panel.

Fitting the 'domes of silence'

Cleaning and finishing

1 If necessary, use a block plane to smooth any edges that are not flush.

2 Cover the heads of the recessed screws with filler. When the filler is dry, sand it flat with abrasive paper wrapped round a flat block.

3 Clean up the whole desk with abrasive paper and soften any sharp edges (*see pages 60–61*).

4 Apply a paint finish, using a primer and undercoat as recommended by the paint manufacturer.

GARDEN BENCH

This project uses interlocking and dowel joints to construct a sturdy bench that can withstand both weather and harsh treatment. Making the bench will give you good practice in using a bench plane.

THIS BENCH should be constructed from a hardwood such as beech or maple. Although hardwoods are not as easy to work with hand tools as softwoods, they are more attractive and are tougher. When you buy the wood, make sure that you get enough to cut and shape all the pieces for the bench. Bear in mind that a considerable amount of wood will be be lost as you prepare and trim the rough-sawn wood into workable sections.

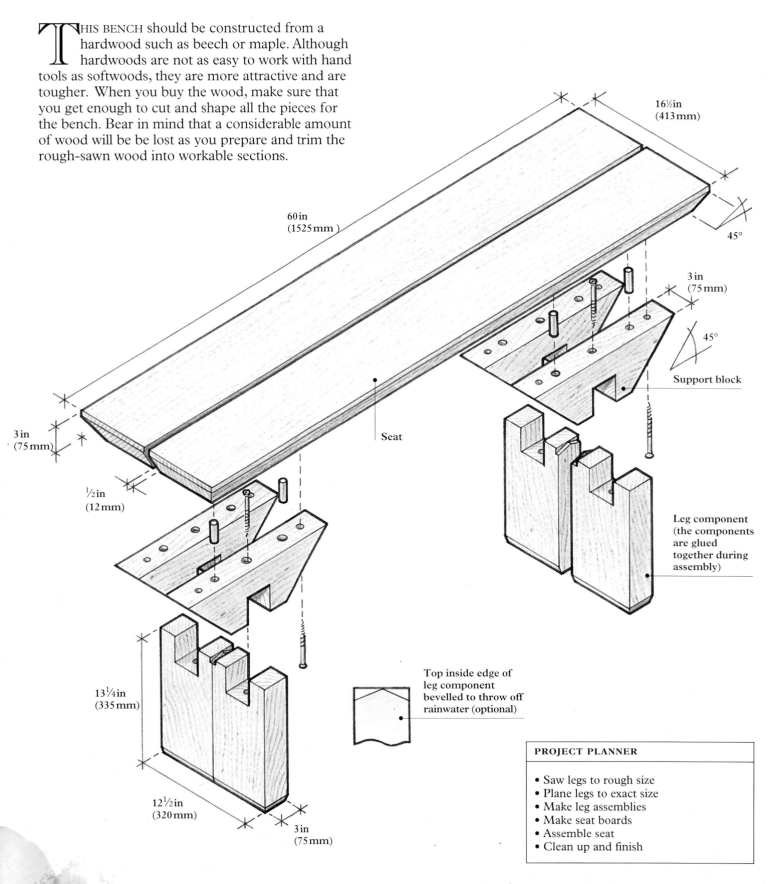

16½in (413mm)

60in (1525mm)

45°

3in (75mm)

45°

Support block

Seat

3in (75mm)

½in (12mm)

Leg component (the components are glued together during assembly)

13¼in (335mm)

Top inside edge of leg component bevelled to throw off rainwater (optional)

12½in (320mm)

3in (75mm)

PROJECT PLANNER

- Saw legs to rough size
- Plane legs to exact size
- Make leg assemblies
- Make seat boards
- Assemble seat
- Clean up and finish

SEE ALSO

SKILLS
- Measuring and marking techniques (*see pages 24–27*)
- Sawing techniques (*see pages 30–31*)
- Drilling techniques (*see pages 34–35*)
- Cutting and shaping techniques (*see pages 38–39*)
- Planing techniques (*see pages 42–45*)
- Clamping techniques (*see pages 48–49*)
- Fixing techniques (*see pages 52–53*)
- Sanding and finishing techniques (*see pages 60–61*)
- Simple joint techniques (*see pages 72–77*)
- Dowel joints (*see pages 78–79*)

WHAT YOU NEED

CUTTING LIST
- Seat: two 60 x 8 x 3in (1525 x 200 x 75mm) lengths of hardwood
- Support blocks: four 16½ x 4¼ x 3in (413 x 110 x 75mm) lengths of hardwood
- Legs: two made up from four 13¼ x 6¼ x 3in (335 x 160 x 75mm) lengths of hardwood
- Dowels: eight ⅜ x 1in (10 x 25mm)
- Screws: twelve 3⅛in (80mm) No. 10 brass countersunk

TOOLS REQUIRED
- Try square and straightedge
- Block plane and bench or power plane
- Protractor and sliding bevel
- Bar clamps

- Circular saw
- Back saw
- Combination square
- Bradawl
- Power drill and bits
- Dowelling pins
- Screwdriver
- Hammer

Shaping the legs

1 Use chalk to mark the approximate outlines of the four leg components on the sawn boards. Make a generous allowance for sawing and planing.

2 Cut out the components, using a power saw if possible. Be careful not to force the saw – 3 in (75 mm) thick hardwood is enough to test even a powerful circular saw (*see pages 64–65*).

Planing the legs to size

1 Set your plane to take fine shavings. If your plane is set fine, planing will take time but it will demand less effort and will enable you to establish a rhythm.

2 Plane a flat face on each piece (*see pages 42–45*). Sharpen the blade regularly and, at frequent intervals, check your progress by laying a straightedge both across the width and along the length of the workpiece.

3 Plane an edge to each piece, working to a straight pencil line and checking regularly that the edge is square to the face.

4 Mark the width of each piece parallel to the first edge and to the finished size. Plane these edges, once again checking regularly that each one is straight and square.

5 After planing three sides on each leg component, set them aside for the time being. The final faces are best left until after the parts have been glued together.

Making the legs

1 Check that the ends to be glued together are flat and square. Clamp them together, if necessary, so that there are no gaps at the joins.

2 Spread waterproof adhesive on the surfaces to be joined and clamp the two components for each leg together. Make sure that the planed faces are flush with each other. Place bar clamps across both the tops and undersides to ensure that pressure is spread evenly along

the joins (*see pages 48–49*). Wipe off any adhesive that is squeezed out.

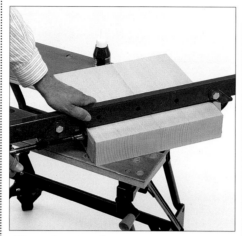

Clamping two leg components

3 When the glue is dry, plane the remaining rough faces flat. Check that the edges are still square and plane them down if necessary.

4 Mark and cut the legs to finished size with a panel saw (*see pages 30–31*).

5 Plane a chamfer ⅛in (3 mm) wide around the bottom edges of each leg.

Shaping the support blocks

1 Saw the rough-sawn wood that you are using for the support blocks into approximate lengths. Plane down all four faces of each length until they are flat and square to each other.

2 Carefully mark the 45° bevels on the ends of each block with a combination square.

Marking the bevel on a support block

3 Use a try square to mark out the half-lap joints on the legs and support blocks (*see pages 72–77*). The center lines of the joints should be under the center lines of the seat boards – 8¼in (206 mm) apart – and the housings should be of equal depth and wide enough for the parts to fit together using hand pressure only.

4 Cut out all the housings with a back saw and tidy them up with a sharp chisel.

Sawing out a housing

5 After cutting out the housings on the support blocks, saw the bevels and clean up the end grain with a block plane.

Assembling the legs and supports

1 Assemble the interlocking joints and check that the supports lie flush with the tops of the legs.

2 Drill countersunk clearance holes in the middle of the support blocks and mark through them into the legs with a bradawl. Drill pilot holes into the legs.

3 Drill two ⅜in (10 mm) dowel holes in the top of each support block (*see pages 78–79*). The holes should be centered and 3⅛in (80 mm) from each end of the support blocks.

4 The last holes to be drilled in the support blocks are for the screws that anchor the seat. Drill these clearance holes vertically, 1⅝in (40 mm) from both ends of each block. Countersink the bevelled faces where the clearance holes merge.

5 When you have drilled all the holes in the support blocks, screw them to the legs.

Screwing the support blocks

Making the seat boards

1 Saw the boards to approximate size, and then plane all the faces square and flat.

2 Mark a 45° bevel along one edge and across both ends of each board. However, leave a ⅜in (10mm) square along the top edges.

3 Plane the bevels off the long edges with a bench plane but use a block plane to shape the ends.

Planing the bevel

4 Finally, use a sliding bevel to check the angle of the bevels. Run the bevel along the full length of the boards to check that the bevels are consistent.

Checking the bevel angle

Assembling the seat

1 Use dowelling pins to mark the underside of the seat boards. Slot the pins into the dowel holes in the support blocks.

Fitting the dowel pins

2 Lay the seat boards upside down, and place ½in (12mm) spacers between them. Check that the ends of the boards are level.

3 Position the leg assemblies upside down on the boards and tap them gently so that the dowelling pins leave marks.

4 With the legs in place, drop screws through the clearance holes in the support blocks and tap them gently to leave small marks for pilot holes.

5 Remove the blocks and then drill both the dowel holes and the pilot holes into the undersides of the seat boards.

6 Before you insert the dowels, cut grooves along them so that excess glue can flow out. If you are using fluted dowels, you do not have to cut the grooves.

7 Spread glue on the dowels and into their holes. Tap the dowels into the leg assemblies and then fit these into the underside of the seat boards, using a mallet.

Tapping in the dowels

8 While the glue is still wet, screw the legs in place. Wipe away excess glue with a damp cloth.

Securing the legs

Finishing

1 Clean the seat up with abrasive paper, softening any sharp or rough edges where necessary (*see pages 60–61*).

2 Coat the whole seat with at least two coats of clear weatherproof varnish.

COMPUTER WORKSTATION

This practical workstation is perfect for the home or office. It can be adapted to suit different types of computer, and uses dowel and simple housing joints in its construction.

THE WORKSTATION has a low work surface so that you don't strain your wrists or arms while working at a keyboard. If you want you can make it wider or deeper, but be sure to work out the changed dimensions before you start the project. Details, such as the location of the cable management slots and the height of the monitor platform, can also be adapted. All the MDF components for the illustrated example can be cut from one 8ft x 4ft (2440 x 1220mm) sheet.

14in (355mm)

Monitor platform

24in (610mm)

7in (178mm)

Cut-out for cable management

Work surface

Rail

4½in (112mm)

2in (50mm)

Base post

Base panel

4in (100mm)

43½in (1100mm)

24in (610mm)

21½in (546mm)

33½in (850mm)

5in (125mm)

25½in (648mm)

6in (150mm)

Front elevation

34½in (876mm)

PROJECT PLANNER

- Prepare components
- Make base unit
- Fit rails to base units
- Make monitor platform
- Make work surface
- Assemble components
- Clean up and finish

SEE ALSO

SKILLS
- Measuring and marking techniques *(see pages 24–27)*
- Sawing techniques *(see pages 30–31)*
- Drilling techniques *(see pages 34–35)*
- Cutting and shaping techniques *(see pages 38–39)*
- Planing techniques *(see pages 42–45)*
- Clamping techniques *(see pages 48–49)*
- Fixing techniques *(see pages 54–55)*
- Hanging and fastening techniques *(see pages 56–57)*
- Sanding and finishing techniques *(see pages 60–61)*
- Simple joint techniques *(see pages 72–77)*
- Dowel joints *(see pages 78–79)*

WHAT YOU NEED

CUTTING LIST
- Base panels: four 24½ x 21½ x 1in (625 x 546 x 25mm) lengths of MDF
- Work surface: one 43½ x 24 x 1in (1100 x 610 x 25mm) sheet of MDF
- Monitor platform: one 24 x 14 x 1in (610 x 355 x 25mm) length of MDF
- Rails: three 39⅜ x 4¼ x 1in (1006 x 110 x 25mm) lengths of softwood
- Base posts: four 24½ x 4 x 2in (625 x 100 x 50mm) lengths of softwood
- Platform supports: two 7 x 8 x 2in (178 x 200 x 50mm) lengths of softwood
- Fixing blocks: three knock-down blocks and suitable screws
- Dowels: four ⅜in (10mm)
- Finish nails: 2½in (63mm)
- Screws: thirty 2in (50mm) No. 8 countersunk

TOOLS REQUIRED
- Try square and straightedge
- Jigsaw
- Back saw
- Bench plane
- C-clamps
- 1in (25mm) chisel
- Hammer and nail set
- Bradawl and screwdriver
- Power drill and bits
- Dowelling pins

Preparing the components

1 Mark out the tops and the panels for the base units on a sheet of MDF. Cut out the components, slightly oversize, using a jigsaw (*see pages 64–65*).

2 Cut the wooden rails and posts to length and plane the edges flat to the finished dimensions (*see pages 42–45*). Make sure that the edges of the posts are parallel with each other.

Making the base units

1 Plane the edges of the MDF panels to the finished dimensions and check that the edges are square.

2 Mark out the simple housing joint in the four panels. Each housing should match the thickness and width of a rail. The housings for the top rail should be set back from the front edge by twice the thickness of a post.

3 The easiest way to mark the housings is to use a rail as a template. Clamp the panels together and use a rail to mark the width of all the housings across all four edges.

Release the clamps and then use the rail to mark the depth of each individual housing.

Marking the depth of a housing

4 Cut the bulk of the waste from the housings with a jigsaw and then clean them up with a chisel (*see pages 38–39*).

5 The next step is to join the panels to the posts. Line up the two back posts with the edges of the housings in the back of the panels; set back the two front posts by the thickness of a post from the front edges of the panels.

6 Mark the center line of the posts down the outside of the panels to show where to drive in the nails.

7 Spread a little glue on the edges of the posts before hammering in the nails. If you find that the components slip about after you add adhesive, clamp them together to ensure that they are correctly positioned.

8 Space the nails about 4 in (100 mm) apart and knock them in with a lightweight hammer.

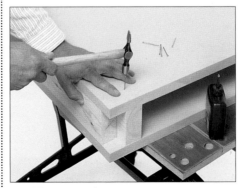

Nailing panels to a post

9 Use a nail set to sink the nail heads below the surface of the MDF. Cover the nail heads with filler (*see pages 60–61*).

Fitting the rails to the base

1 Mark the top rail for clearance holes so that the rail projects 2 in (50mm) past the base units.

2 Drill and countersink clearance holes and then use a bradawl to mark through them into the housings in the edges of the MDF panels.

3 Drill pilot holes at your marks and carefully screw the top rail in place. If you find that the MDF starts to split or expand when you drive in the screws, drill out slightly larger pilot holes.

Fixing the top rail

4 Mark the two back rails for clearance holes – these rails are screwed to the posts, not the MDF. Drill and countersink clearance holes and mark the positions of the pilot holes in the posts with a bradawl. Drill the pilot holes and screw the rails in place.

Making the monitor platform

1 Cut out the shape of the monitor platform with a jigsaw. The easiest way to mark the curve of the front edge is to bend a thin strip of wood – for example, a length of thin dowel – into a suitable arc and to anchor each end with a C-clamp. Run a pencil against the bent strip and use this line as a guide. Do not force the saw, as this could lead to an inaccurate cut.

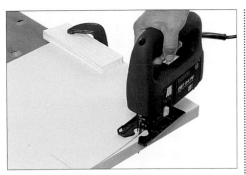

Cutting the curved edge

2 Plane down the straight edges of the platform and smooth down the curve with abrasive paper.

3 Mark the position of the cable management slot. It should be about 4in (100mm) long and 1in (25mm) wide. The exact dimensions and position of the slot will depend on what type of monitor you have. Once you have marked out the slot, mark centers at each end.

Marking centers at the ends of the slot

4 Choose a drill bit that matches the width of the slot and drill holes through the platform.

5 Cut between the two holes with a jigsaw, keeping the blade to the waste side of the lines.

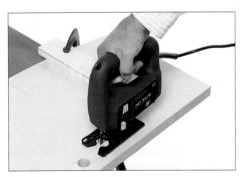

Sawing out the slot

6 Saw the two platform supports to length and check that the ends are square. Mark the tops of the

supports for dowel centers 1¼in (32mm) from each end. Drill the dowel holes and tap in dowelling pins (*see pages 78–79*).

Drilling the dowel holes

7 On the underside of the monitor platform, mark the positions of the supports. They should be flush at the back of the platform and 2in (50mm) in from each end.

8 Position the supports with the pins in place and tap them with a hammer to give drilling centers in the MDF.

Marking the dowel holes with pins

9 Drill holes for the dowels in the MDF, making sure that the total depth of the two holes is slightly more than the length of the dowels.

10 Spread glue on the dowels and join the supports to the monitor platform. Use clamps to pull the joints tight and check that they are square.

Making the work surface

1 Mark out and saw the work surface to size. As with the other pieces, plane the edges smooth.

2 Cut the cable management slot in a position that suits your computer set-up in exactly the same way as you did for the slot in the monitor platform.

Assembling the top

1 Fit the three knock-down fittings to the top of the back rail (*see pages 56–57*) and then drill three countersunk clearance holes on the underside of the front rail – one in the center and one at each end.

2 Turn the work surface upside down and place the base assembly in position. The work surface should overhang 1in (25mm) at the back.

3 Mark through the clearance holes, remove the base, and drill pilot holes in the MDF.

4 Reposition the base on the work surface and screw the two components together.

5 Stand the workstation the right way up and place the monitor platform in position. The platform can go in any position you like, to one side or in the center. Mark around the platform supports.

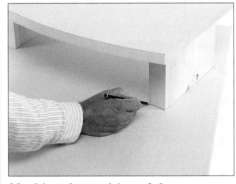

Marking the position of the monitor platform

6 Drill two clearance holes through each of your outlines for the platform supports and countersink them on the underside. Mark through the clearance holes into the bottoms of the supports with a bradawl and then carefully drill out small pilot holes.

7 Secure the supports with screws driven up from the underside of the work surface.

Finishing

1 Clean up all the surfaces with abrasive paper and paint the workstation.

PICNIC TABLE

This compact seating arrangement can be placed outside for informal garden meals, or inside in a screened porch. It is mainly bolted together, but also uses what are called bird-mouth joints.

THIS TABLE can be made from any solid wood. Pressure-treated lumber, cedar, redwood, or cypress, will withstand outdoor conditions best. Before you start on the project, you need to make accurate, full-size drawings of the side and end elevations. These can be made on any large pieces of sheet material – thin MDF is ideal. By making precise drawings first, you can check the accuracy of the various components before you assemble them.

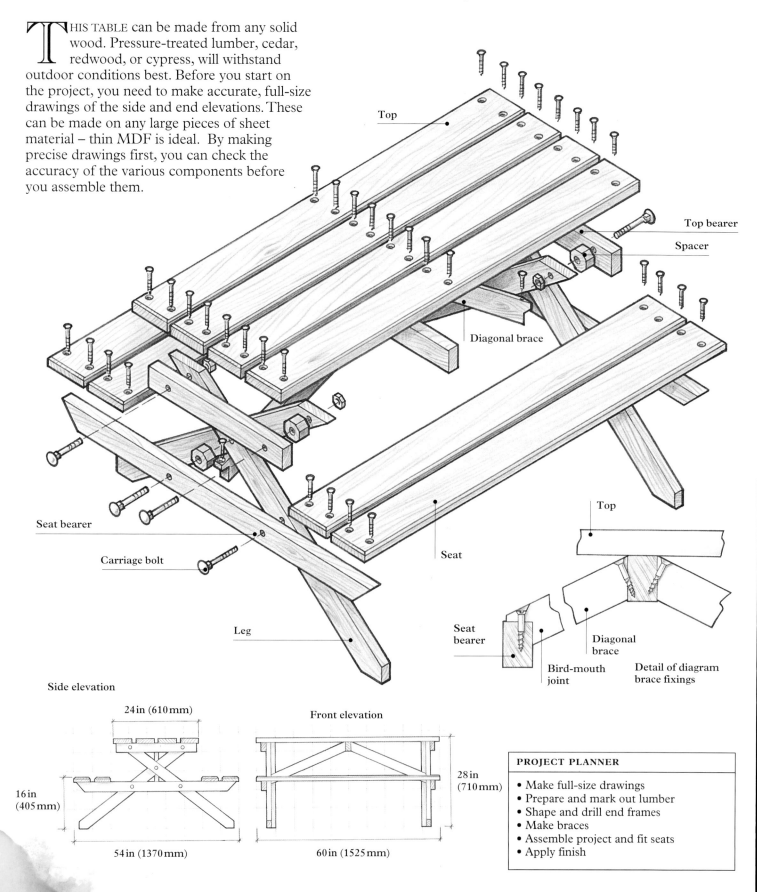

Top

Top bearer

Spacer

Diagonal brace

Seat

Seat bearer

Carriage bolt

Leg

Top

Seat bearer

Bird-mouth joint

Diagonal brace

Detail of diagram brace fixings

Side elevation

24 in (610 mm)

16 in (405 mm)

54 in (1370 mm)

Front elevation

28 in (710 mm)

60 in (1525 mm)

PROJECT PLANNER
• Make full-size drawings
• Prepare and mark out lumber
• Shape and drill end frames
• Make braces
• Assemble project and fit seats
• Apply finish

144

SEE ALSO

SKILLS
- Measuring and marking techniques
  (*see pages 24–27*)
- Drilling techniques (*see pages 34–35*)
- Cutting and shaping techniques
  (*see pages 38–39*)
- Planing techniques (*see pages 42–45*)
- Clamping techniques (*see pages 48–49*)
- Fixing techniques (*see pages 54–55*)
- Sanding and finishing techniques
  (*see pages 60–61*)
- Simple joint techniques
  (*see pages 72–77*)

WHAT YOU NEED

CUTTING LIST
- Legs: four 46 x 3 x 1½in (1170 x 75 x 38mm) lengths of softwood
- Seat bearers: two 53 x 3 x 1½in (1345 x 75 x 38mm) lengths of softwood
- Top bearers: three 24 x 2½ x 1½in (610 x 63 x 38mm) lengths of softwood
- Braces: two 32 x 2½ x 1½in (815 x 63 x 38mm) lengths of softwood
- Seats: four 60 x 5½ x 1¼in (1525 x 140 x 32mm) lengths of softwood
- Table top: four 60 x 5½ x 1¼in (1525 x 140 x 32mm) lengths of softwood
- Bolts: eight ⅜in (10mm) carriage bolts at least 6in (150mm) long, complete with nuts and washers

- Screws: forty-four 1¾in (45mm) No. 8 countersunk brass for exterior use
- Material for drawings: cardboard, thin MDF or plywood, large enough for full-size side and end elevations

TOOLS REQUIRED
- Try square and long ruler
- Sliding bevel and protractor
- Bench plane
- Panel saw
- Power drill and bits
- Bradawl, screwdrivers and spanner
- C-clamps

Making the drawings

1 Make full-size drawings of the side and front elevations on a sheet of MDF, plywood, or cardboard, scaling them up from the drawings on page 144. For this you will need a square and a long ruler. These drawings will establish the angles of the legs and braces and the exact positions of the bolts that fasten the end frames.

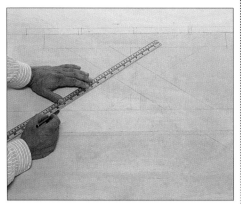

Setting out a drawing

2 On the drawings, make sure that those components that are square to each other are truly at right-angles. You will then be able to check each component for accuracy before you fit them together.

Preparing the lumber

1 Plane all the lumber to the finished widths given in the cutting list and clean up the faces of all the components (*see pages 42–45*).

2 Cut to length the boards for the table top and the seats, and chamfer their edges.

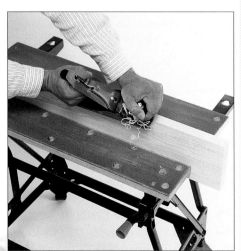

Planing the chamfers

Preparing the end frames

1 Mark the angles at the top and bottom of the leg pieces from one drawing, and mark the centers for drilling the bolt clearance holes. Also mark out the top and seat bearers.

Marking out a leg

2 Saw the legs and bearers to size and cut two spacers for each frame from the waste material – these must be the same thickness as the other components. The spacers need to be approximately 4 in (100 mm) square, but you can cut them into octagons so that they look neater and are less obtrusive. Drill a clearance hole for a bolt through the center of each spacer.

3 Holding the workpieces securely, drill all the clearance holes in the legs for the bolts. Make the holes slightly tight so that the bolts have to be tapped through with a hammer (*see pages 34–35*).

Hammering in a bolt

Making the braces

1 Mark the two diagonal braces carefully off your drawing. It is important to make these components accurately or they will not do the job of locking the whole structure rigid.

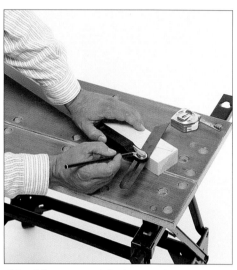

Marking out a bird-mouth joint

2 Carefully cut out the bird-mouth joints in the ends of the diagonal braces. Cutting out a bird-mouth joint is similar to cutting a rabbet joint (*see pages 72-77*), except that the cuts are not made parallel to the edges of the wood. As accuracy is important, firmly anchor each brace to your workbench before making the cuts with a back saw.

Sawing a bird-mouth joint

3 Also take care when making the angled cuts at the other ends of the braces. To reduce the chances of mistakes, make these cuts after shaping the bird-mouth joints.

4 Use a sharp chisel to pare away slivers of wood until both ends of each brace match the outlines on your drawing perfectly. Also check that the faces of the joints are square – if they are not square, they could allow the finished picnic table to rock sideways.

5 After cutting out the two braces, confirm that they are accurate by comparing them for length against your drawing.

Checking the accuracy of a brace

6 Drill a countersunk clearance hole through the top of each bird-mouth joint, making sure that the angle for screwing into the seat bearers is correct. At the same time, drill an angled countersunk clearance hole at the top of each brace for fixing into the central top bearer.

Assembling the frames and top

1 Bolt the top and seat bearers to the legs, making sure that you insert spacers where necessary. Slip washers over the bolts before tightening the nuts.

Bolting the frame together

2 When you have assembled both end frames, mark out the centers for the clearance holes in the four boards for the table top. There should be two screw fixings in both ends of each board, and two in the middle for the center bearer.

3 Drill countersunk clearance holes at each of your marks and place the table top boards in position, making sure that they are evenly spaced. Mark through the clearance holes with a bradawl, and then drill small pilot holes into the three bearers. You may need to enlist the help of an assistant. If you want, you can slide 'cups' (small brass rings) onto the screws before driving them home. If you do use cups, do not countersink the holes as the screw heads lie above of the surface.

4 Screw the table top boards to the bearers, making sure that all the boards stay parallel to each other.

5 At this stage everything will be a little loose and vulnerable, so clamp one of the seat boards to each end of the seat bearers.

6 Position the two braces, making sure that the end frames are square to the top and the ground. Adjust the alignment of the clamped board if necessary.

7 Check that the bird-mouth joints fit neatly and mark through the clearance holes in the braces. Drill pilot holes into the bearers and screw the braces in place.

Securing a bird-mouth joint

Fitting the seats

1 Remove the clamped board and lay out all the seat boards on the seat bearers. Drill countersunk clearance holes and clamp all four boards in their correct positions. As with the table top boards, you can slide cups onto the screws before tightening them up. The advantage of using cups is that you do not have to countersink the holes and there is less chance of the holes creating splinters when the seats are used. You may find it helpful to use a scrap of wood to space out the boards equally and to make sure that they are parallel with each other.

2 Drill pilot holes into the bearers and screw the seats in place. When you have fixed the seat boards, double-check that all the screws are tight.

Screwing the seat boards

Finishing

1 Go over the whole table with abrasive paper to round off any sharp corners and to remove pencil marks. Pay particular attention to the ends of the seat boards where there could be splinters. When you sand off pencil marks, wrap your abrasive paper around a square block and rub it along the grain of the wood. If you rub against the grain you will inevitably score the surface.

2 Apply a suitable finish. If you intend to leave the table outdoors permanently, use a weatherproof varnish or tinted preservative.

CORNER CUPBOARD

*This cabinet fits well in a country-style kitchen or in a corner of a dining
room or bedroom. It is a good exercise in assembling panels from
solid wood, and in hanging doors.*

T HIS IS A VERY simple way of building a
wall-hung corner cabinet as the carcass
doesn't have sides; instead, the walls
form the sides of the cupboard. Some of the
detailing, such as the cornice, can be made to
suit features that already exist in the room. You
could use a hardwood to make the cupboard,
but a softwood such as redwood fits with the
simple style and takes a stained finish well.
Whatever wood you use, all the boards should
be cut overwidth and the edges planed so that
they fit together neatly.

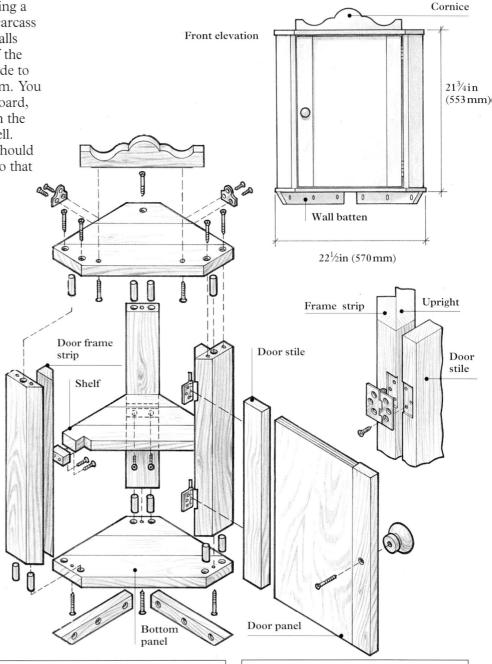

Cornice

Front elevation

21¾in
(553 mm)

Wall batten

22½in (570 mm)

Frame strip

Upright

Door stile

Door
stile

Door frame
strip

Door stile

Shelf

Bottom
panel

Door panel

WHAT YOU NEED

CUTTING LIST
- Door stiles: two 21¾ x 2⅜ x 1 in
  (553 x 60 x 25 mm) lengths of softwood
- Door panel: one 21¾ x 11 in
  (553 x 280 mm) length of ¾in (19 mm)
  plywood
- Top and bottom panels: lengths of
  softwood to make two 22½ x 11½ x
  1¼in (570 x 290 x 32 mm) panels
- Shelf: softwood for one 21¾ x 9½ x
  1¼in (553 x 240 x 32 mm) panel
- Uprights: three 22 x 8 x 1¼in (560 x
  200 x 32 mm) lengths of softwood
- Door frame strips: two 22 x 3 x 1¼in
  (560 x 75 x 32 mm) lengths of
  softwood
- Cornice: one 15¾ x 3⅛ x 1¼in
  (400 x 80 x 32 mm) length of softwood
- Wall battens: two 9 x 1½ x 1¼in
  (230 x 38 x 32 mm) lengths of softwood
- Butt hinges: one 50 mm (2 in) pair and
  fixing screws
- Door knob: one from matching
  softwood (optional)
- Catch: one magnetic for door
- Dowels: ten 2 x ⅜in (50 x 10 mm)
- Screws for shelf support blocks: six
  1½in (38 mm) No. 8 countersunk
- Screws for support battens: six 2⅜in
  (60 mm) No. 10 countersunk
- Screws for cornice: two 1½in (38 mm)
  No. 8 countersunk
- Screws for carcass: eight 2 in (50 mm)
  No. 8 countersunk

TOOLS REQUIRED
- Try square and straightedge
- Combination square
- Tape measure
- Back saw and jigsaw
- Bench and block planes
- Bar clamps
- Power drill and bits
- Mallet and ½in (12 mm) chisel
- Spirit level

PROJECT PLANNER
- Make carcass components
- Make top and bottom panels
- Assemble carcass
- Make door
- Make and fit cornice
- Hang door
- Apply finish
- Install cabinet in corner

SEE ALSO

SKILLS
- Measuring and marking techniques
  (*see pages 24–27*)
- Drilling techniques (*see pages 34–36*)
- Cutting and shaping techniques
  (*see pages 38–39*)
- Planing techniques (*see pages 42–45*)
- Clamping techniques (*see pages 48–49*)
- Hanging and fastening techniques
  (*see pages 56–57*)
- Sanding and finishing techniques
  (*see pages 60–61*)
- Dowel joints (*see pages 78–79*)

Making the top and bottom panels

1 Measure and cut the boards over-length, and plane the edges that are to be glued together (*see pages 38–39 and 42–45*). Check that the edges are both straight and square.

2 Apply glue to the edges to be joined and use bar clamps and packing pieces to hold the boards in place while the glue dries (*see pages 48–49*). Check that the boards are flat while they are clamped, and wipe off excess glue with a damp rag.

Clamping the boards

3 When the glue is dry, use a bench plane to flatten both the panels to an even thickness (*see pages 42–45*).

Making the front uprights

1 Glue and clamp door-frame strips to the inside faces of the front uprights. These will form the sides of the door frame.

2 Once the glue has set, mark and cut the ends of the uprights to the finished length. Check that the ends are square.

3 Mark the outlines of the 45° bevelled edges on both ends of each front upright, using a combination square (*see pages 24–27*). Join the marks from end to end with pencil lines and then plane the bevels to the lines, using a bench plane (*see pages 42–45*). Do not plane beyond the lines.

Planing the bevels

Making the top and bottom

1 Mark out the identical shapes of the top and bottom accurately on the two prepared panels. The front angles should be marked at 45° and the back edges of the panels must be parallel to the front edges.

Marking the bottom using a combination square

2 Saw the waste from the two pieces and finish by planing the panels to the finished size.

Assembling the carcass

1 Cut the back upright to match the length of the two front ones, and plane the ends square with a block plane.

2 Mark the location of the three uprights on the top face of the bottom panel and the underside of the top panel. Make sure the uprights overhang the perimeter of the panels by ½in (12mm) as these make it easier to fit the cupboard to corner walls.

3 Drill the dowel holes in the end grain of the uprights, making sure you hold the drill vertically, then drill corresponding dowel holes in the top and bottom panels (*see pages 78–79*).

Drilling the dowel holes

4 Drill countersunk clearance holes for the screws in the top and bottom panels (*see pages 34–36*). Mark through the holes with a bradawl into the end grain of the uprights, and drill out pilot holes.

5 Apply glue to the dowel holes, tap in dowels, and knock the carcass gently together. Insert the screws and tighten them up. Check that the opening for the door is perfectly square.

Screwing the top panel to the uprights

Fitting the shelf

1 Cut three small blocks, measuring approximately 2 x 1 x 1in (50 x 25 x 25mm), from waste wood, and drill two countersunk clearance holes in each for fixing them to the uprights.

2 Mark off the height of the shelf halfway up the inside of each upright, and glue and screw the blocks in place to support the bottom of the shelf.

3 Measure and cut the shelf to fit around the strips glued to the front uprights, then plane it at the front and back so that it fits snugly into the carcass.

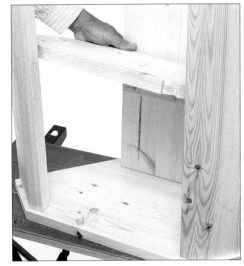

Fitting the shelf

4 After you have fitted the shelf, double-check that the door opening is square. The easiest way of doing this is to compare the diagonals of the opening – they should be the same.

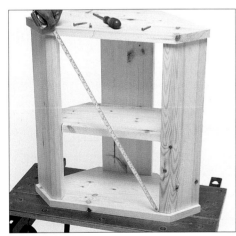

Checking the diagonals of the opening

Making the door

1 Cut and plane the plywood panel to width, leaving clean, square edges. Plane the two door stiles so they also have square parallel edges, but leave them slightly overwidth.

2 Spread glue on the edges to be joined and clamp the stiles to the panel. Make sure that the back of the panel is flush with the backs of the stiles, then clean off surplus glue.

Clamping the stiles to the door panel

3 When the glue has dried, plane the tops and sides of the door to fit closely to the opening in the cupboard carcass.

Making and fitting the cornice

1 Draw the outline of the cornice full-size on paper or thin MDF, then cut it out and transfer the shape to the wood.

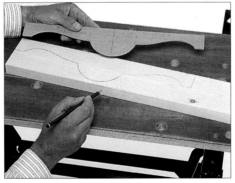

Marking the profile of the cornice, using a template

2 Cut out the profile of the cornice with a jigsaw (*see pages 38–39*), and clean up the edges with a fine abrasive paper.

3 Drill countersunk clearance holes in the underside of the front edge of the top panel so that the cornice stands slightly back from the leading edge.

4 Mark through the holes with a bradawl into the bottom edge of the cornice, and drill pilot holes. Apply glue thinly to the underside of the cornice and screw it in place.

Screwing the cornice in place

Hanging the door

1 Mark the hinge positions 2 in (50 mm) from the top and bottom edges of the door. Cut hinge recesses in the door and in the right-hand upright, using a sharp chisel (*see pages 56–57*).

2 Screw the hinges in place, adjusting them as required until the door hangs correctly. Fit the knob and catch.

Finishing

1 Clean up all the components and soften all sharp edges with abrasive paper (*see pages 60–61*).

2 Apply a wood stain followed by one or more coats of varnish. Alternatively, paint the cupboard to match other room furniture.

Hanging the cabinet

1 Cut the wall battens to length, and plane 45° bevels on the front ends. Drill three countersunk clearance holes for the fixing screws in each batten.

2 Mark the corner walls so that the battens are horizontal and level (*see pages 24-27*), then drill the wall and fit suitable wallplugs (*see pages 56–57*). Screw the battens to the wall.

3 Screw a pair of mirror plates to the back edges of the cupboard top. Place the cupboard on top of its battens and mark holes to be drilled in the walls for the mirror plates.

4 If necessary, scribe the overhanging edges of the carcass to get the cabinet to fit neatly to the walls (*see pages 24-27*). Drill the wall, fit wallplugs, and screw the cabinet in place.

HARDWOOD STOOL

*This robust three-legged stool is made from solid lumber and has wedged tenon
joints that lock the whole construction together. The stool makes an ideal
occasional seat in a living room, kitchen or child's bedroom.*

CHOOSE A STURDY hardwood from which to
make the stool, as a softwood is more likely
to split when the joints are assembled.
The illustrated example is made from oak, but
you could use maple or beech if you prefer
paler wood.

This is an extremely satisfying project to make
because no pins or screws are used to secure the
joints. Instead, wedges are tapped into the tenons
to anchor them in the mortises. Set aside plenty
of time to make the stool, as the apparently simple
design is deceptive.

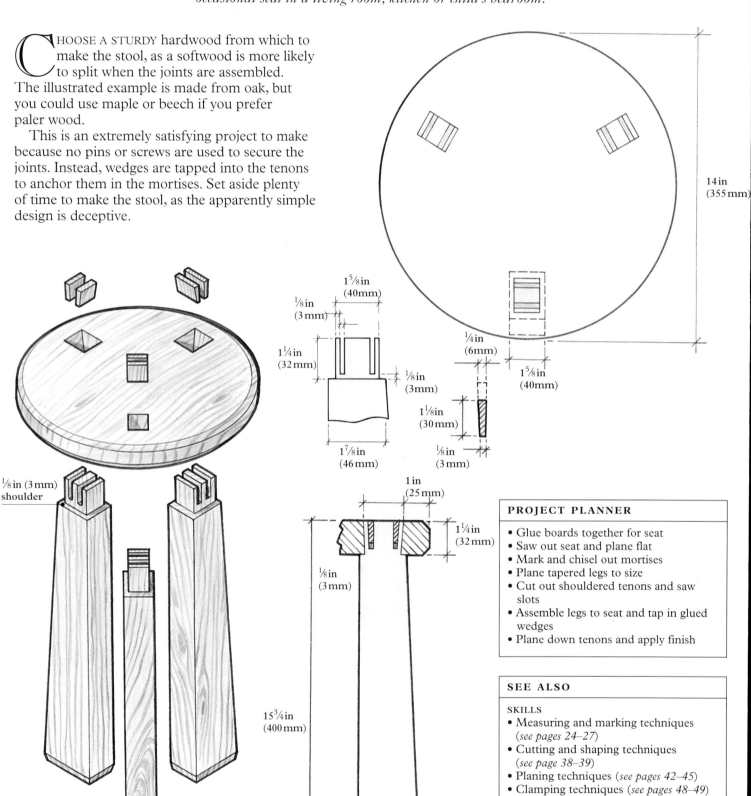

14 in
(355 mm)

1⁵⁄₈ in
(40 mm)

⅛ in
(3 mm)

1¼ in
(32 mm)

⅛ in
(3 mm)

¼ in
(6 mm)

1⁵⁄₈ in
(40 mm)

1⅛ in
(30 mm)

1⁷⁄₈ in
(46 mm)

⅛ in
(3 mm)

⅛ in (3 mm)
shoulder

1 in
(25 mm)

1¼ in
(32 mm)

⅛ in
(3 mm)

15¾ in
(400 mm)

PROJECT PLANNER

- Glue boards together for seat
- Saw out seat and plane flat
- Mark and chisel out mortises
- Plane tapered legs to size
- Cut out shouldered tenons and saw
  slots
- Assemble legs to seat and tap in glued
  wedges
- Plane down tenons and apply finish

SEE ALSO

SKILLS
- Measuring and marking techniques
  (*see pages 24–27*)
- Cutting and shaping techniques
  (*see page 38–39*)
- Planing techniques (*see pages 42–45*)
- Clamping techniques (*see pages 48–49*)
- Sanding and finishing techniques
  (*see pages 60–61*)
- Power saws (*see pages 64–65*)
- Simple joint techniques
  (*see pages 72–77*)

WHAT YOU NEED

CUTTING LIST
- Seat: sufficient 1¼ in (32 mm) thick hardwood to make 14 in (355 mm) disk
- Legs: three 17 x 3 x 1½ in (430 x 75 x 38 mm) lengths of hardwood
- Wedges: offcuts of hardwood

TOOLS REQUIRED
- Jigsaw
- Back and rip saws
- Try square and straightedge
- Tape measure or rule
- Marking gauge and protractor
- ¾ in (19 mm) chisel and mallet
- Block and bench planes
- Light (pin) hammer and compass
- C-clamps

Preparing the seat

1 Unless you are fortunate enough to have a piece of wood at least 14 in (355 mm) square, you will have to join two boards together to make the seat.

2 Glue and clamp together the boards (*see pages 48–49*), making sure that the joining surfaces are perfectly flat.

3 When the adhesive has set hard, mark out the diameter of the seat – 14 in (355 mm) – using a compass.

4 Cut out the seat using a jigsaw, keeping the blade to the waste side of the cutting line. Make sure the workpiece is securely clamped and do not force the saw.

Cutting the seat

5 When you have cut out the seat, clean up the sawn edge with a block plane and abrasive paper.

When you have done this, level the top and bottom faces with a bench plane (*see pages 42–45*).

Cutting the mortises

1 Mark the three mortises on both faces of the seat. Divide the circle in three with a protractor and mark round the edge so that the radii on the top and bottom are in line.

2 Using the radii as the center lines of the mortises, mark the outlines of the mortises on both sides of the seat. The mortises should measure 1⅜ x 1 in (35 x 25 mm) square and should be positioned 1 in (25 mm) in from the edge of the circle. On the top only, mark in two wedge allowances on each mortise. Each allowance should be ⅛ in (3 mm) wide.

3 Cut out the mortises using a chisel and mallet (*see pages 72–77*) and carefully pare away the wedge allowances which should taper from the top to the bottom.

Removing the waste

Making the legs

1 Saw the leg pieces ¼ in (6 mm) overlength. This is so that the tenon can be left slightly longer than necessary and planed down flush with the seat after assembly to make a neat finish.

2 Mark the taper on each leg – from 3 in (75 mm) wide at the bottom to 1⅞ in (46 mm) at the shoulder, using a hard pencil and a steel straightedge.

Marking out the legs

3 Saw off the waste wood from each leg, then chamfer the bottoms of the legs and plane down rough surfaces. All three legs must be identical.

4 Mark the tenons on each leg with a marking gauge (*see pages 24–27*) remembering to allow each tenon to be ¼ in (6 mm) longer than necessary. The tenons have ¼ in (6 mm) shoulders all around (⅛ /3 mm each side) that support the seat as well as anybody sitting on it.

5 Carefully cut out the tenons with a back saw (*see pages 72–77*). It is crucial that the four shoulders to each tenon are level.

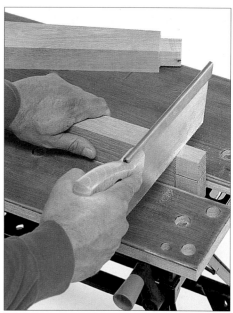

Cutting the tenons

6 To cut the slots in a tenon, first clamp a leg vertically in your workbench. Each slot should be about ⅛in (3mm) in from the ends of the tenon and should be about ⅛in (3mm) wide. Cut the slots with a back saw to just above the shoulders. Carefully saw out two slots in each tenon, making sure that they are all vertical.

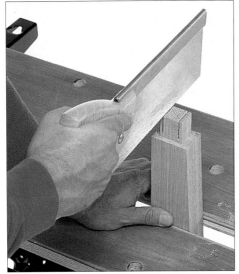

Cutting the slots

7 You can cut the wedges from offcuts of the hardwood you are using. They need to be slightly longer than the depth of the slots and should match the thickness of the tenons exactly. The wedges should taper from approximately ¼in (6mm) at the top to ⅛in (3mm) at the bottom. It is crucial that the tips of the wedges are not broader than the bottoms of the slots otherwise they won't tap in.

Making the wedges

Gluing up and finishing

1 Test the tenons in the mortises and when you are satisfied that they all fit, neatly label them.

Checking for fit

2 Clean up the seat and legs with abrasive paper – dirt and marks are easier to get rid of before the components are assembled.

3 Smear PVA adhesive to both the tenons and the mortises and assemble the stool, one leg at a time. The tops of the tenons should protrude about ¼in (6mm) above the level of the seat.

Fitting the legs

4 Stand the stool upright and, making sure that the seat is resting on the shoulders of the tenons, smear the wedges with glue and insert them into the slots.

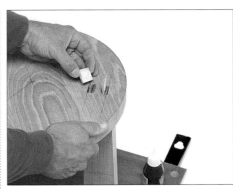

Inserting the wedges

5 So as not to shatter the wedges, place an offcut over them as you tap them home with a hammer. When you drive home the wedges, the sides of the tenons bend to fill the allowances cut for them and lock the joint tight. Tap in the wedges as far as they will go and wipe off any surplus glue that oozes out.

6 When you have tapped in all the wedges, allow the adhesive to set for a few hours. Then plane down the protruding tops of the tenons (and their wedges) with a block plane (*see pages 42–45*) until they are flush with the top of the seat.

Planing the joints flush

7 Chamfer the edges of the seat to make it more comfortable to sit on. To ensure that the chamfers are equal all the way around, use a marking gauge set to about ¼in (6mm) to scribe guide lines around the circumference. Use a block plane for making the chamfers, but be careful not to plane against the grain of the wood, as it may splinter.

8 Give the edges and top a light sanding, and check that all marks and scratches have been removed before applying a clear varnish or Danish oil (*see pages 60–61*).

GLOSSARY

Allen screw
A **machine screw** with no head. It is twisted with a special key that is slotted into an octagonal recess in the top of the screw.

Bevel
A sloping surface. For example, a bevel-edge chisel has sloping faces down each side of the blade.

Chamfer
A narrow, flat surface on the edge of a length of timber. It is usually planed at an angle of 45° to the two adjacent surfaces and makes the edge less sharp.

Chuck
The part of a drill that holds a bit. The jaws inside a chuck grip the bit and are opened and closed by turning the outside ring while keeping the drill steady. Most chucks are tightened by a purpose-made key, but with 'fast-action' power drills a key is not required.

Clearance hole
A hole drilled through a piece of wood that allows the threads of a screw to pass through without biting into the wood. A clearance hole should match the diameter (gauge) of the screw shaft.

Counterbore
A hole drilled into wood to widen the entrance to a screw or bolt hole so that the head of the screw or bolt can be positioned deep inside the wood. The size of a counterbored hole should be just sufficient to accommodate the head of the screw or bolt. Counterbored holes are usually made to hide the head of a screw or bolt, but they are also sometimes used to make sure that a short screw or bolt protrudes far enough out of the edge of the wood to make a strong fixing.

Countersink
The tool used to make a cone-shaped recess at the entrance to a screw hole so that the head of a countersunk (flat-topped) screw can lie below the surface of the wood and be covered with filler.

Dry wall
A man-made board comprising a layer of plaster that is faced on both sides with card or thick paper. Dry wall sheets are nailed to a lumber framework to create cavity walls.

End grain
When wood is cut across the **grain**, the exposed timber is described as 'end grain'.

Fence
A mechanical device used to guide a tool in a straight line. With a power saw, for example, a purpose-made fence can be clamped to the side of the tool – the fence runs along the straight edge of the timber so that the saw cuts along a parallel line. You can improvize your own fence by clamping a straight batten to the workpiece and running the tool you are using along it.

Finish
This can refer to opaque or clear paints, varnishes, lacquers and oils, or the smoothness of a piece of wood.

Finish nail
A type of nail that has a small head. The head can be punched below the surface of wood so that it is almost invisible.

Frog
The (usually) steel support for the blade in a plane; the frog is attached to the **sole plate**. A frog can also mean the indent in the top of certain types of bricks.

Grain
The alignment or direction of wood fibers. 'With the grain' means parallel to the direction of the fibers.

Grub screw
A small **machine screw** that is used to secure a metal collar to another part of machinery. Grub screws have small, recessed heads or are **Allen screws**.

'Hammer' action
A facility found on some power drills that makes the drill bit vibrate backwards and forwards as it turns. This makes drilling into brick, concrete and other masonry material quicker and easier.

Hone
To sharpen to a fine, clean edge.

Kerf
The cut made by a saw.

Knock-down fitting
A fitting used to join together two pieces of wood or board at right-angles. Knock-down fittings are easy to take apart.

Knot
The remnants of a branch outgrowth found some milled woods. In certain types of wood knots are considered attractive, but in others they are considered flaws.

Lacquer
A tough, glossy finish that is usually made from natural resins or cellulose products. Lacquer is extremely hard and durable and gives an elegant sheen but it can be difficult to apply. It is best to spray it on, as brushes tend to leave trail marks when the volatile **solvent** evaporates. Lacquer can be dangerous to work with; wear a respirator face mask and keep your work area well ventilated.

Machine screw
A type of screw that is used for fixing into metal. Unlike woodscrews, the threads are shallow and narrowly spaced, and they do not taper to a point.

Miter
Strictly speaking, a miter joint is any corner joint where the two pieces of wood are cut to equal angles. In most instances, however, the two pieces are cut to 45°.

Moulding
This is the term for a strip of wood that has a shaped profile or outline. Both hardwoods and softwoods are used to make mouldings.

Movement
This is the shrinkage or expansion of lumber as it loses or absorbs moisture. All wood 'moves', even if it is only by a tiny amount, according to variations in atmospheric conditions.

Offcut
A scrap or remnant of wood that has not been shaped for a particular purpose. Offcuts are not always worthless, however. For example, an offcut can be used to shield or protect a workpiece from being bruised or dented by the jaws of a clamp.

Oilstone
A stone with a fine grain that is used for sharpening chisels and other sharp tools. Most oilstones are man-made composites. The name comes from the fact that the surface of the stone is lubricated with oil when being used.

Pare
To take fine shaving off wood with a chisel. Paring is usually done by manipulating the chisel with the hands alone; the chisel is not struck with a mallet.

Patina
The sheen, color and texture acquired by lumber after prolonged handling or polishing.

Pilot hole
A small hole drilled into wood to accept the threads of a screw. A pilot hole reduces the chances of the wood splitting as a screw is driven home but, to be effective, it must have a diameter narrower than the diameter of the screw threads.

Power tool
Any tool that is driven by an electric motor, for example, a power drill, power plane, or power saw. These tools can dramatically reduce the time required to complete a project.

Rabbet
This is a recess cut along the end edge of a board. Rabbets are most often rectangular in cross-section.

Rough-sawn lumber
Boards that have been sawn but not planed. Rough-sawn wood has coarse, splintered surfaces. Most home centers sell only S4S boards, some lumber yards sell rough-sawn hardwoods and softwoods.

Shoe
A **sole plate** with a slot through which the blade of a power saw protrudes. The forks on each side of the slot help to prevent the lumber from splintering as it is cut. Most jigsaws have shoes.

Sole
The flat base of a tool that is designed to slide along the surface of wood – for example, the sole of a plane is the smooth, flat bottom of the plane.

Sole plate
A flat-bottomed sheet of moulded steel that is screwed or bolted to a power saw so that the tool can be moved along the surface of the wood at a constant level as the blade cuts the wood. With most power tools, the sole plate can be tilted to vary the angle of cut.

Solvent
A solvent is any liquid that can be used to dissolve a substance. However, in woodworking terms, solvent usually refers to a petrochemical liquid that is used as the base for certain paints and stains. A solvent-based paint has pigments dispersed in a petrochemical liquid. Solvent-based paints can be thinned with mineral spirits (another solvent) but can be harmful to the environment.

Stile
The vertical side parts of a door or window frame.

Stock
The body, handle or main part of a tool that is often made from hardwood. The stock of a try square is the handle to which the blade is secured; the stock of a marking gauge is the part that slides up and down the shaft.

Straightedge
This is a rule that has at least one perfectly level edge to it. A straightedge is used to test the flatness of a piece of lumber and as a guide for marking lines. It does not necessarily have to have measurements marked on it, although this can be extremely useful. Steel straightedges are the most reliable for woodworking as plastic, aluminium and wooden versions are easily chipped, bent or warped out of shape.

Surfaced four sides (S4S)
A term used to describe a board that has had its two faces and two edges planed before being sold. The dimensions given for S4S lumber are usually those of the **rough-sawn** wood before it was planed .

Tang
A sharp metal spike, often found on chisels and rasps, to which a handle is fixed. Never use a tool with an exposed tang as it could cause a nasty gash if your hand slips forward.

Template
A pattern or shape that is used as a guide when marking out parts accurately. A template is marked and shaped to exact size and then laid over the wood to be cut. A template can be made from card, hardboard or any thin but rigid material. There are two advantages to using a template: details can be corrected or adjusted before the part is cut, and the template can be used several times to mark out identical shapes or profiles.

Tongue-and-groove
A type of joint used to join boards together. A narrow strip (the tongue) along the length of one edge of a board slots into a groove along the edge of another board.

True
As a verb, this means to flatten or smooth down to a perfect level with a plane or chisel. As an adjective, it means exact or precise – for example, a true vertical is an exact vertical.

Wallplug
A plastic, fibrous or metal fitting that helps a woodscrew grip when it is driven into a wall. Different types of wallplug are used in masonry and drywall walls.

Warp
A swelling or twist in lumber, usually caused by wood shrinking or expanding as it dries out or absorbs moisture.

Wire
The thin strip of waste metal that is formed along the edge of a blade as it is sharpened. After sharpening, the wire can be removed to leave a clean edge.

Workpiece
Any project or piece of wood that is being drilled, sanded, painted, chiselled and so on.

A

abrasive paper 58, 60, 71
adhesives 48, 52, 54
all-in-one bit 33
allen screw 156
aluminium-oxide paper 58
ash 15
auger bit 33, 35
Auraucaria angustifolia 12

B

back saw 21, 28, 30
ball-peen hammer 51
bar clamp 47
bark 10, 11
beech 15
belt sander 66
bench hook 21
bench plane 21, 40, 41, 42–43
bevel 156
bevel-edged chisel 36, 37
bird box 82–83
bird feeder 90–91
bird-mouth joint 146–147
blanket chest 128–131
block plane 40, 41
blockboard 16
boards
    cutting 24, 30
    from planks 48–49, 76
    joining 57
    man-made 16–17
    planing 44
    sawing from logs 10
bolts 53
bookshelves 96–99
bowing 11
brace and bit 33, 35
bradawl 32, 57
brushes 20, 59
buffing mop 71
bulletin board 84–85
butt joint 72

C

C-clamp 21, 46, 49
carriage bolts 55
catches 53
cavity wallplugs 53, 57
cedar
    of Lebanon 12
    Western red 12, 13
Cedrus libani 12

chamfer 68, 156
cherry 15, 62, 63
child's desk 132–135
child's toy chest 116–119
chipboard 17
chiselling 38–39, 57
chisels 20, 36–37
    sharpening 37, 39
Chlorophoro excelsa 14
chuck 32, 33, 71, 156
circular saw 64
clamp heads 47
clamping 30, 48–49
clamps 21, 46–47
clawhammer 20, 51
clearance hole 156
combination square 22, 26
computer workstation 140–143
Continental-pattern hammer 51
coping saw 28, 31
corner brackets 53
corner cupboard 148–151
corner lap joint 73
corners
    marking levels 27
    sanding 66
counterbore 156
countersink 32, 33, 55, 156
countersunk screw 52
cross-cut saw 21, 28, 29, 30
cross-lap joint 73
cupboard, corner 148–151
curved edges
    cutting 31, 65
    planing 41, 45
    sanding 71
cushion corner 13
cutting *see* chiselling; sawing

D

dado 13
Danish oil 63
depth stop 33, 34
desk
    child's 132–135
    computer workstation 140–143
detail sander 66
dish rack 124–127
Douglas fir 12
dowel 13
dowel joints 33, 78–79, 124
drilling 34–35, 56
drills 21, 32–33
    attachments 70–71

bits 21, 32–33
    brace and bit 33, 35
    depth stop 33, 34
    hammer action 32, 156
    stand 35
drum sander 70, 71
dry wall 53, 156
dust bags 66, 67

E

edge-to-edge joint 76
egg and spice rack 94–95
elm 15
end grain 156
    planing 45
    staining 61
end splits 11
English oak 15, 63
Entandrophragma
E. *cylindricum* 14
E. *utile* 14
European redwood 12, 62

F

face mask 21
Fagus spp. 15
fastening techniques 56–57
fence 64, 156
fiberboard 17
filler 58, 60
finish nail 156
finishes 62–63, 156
finishing
    techniques 60–61
    tools 58–59
firmer chisel 36, 37
fittings 52–53
fixing
    techniques 54–55
    tools 50–51
fixings 20, 52–53
flakeboard 17
flat-sawing 10
flint paper 58, 71
frames 49, 88–89
Fraxinus spp. 15
frog 156

G

garden furniture
    bench 136–139
    picnic table 144–147

planter 100–103
trellis 120–123
garnet paper 58
gauge
    marking 20, 22, 25, 73
    mortise 20, 26
    profile 22, 27
gimlet 32
glass paper 58
gloss paint 63
glossary 156--157
gloves 21
gluing 48, 52, 54
goggles 21
grain 42, 156
grub screw 156

H

half round 13
half-lap joint 38, 73–74, 124
'hammer' action drills 32, 156
hammers 20, 51
hand brace 33, 35
hand drill 32
hanging techniques 56–57
hardboard 17
hardwood 14–15
    veneer 17
hemlock 12, 62
hinge-cutter 33
hinges 53, 56, 57
hole saw 70
holes
    drilling 34–35
    filling 60
hollow walls, fixings 57
honeycomb checks 11
honing 39, 43, 156
honing guide 39, 43
horizontals 27
hot-melt glue 52

I

interlocking joint 77
iroko 14

J

jack plane 41
jig, dowelling 79, 98
jigsaw 65
jointer plane 40, 41
    lap 38, 73--74, 124

joints 72–79
  bird-mouth 146–147
  butt 72
  clamping 49
  cutting 38
  dowel 33, 78–79, 124
  edge-to-edge 76
  fixing 54–55
  half-lap 38, 73–74, 124
  interlocking 77
  knock-down fittings 53
  lap 73–74
  mitered butt 72
  mortise and tenon 74–75
  rabbet 77
  skew-nailing 55
  through dado 76

K
kerf 156
key-hole saw 28
Khaya spp. 14
knife block 92–93
knives
  marking 22
  putty 58, 60
  utility 21, 24
knock-down fittings 53, 56, 57, 156
knots 11, 13, 156
  sealing 61

L
lacquer 156
laminates 16–17
laminboard 16
lap joints 73–74
lumber
  defects 11, 15
  end grain 45
  grading 11
  hardwood 14–15
  planed 11, 157
  planing square 44
  reclaimed 11
  renewable sources 12, 15
  rough-sawn 11, 15
  sawing planks 10
  selecting 11, 13, 15
  shrinkage 10
  softwood 12–13
  squaring up 25, 44

M
machine screw 156
mahogany, African 14
mallet 21, 37, 54
man-made sheet 16–17
marine board 16
marking
  gauge 20, 22, 25, 73
  techniques 24–27
  tools 22–23
masonry
  drill bit 32, 56
  wallplugs 53
MDF see medium-density fiberboard
measuring
  techniques 24–27
  tools 22–23
medium-density fiberboard (MDF) 17, 116, 132, 140
melamine-faced chipboard 17
metal
  drilling 32
  shaping 51
mineral spirits 59, 61, 157
mirror plates 53
miter 156
  cutting 31
  marking 26
miter block 29
miter box 21, 29, 31
miter clamp 47, 49
mitered butt joint 72
moisture resistant boards (MR) 16
mortise
  marking 26, 74
  measuring 74
  removing waste 75
  'stub' 112, 114–115
mortise chisel 36, 37
mortise gauge 20, 26
mortise and tenon joint 74–75
mouldings 13, 84, 156
  marking around 27
movement 156
multi-purpose saw 29

N
nail set 51
nails 20
  finish nail 156
  removing 51
  skew-nailing 55

O
oak 15, 63
occasional table 104–107
offcut 156
oil, finishing 63
oilstone 37, 39, 43, 157
one-handed clamp 47
orbital sander 66, 67

P
paint 63
panel nails 20, 51, 54
panel saw 21, 28, 29, 30
Parana pine 12
paring 38, 39, 57, 157
particle boards 16–17
parting bead 13
patina 157
pencils 21, 24
Phillips-head screw 52
Phillips-head screwdriver 50, 71
picnic table 144–147
picture frame 88–89
pilot hole 157
pin hammer 51
pincers 51
Pinus sylvestris 12, 62, 63
planed lumber 11, 44, 157
planer file 41
planes 40–41
  bench 21, 40, 41, 42–43
  block 40, 41
  jointer 40, 41
  power 68–69
  sharpening 43
planing 42–45
planks see boards; lumber
plug cutter 33
plumbline 23, 27
plywood 16
polyvinyl acetate adhesive (PVA) 52, 54
power tools 157
  attachments 70–71
  drills 21, 32
  planes 68–69
  sanders 66–67, 70, 71
  saws 64–65
  screwdrivers 50, 71
preservatives 62
profile gauge 22, 27
projects
  bird box 82–83
  bird feeder 90–91

blanket chest 128–131
bulletin board 84–85
child's desk 132–135
child's toy chest 116–119
computer workstation 140–143
corner cupboard 148–151
dish rack 124–127
egg and spice rack 94–95
garden bench 136–139
garden planter 100–103
hardwood stool 152–155
knife block 92–93
occasional table 104–107
picnic table 144–147
picture frame 88–89
shelving unit 96–99
shoe storage rack 86–87
towel rack 108–111
trellis 120–123
workbench 112–115
protractor 23
Prunus spp. 15, 62, 63
Pseudotsuga menziesii 12
putty knife 58, 60
PVA adhesive see polyvinyl acetate adhesive

Q
quadrant 13
quarter-sawing 10
Quercus robur 15
quick-action clamp 46

R
rabbet 157
rabbet joint 77
raised head screw 52
rasps 41, 45
reclaimed wood 11
redwood 12, 62, 63
rip saw 28, 29
rotary sander 66, 67
rough-sawn lumber 11, 15, 157
roundhead screw 52
ruler, collapsible 22

S
S4S see surfaced all sides
safety
  equipment 21
  power tools 65, 67, 68
sanding 60–61

block 21, 58
disks 67, 71
drill attachments 70–71
power sanders 66–67
sealer 59
sapele 14, 16
sawing 30–31
boards 10
cutting line 24, 65
saws 21, 28–29
circular 64
coping 28, 31
cross-cut 21, 28, 29, 30
hole saw 70
jigsaw 65
key-hole saw 28
multi-purpose 29
panel 21, 28
rip saw 28, 29
teeth 29, 64
tenon 21, 28
scotia 13
screwdrivers 20, 50, 71
screwing 55, 57
screws 20, 52, 56
scribing 26, 27
sealers 59, 60, 61, 63
shakes 11
shapes, cutting 31, 65
sharpening
chisels 37, 39
plane blades 43
saws 28
sheet materials 16–17
from planks 48–49, 76
shelving unit 96–99
shoe 157
shoe storage rack 86–87
shrinkage plate 53
skew-nailing 55
sliding bevel 23
slot-head screwdriver 50, 71

slotted screw 52
smoothing plane 41
softwood 12–13
sole 45, 157
sole plate 157
solvent 157
spade bit 32, 33, 35
spirit level 23, 27
squares
combination 22, 26
try 21, 23, 24, 29
squaring up 25, 44
stain 61, 62, 63
steel wool 58, 61, 63
stile 157
stock 157
stool, three-legged 152–155
straightedge 23, 26, 157
stubby screwdriver 50
surface checking 11
surfaced four sides lumber
(S4S)11, 157
Surform 45

T
T-lap joint 74
tables
occasional 104–107
picnic 144–147
tang 36, 157
tape measure 21
retractable 22, 23, 24
Taxus baccata 12, 13
teak 14
techniques
chiselling 38–39
clamping 48–49
drilling 34–35
fastening 56–57
finishing 60–61
fixing 54–55

hanging 56–57
joints 72–79
marking 24–27
measuring 24–27
planing 42–45
sanding 60–61
sawing 30–31
Tectona grandis 14
template 157
tenon 31, 74, 75
3-ply board 16
through dado joint 76
through-and-through sawing 10
Thuja plicata 12, 13
timber see lumber; wood
tongue-and-groove 100, 157
toolbox 20
tools 20–21
chisels 20, 36–37
clamps 21, 46–47
drills 32–33, 35, 70–71
finishing 58–59
fixing 50–51
hammers 20, 51
maintenance 22, 23, 28, 36, 39,
45
marking 22–23
measuring 22–23
pincers 51
planes 40–41
rasps 41, 45
sanding 58–59, 66–67
saws 21, 28–29
screwdrivers 20, 50, 71
storage 22, 36, 40, 50
towel rack 108–111
toy chest 116–119
trellis 120–123
true 157
try square 21, 23, 24, 29
Tsuga heterophylla 12, 62
twist drill 33

U
Ulmus spp. 15
uneven surfaces, marking 27
urea-formaldehyde glue 55
utile 14
utility knife 21, 22, 24

V
varnish 59, 62, 63
veneers 17
verticals 27
vises 46–47

W
wallplugs 53, 56–57, 157
warping 10, 11, 48, 157
water and boil proof boards
(WBP) 16
waxing
plane sole 45
wood 49, 58, 59, 61, 63, 71
web clamp 47, 49
Western red cedar 12, 13
wire 39, 43, 157
wire wool 58, 61, 63
wood
preservatives 62
sealing 59
selecting 11, 13, 15
structure 10
types 10–17
workbench
folding 46, 49
project 112–115
workpiece 157
wrench, adjustable 20

Y
yew 12, 13

ACKNOWLEDGMENTS

The publishers would like to thank the following for their help and co-operation in the publication of this book.

Power Tools
Robert Bosch Limited
P.O. Box 98,
Broadwater Park
North Orbital Road
Denham
Uxbridge, UB9 5HJ
England

Specialist hand tools
John Boddy's
Riverside Sawmills
Boroughbridge
North Yorkshire
YO5 9LJ
England

General woodworking tools
The Tool Bar
96-97 Lower Marsh
Lambeth
London
SE1 7AB
England